TOUGH TIMES WON'T LAST

BUT TOUGH PEOPLE WILL

Chicken Soup for the Soul: Tough Times Won't Last But Tough People Will
101 Stories about Overcoming Life's Challenges
Amy Newmark

Published by Chicken Soup for the Soul, LLC www.chickensoup.com
Copyright ©2021 by Chicken Soup for the Soul, LLC. All Rights Reserved.

The publisher gratefully acknowledges the many publishers and individuals who granted Chicken Soup for the Soul permission to reprint the cited material.

Front cover illustration of faces courtesy of iStockphoto.com/frimages (©frimages)
Back cover and interior illustration of faces courtesy of iStockphoto.com/frimages (©frimages), Thumbs Up illustration courtesy of iStockphoto.com/blackred (©blackred)
Photo of Amy Newmark courtesy of Susan Morrow at SwickPix

Cover and Interior by Daniel Zaccari

Publisher's Cataloging-In-Publication Data
(Prepared by The Donohue Group, Inc.)

Names: Newmark, Amy, compiler.
Title: Chicken soup for the soul : tough times won't last but tough
    people will : 101 stories about overcoming life's challenges /
    [compiled by] Amy Newmark.
Other Titles: Tough times won't last but tough people will : 101
    stories about overcoming life's challenges
Description: [Cos Cob, Connecticut] : Chicken Soup for the Soul,
    LLC, [2021]
Identifiers: ISBN 9781611590760 (print) | ISBN 9781611593167 (ebook)
Subjects: LCSH: Resilience (Personality trait)--Literary
    collections. | Resilience (Personality trait)--Anecdotes. |
    Fortitude--Literary collections. | Fortitude--Anecdotes. |
    Determination (Personality trait)--Literary collections. |
    Determination (Personality trait)--Anecdotes. | LCGFT: Anecdotes.
Classification: LCC BF698.35.R47 C45 2021 (print) | LCC BF698.35.R47
    (ebook) | DDC 155.24--dc23
Library of Congress Control Number: 2021944751

PRINTED IN THE UNITED STATES OF AMERICA
on acid∞free paper

25 24 23 22 21   01 02 03 04 05 06 07 08 09 10 11

TOUGH TIMES WON'T LAST

BUT TOUGH PEOPLE WILL

101 Stories about
Overcoming Life's Challenges

Amy Newmark

Chicken Soup for the Soul, LLC
Cos Cob, CT

Changing your life one story at a time®
www.chickensoup.com

Table of Contents

❶

~The New Normal~

❷

~Count Your Blessings~

❸

~Find Your Inner Strength~

❹

~It Takes a Village~

❺

~Coping with COVID~

❻

~Attitude & Perspective~

❼

~Moving Forward~

❽

~Meet the New You~

❾

~Face Your Fears~

❿

~Loss, Grieving, and Healing~

The New Normal

Andrà Tutto Bene

May you always have courage to take a chance.
~Irish Saying

I'm so good at worrying that I've considered adding it to the skills section on my resume. I'm the best there is at fretting over the little things, like how I'll manage a left turn at a light that has no green arrow, and the irrational, like wondering if a human has ever died from the shock of encountering a large insect in the kitchen.

I worry about big things, too. For the last decade, I was a graphic designer, a longtime employee at a company that struggled financially for years. Layoffs were frequent, and I lost count of how many talented employees were shown the door. It was a depressing place. There wasn't time for creative thinking, as we leftovers had to pick up the extra work. It was no longer the career I had loved.

I found a solution that allowed me to enjoy being creative again. I started making handmade jewelry as a hobby and selling it on Etsy. At first, I sold only one or two items a month. But I got a kick out of hearing the sales bell chime on my iPhone, and it felt good to put my energy into a project where the underlying motivation wasn't fear.

I developed new items to sell whenever I had time, and my little shop grew. After eight months, I was making enough cash on the side to pay for an occasional weekend trip or a fancy dinner. And as the stress level at my day job increased, my Etsy shop was a lovely contrast to all that — a steady nightlight in a dark house.

When the COVID pandemic hit, I did what I do best and found something new to worry about — that my Etsy sales would stop. But, to my surprise, the opposite happened — my weekly numbers actually doubled. In fact, my sales were a little too good. I was struggling to keep up. In a fleeting moment of excitement, I contemplated quitting my day job to run my Etsy shop full-time. But there were too many worries: No health insurance. No 401k match. These were the important things, I had been taught. Better to stay put.

And then I got a call from the company — they were reducing my hours by fifty percent in light of even more financial struggles from the pandemic. But they were maintaining my benefits. It should have been bad news, but the universe had thrown me a curveball when I was batting really well. I would have the time I needed to work on my shop.

I squeezed the life out of every extra minute I was given, creating new products to sell. One I particularly loved was a bracelet with letters that spelled "Andrà Tutto Bene." It was an Italian phrase I had seen in photographs from Venice, one of my favorite travel spots, where quarantined citizens had banners with the phrase hanging from their windows. The translation: "Everything will be fine." It was a beautiful sentiment, not only for the world suffering in a pandemic, but for a perpetual worrywart like me.

The bracelets didn't sell, but I had a soft spot for them, so I kept paying to list them anyway. And other items sold well over the next several months. I was hitting my stride. My weekly sales doubled, again. I wondered how I would manage, again. And the universe threw me a curveball, again.

This one I wasn't sure I could hit.

Another call from the day job. This time, it was the HR director telling me that my position had been eliminated. It was my turn. "Please don't take it personally that we've personally selected you to get rid of."

It was a miserable call to get, no matter how much I disliked my job. I felt guilty as I thought of my newlywed husband, an incredible man who had made approximately one billion sacrifices for me already. In return, I would have to burden him with the sole responsibility of paying our bills. As I waited for the HR director to get through the script, the sales bell chimed on my iPhone. Maybe I shouldn't have picked it up in the midst of what was happening, but I did — and saw that a customer had bought two of my Andrà Tutto Bene bracelets.

For most, this would be a sign that this order came in at the exact moment I was losing my job. But as a skilled worrier, I had no time for that. How much did health insurance cost? What if I never found another job? What if I never got a left-turn green arrow again?

The call ended. I sat at my desk for a while thinking. Fifteen minutes later, my sales bell chimed again.

It was the same customer. She bought three more bracelets. The universe: *Okay, idiot, you didn't get it the first time. How about now?*

I made the five bracelets the next day. I debated telling the customer about the unusual circumstances but didn't want to be a creepy over-sharer. I sent the order off and started wading through the things you do when you get laid off.

Worriers need constant reinforcement. People don't always know that, but the universe does. And it brought me the same customer when I needed her. As I negotiated my severance package, she ordered three more bracelets. As my husband and I figured out our health-insurance plan, three more. With every new tidal wave of worry, she threw me a raft to hang onto.

Once I got things sorted, her orders stopped. But others came, in numbers I wouldn't have dreamed possible. My customers are mostly women, and I wondered how many of them might be struggling like me and in need of a similar boost. How many were stuck in a miserable job, or stressed by the pandemic, or upset by the tense political landscape? There were a lot of reasons to worry, even if you weren't normally a worrier.

I did my best to pay it forward. I included personalized touches with each order. I wrote handwritten messages and added small gifts. I told people to have a great day. I called them fabulous. They are.

The response was overwhelming. I started receiving sweet e-mails and even a few handwritten thank-you notes in return. "When I opened your package, I had the biggest smile on my face... It made my day after having a really bad mental-health day today... It's so heartwarming and appreciated to have someone put in a little extra right now." It felt so good to be enveloped in positivity after all the years of professional gloom and doom.

Today, my shop has more than 10,000 sales and my weekly earnings exceed what I was making at my previous job. A worrier like me would never have thought that possible. But the best part is the joy I get from taking care of my customers, and how lucky I've been to have them take care of me in return. Everything is fine, and so much more.

— Jenine Zimmers —

Broken Vessel

Freeing yourself was one thing, claiming
ownership of that freed self was another.
~Toni Morrison, Beloved

I woke to another day of feeling lonesome. Comfort came in the form of my four-year-old daughter, who climbed onto my chest for her last twenty minutes of sleep. Gently, I rested a palm on her head full of even cornrows. Her deep, contented breathing was a reminder that I had to figure out something to ensure she could feel that peace for days to come. I could not rest.

After all, I was the one who had revolted against a marriage marred by fear, disrespect, and isolation. This was my choice, but now I faced the consequences and the need to protect my children.

The two years of separation from my spouse had passed quickly, and I found myself without a car or a job, sleeping in my soon-to-be ex-father-in-law's family room. I'd decided to walk away without requesting alimony, child support, or even the family vehicle, thinking that would mollify my ex. I wanted him to accept the divorce, but after he failed to show several times for court appearances, I wasn't any closer to complete liberty and safety.

As I awaited the finalization of my divorce, I was overwhelmed by negative thoughts. My father-in-law didn't help, telling me I had ruined my marriage. I was at rock bottom, filled with self-doubt and blaming myself. Why was I unlovable? Wasn't I good enough?

I was broken. Beyond repair. Or so I thought.

There is a process in Japanese art called *kintsugi* in which broken pottery pieces are put back together with gold. On this morning, after rising from the sofa, that process began in my life. I decided to return to church. Pastor Elwood Matthews began to lead me through the lower levels of my rock bottom up to a middle ground. I was shown how to embrace my imperfections in order to yield a more beautiful piece of art. He spearheaded the process to rebuilding a stronger me held together by the pure gold of love, patience, self-control, and understanding.

That was only the beginning.

I decided that the best place for us to rebuild our lives was somewhere else. A few weeks later, I moved from Maryland to California. It was the first time I had been away from my children in thirteen years, but this leg of the journey had to be taken alone. I arrived in California in June 2018. At first, I stayed with a college friend who lived in North Hollywood, sleeping on an air mattress. After two months, my elder daughter arrived, and I relocated us to a motel for two more months.

At times, my angel of a friend, Emmanuel, brought us meals. I'd met him through a former bandmate in the band my ex-husband managed. My daughter and I had exhausting, long commutes to school and work, yet we trudged on.

When I couldn't afford the motel anymore, Emmanuel insisted we stay with him. Two months passed, and we found a one-bedroom apartment in Temple City. Finally, we had a home. My other two children flew in, two more pieces of my vessel as it was repaired with seams of gold.

After months of navigating public transit in the worst cold and rain that many in California said they had seen in years, I purchased a car.

Piece by piece, I began to stand again. It all happened as slowly as the tears that trickled down my face each night. I knew if I could just make it through the pain and work of rebuilding, we would be okay.

I began to feel droplets filling my newly repaired vessel. I found encouragement at work and throughout my new life. The dark clouds lightened, outlined with silver. We all navigated a year of distance learning together in 2020. By 2021, I was approved for a mortgage for my first home. I was able to give my daughter that first car I'd purchased and get myself a new one. I got a new job as a regional manager hiring coaches for L.A. County schools.

I couldn't see any of this on the horizon when all my pieces lay in shards. I woke up in pain each day and went to sleep filled with anguish. Yet something urged me to fight. I found my inner fortitude and resilience and I pushed on, one day at a time.

I am still a work in progress with sparkles of gold crisscrossing my frame. Now I know that I have always been worthy. I have always been lovable. I am enough.

— Gold Meadows —

The Empty Room

*It does not take much strength to do things, but it requires
a great deal of strength to decide what to do.*
~Elbert Hubbard

ne room in our house remained unfinished. Nearly
three years after we traded a decade of city living for the
suburbs, the empty bedroom still had its original green
paint, and only contained a yoga mat and a discarded
rocking chair.

"And this will be the baby's room," we'd say when we first gave
family and friends the tour. That was, after all, what the move to the
suburbs was for.

I was incredibly dramatic as I pulled my mother aside and let her
know I had stopped taking birth control. I did the same to my sisters-
in-law and was disappointed by their very matter-of-fact response.
Didn't they understand how big a deal this was?

For me, it was a big deal. I thought back to the time I announced
at a college party, when the object of my affection was not paying suf-
ficient attention to me, that I didn't want to get married or have kids,
ever. I thought I might live abroad, that I would never return to the
familiar life of my upbringing.

I laughed at myself when I got married ahead of that guy I had
liked, the one who told me I was "too independent and too much of
a feminist to date." I couldn't wait to hear what all the people who
thought I was "too much," who probably thought I would never be

fit to be a mother, would say.

I quickly became comfortable texting my mother updates on our progress, concerned if my husband was traveling while I was ovulating. I texted my closest friends about vaginal mucus, and I found meaning in every slight change in my body.

Months passed, and nothing happened. Still, I planned the momentous Facebook post in which I would announce my pregnancy. I mulled over the gender-neutral color we would choose when we repainted that empty room, and I chose the quote we would stencil onto the wall. I identified a doula. I read books about birth plans. All of it seemed so far away until it suddenly started to feel like we were behind.

"Just one more month," we kept telling ourselves. Our friends had their second kids, their third, their vasectomies. A lesbian couple we knew got pregnant. Another had their second successful adoption. I lost myself in Google rabbit holes. I took supplements, tried acupuncture, and talked to everyone I knew. "Relax," they'd say. "Give it time." Every day, I'd go to a different extreme — adoption, eschewing parenthood altogether, selling the house and moving halfway across the country, across the world. I just wanted to know, one way or another. Was something wrong?

People have children for a lot of reasons. Sometimes, it's to save them from themselves. I viewed having kids, or at least being pregnant, as a way to motivate myself to do what I knew I should do — quit drinking, eat healthier, write more.

I talked to other couples who were having difficulty conceiving, I'd hear the woman say she wanted kids more than anything. I wanted kids, sure, but more than anything? I told my husband I wasn't sure if I wanted to do IVF — pumping my body with chemicals, not knowing the long-term effects. There were too many horror stories about births gone wrong, too. We even knew someone who died of complications from giving birth.

It felt as if some intuitive truth was trying to break free from deep inside me: Was this what I really wanted or just what I thought I was supposed to do?

We finally made an appointment. I got blood work done and had my first ultrasound. I felt relaxed looking at the screen, even though there was nothing there. We made the jokes about my husband doing his part. We told our families we were finally looking into what was taking so long. Then we waited.

The first doctor told us our only option was IVF. I cried. My husband and I tried not to blame each other, but of course we did a little bit. I stressed out as the woman from the doctor's office kept calling to ask when we wanted to start the process even though she often couldn't remember my name or what tests we had already done. Was this how I wanted to bring new life into the world? Would they implant the wrong embryo? My gut feeling was that this wasn't right for us.

We stopped.

"This is working so far," my husband said one day, motioning at just the two of us. We joked that we hadn't really fought yet as a married couple because we didn't have kids. We busied ourselves with other activities. I started writing and teaching spin class on the side. I stopped drinking. Maybe I didn't need a baby as an excuse to make changes. I deflected concerned co-workers' and friends' questions about how everything was going. "The same," I'd say.

Then, we heard of friends in our situation who didn't have to go as far, so we made another call, another appointment. We were given better news, less invasive options. We celebrated and then dove immediately into our new routine.

I took hormones, did four intra-uterine inseminations (IUIs), and had surgery. Each step felt like increasing the water temperature while the frog slowly boiled alive inside the pot. I started having panic attacks—once with the ultrasound wand inside me. The doctor recommended we take a break. We knew this "easier" solution was no longer working, and IVF would be the next step. It was time to make a choice, but we would give ourselves a year off first to reevaluate how we felt.

The year was 2020. "What if we just... don't?" I ventured. We felt relief, and then, immediately, guilt. We asked ourselves whether we felt anything was missing. We questioned how we might feel in five, ten, and twenty years. We felt thankful for our quiet, clean house as we worked from home for a year during the pandemic. In this one area of our lives, in this unpredictable time, we felt oddly at peace.

Decisions are always easier when they're made for you. The ability to choose is our great freedom and, also, a curse. Still, I live with the haunting question: What if I make the wrong choice?

Typically, you only hear these stories once a couple is at a happy ending with a baby, where they say it was all worth it. But we never talk about this part: the waiting, the questioning. The other decision. And that's why I share this. I know there is someone out there at this part, holding back tears, but not quite sure why.

— Amanda ReCupido —

Lost for Words

*I will love the light for it shows me the way; yet I will
love the darkness for it shows me the stars.*
~Augustine "Og" Mandino

t the age of fifteen, I was a self-proclaimed expert at tying
my father's shoelaces. I bent over, employed the tried-
and-true bunny-ear method, and got to work. When I
stood up, his lips twitched in frustration before falling
into a hard line. He pried his mouth open once again, trying to coax
out the words. Still, they refused to come.

I gave him an encouraging nod and chewed on my tongue until
it bled. The space between us was entirely devoid of sound, save for
the occasional defeated groan. Eventually, he resorted to gesturing:
little pats on his chest followed by a wave in my direction. I forced a
smile — the kind where most of my face remains stationary.

"I love you, too, Dad," I whispered, modulating my tone to cam-
ouflage the cry caught in my throat. A heavy silence settled on us then,
filled with tacit sentiment and burgeoning grief.

Before this, my father had been a corporate sales trainer who
taught presentation skills. He traveled across the world for work and
competed in tennis tournaments on the weekends. "Life is good," he
would say, with a twinkle in his eye.

Everything changed during my sophomore year of high school. A
sudden stroke — caused by a rare autoimmune disease — left my dad
with severe physical and neurological deficits. In addition to sustaining

frontal lobe damage, he was unable to move the right side of his body. But the most drastic debt, amidst so many others, was his loss of speech.

The stroke resulted in a disorder called aphasia, which impairs someone's ability to communicate and understand language. The doctor's prognosis was not lost on me that day. "A full recovery will be extremely difficult," he said gravely.

I learned early on that aphasia does not affect intellect. It was like my father was a prisoner in his own body, unable to do and say exactly what he wanted. I could not even begin to imagine how debilitated and frustrated he felt.

The aphasia also caused my dad to say things he did not mean. He would sometimes cry in the middle of a funny movie and laugh when something tragic happened. I found myself succumbing to embarrassment whenever we were in public. My father would wield his cane like a weapon and shout incoherent yet harmless phrases at passersby. I knew that these actions were byproducts of his stroke, but they still upset me. I hated the stares and hushed comments, even though he did not notice.

One afternoon, I came home to find my dad watching an old video. It was footage of us playing tennis — whipping the ball back and forth while running around the court. What used to be such a simple pleasure was now impossible. I stared at us on the screen, enraptured by that bittersweet memory.

We watched in silence until I couldn't hold in my grief any longer. Everything I had suppressed bubbled up to the surface. I found myself shaking, crying, and heaving while the video played in the background. My heart broke for us both and ached for what we could no longer do together.

His lips moved while he watched me cry. My dad clearly wanted to say something, but he was powerless. There we were — incapable of fixing each other's worst problems. Although his movement was limited, he closed the gap between us and gave my hand a comforting squeeze. I looked up, struck by how the littlest thing could mean so much.

We were both lost for words for vastly different reasons. At any time, he could have another stroke. There was no guarantee — no promise of tomorrow. I felt overcome by fear, both for my family and for my father. Amidst so much uncertainty, was life truly worth living? That question hung over me, coloring formative experiences during my adolescence and clouding otherwise blissful days.

I finally found my answer. When my family took a weekend trip to Tahoe, my dad saw a group of people parasailing on the lake. He and I had gone a few times before his stroke, but years had passed since then.

"You and me!" he managed to say.

We floated high above the water, eyes fixed on the setting sun. Just after the sky put out its last flicker of pink, my dad looked at me with a familiar expression. "Life... good."

It may have been his bright smile, or a rush of warm air, or the ripe burst of colors enveloping us. But in that precious moment, I understood exactly what he meant.

"Yes," I whispered back. "It really is."

I did not know then what I know now. I did not realize how tirelessly my father would work to recover what he lost, or that he would go on to regain a fair amount of his speech. I could not comprehend how much he would inspire me to move forward in the face of fear. I did not know I was about to lose him forever.

After an autoimmune flare-up landed my father in the hospital, he suffered another series of massive strokes. Over the course of one month, he would fall into a coma and ultimately pass away. It all happened so suddenly.

I still wish we could have had one last conversation. The biggest thing I continue hanging onto is something my dad said over the phone shortly before he died.

"Life is good." Three simple words: a cliché in any other context. But he injected true meaning into the phrase by refusing to let his sickness overshadow the days he had left.

One evening toward the end of my father's coma, I sat at his bedside until everyone else had left the room. Then I spoke softly into his ear. I told him how scared I was before asking the question that eclipsed every other: *What if you never wake up?* As soon as it departed my lips, I knew I already had the answer.

I gave his hand one last squeeze before leaving the hospital. On my way home, I paused to look up at the August night sky. A black expanse with scattered bits of brightness stared back at me. I let myself linger for a while, taking in the brilliant panorama.

How beautiful is it that we need darkness to see the stars?

—Danielle M. Wong—

Letting Annie Go

When you put love out in the world it travels,
and it can touch people and reach people
in ways that we never even expected.
~Laverne Cox

My daughter, Annie, called me on one of the first warm days of spring two years ago. I had just made a cup of tea and set it on my writing table outside next to the vegetable garden, desperate to feel sun on my pale winter arms and shoulders. I had picked a quirky number by Björk for Annie's ring, and it made me laugh because it was so different from any of my music. Annie was urging me again into the twenty-first century.

Her voice and mood could differ drastically from day to day, and I was always prepared for anything. She might be "meh," which meant just okay, or upset, maybe crying, or upbeat and silly. Today, I knew something was very wrong. She started off hesitantly, like she was afraid to tell me something.

"It's Megan," she said. "She killed herself."

It was one of those moments when your mind starts racing, but at the same time you feel hot and dizzy and very present. The steam from the blue teacup swirled into the humid air, and I wanted to go back in time to the calm moment before the call when I was about to sip my tea — as though that would change the call, and Megan would be alive and well.

"But I just heard from her. She texted me." Megan had texted me a few days earlier asking if I would come pick up some things that Annie had left at their apartment in Minneapolis. I hadn't gotten around to answering her. "When did this happen?"

"Friday. Her roommates found her. She hung herself." Annie was sobbing now.

Megan and Annie were both transgender. The vulnerability of that hit me hard and made me want to have Annie back at home, a little boy at age six, laughing at me reading Shel Silverstein poems aloud. But Annie was 2,000 miles away in San Francisco, having moved out of state for the first time at age twenty-five to get away from the cold Minnesota winters and uptight people. Her pain felt so palpable that I could imagine holding her thin body. The empty spot left in me when she moved away ached.

Megan and Annie had been roommates and dated for a while in Minneapolis. They supported each other on this journey, two young adults trying to find their way in the world like all twenty-somethings but with the added burden of being transgender.

I said, "But after all she just went through? The surgery? I don't understand. She's only been back for, what, two months, not even fully recovered. Why?"

I had met Megan a few months before she went to Thailand for reassignment surgery. She had been warm and gracious to me at a time when Annie had been ambivalent and testy. Annie and I had normal communication problems made more complicated by me trying to learn the new language of cis, non-binary, gender queer, and all the nuances that went along with that. Megan was spunky and had a throaty, enthusiastic voice. She and I had clicked right away and texted almost daily while she was in Thailand. Her parents lived in Virginia, and she was out of touch with them. I tried to fill that gap, and Megan responded.

Annie said, "She had tried it once before I met her. I knew she had real problems, and I tried to get her to go to therapy, but she didn't trust anybody. She thought everybody was out to get her."

I started to shiver in the sunshine, and my stomach was a hard knot. I imagined Megan strutting around with her little kid's bouncy walk. The bedroom that had once been Annie's with the loft bed where the roommates had found her hanging. And her text message to me left unanswered. Again, I had the sensation of needing time to stop and go back before it happened so the outcome could be different.

Annie said, "Are you okay? I know you felt close to her. I didn't want to shock you."

The role reversal struck me because I had always been the one to console Annie, to take care of her, and now she was worried about me. Something had shifted between us, feeling different, like when an optical illusion reveals itself.

"I'm worried about you. Are you okay?" Since Annie had moved, I allowed myself to relax a little in my ever-present worrying about her. I thought California was a good place for a transgender person to be. From her calls, I knew she was having some issues, but she didn't seem as depressed as she often had at home. Yet Megan, who had seemed so stable and self-assured, had killed herself, so what did that mean for Annie? She was thousands of miles away from my home in Wisconsin, living in a place I'd never seen with roommates I'd never met.

"Yeah, I was really upset at first. I found out yesterday, but I guess I'm not really shocked. I think it was an impulse. Not planned out or anything."

Annie made it sound like Megan's suicide was a whim, like choosing an ice-cream flavor to see what it tastes like. It was as though we were having a conversation about kids dropping out of high school, like it was one of those things that happens to troubled youth.

"But it doesn't make any sense. I mean, she seemed like she was doing so well," I said. I had seen Megan once since Annie left, and she seemed fine, a bit awkward and distracted, but not desperate. "What about you? Are things going better?" I had talked to Annie a couple of weeks earlier. She was having trouble getting along with roommates, and the medical clinic didn't take her insurance.

"Yeah. It's okay. Listen, I have to go, but we can talk later if you need to, okay?" There it was again: *if* I need to talk. It reminded me of when she and her brother, Brian, were little. When I was tired or had a cold, they might put a hand on either side of my face and ask me what was wrong. She hung up before I asked her if she'd called Brian. He would be upset, too. Brian had met Megan when he came to Minneapolis from New York to help Annie move. He had really liked her.

I found my husband, John, icing his back in bed and watching an episode of *The Sopranos*. At first, he didn't remember Megan; he'd only met her once.

"Oh, that's terrible. I know how much you liked her. How's Annie?"

I was grateful he asked. Annie is John's stepdaughter, and they've never lived together. When we met, she had been having a hard time and was living with me. He was there during her transition as I tried to help her with doctors, therapists, and social workers. Then we helped take care of her after her bike accident and knee surgery. Her biological dad, my ex, had not been very involved in her life for a while. He seemed more fixated on Annie getting a degree and a job than with her being transgender.

"I don't know. She seems okay. She's so far away that I can't even imagine how she feels."

John held me as images of Megan went through my mind, living images of her bouncy walk, her warm laugh and smooth vowels. Then I imagined her body hanging lifeless and cold from that loft bed. It was agonizing. I was heartbroken and scared.

I had been scared ever since Annie brought up the transgender thing. It was 2006, and I had never heard the words cis, non-binary or gender queer. I had seen the films, *Boys Don't Cry* and *The Crying Game*, and I knew that it would not be an easy life and could be dangerous. But the more I sat with the idea, the more it made sense.

As a little boy in preschool, Annie had not moved from parallel play to interactive play at the right time. Annie's first-grade teacher declared that Annie never spoke out in class and had classic ADHD behavior. Teachers in the gifted program complained that she had no curiosity or imagination. Then she'd come home and ask questions and talk non-stop to me for two hours. Friendships had been difficult. None of it at the time seemed related to her gender, but in retrospect

I thought being transgender could be a good explanation.

Weeks went by, and my sadness became agitation and anxiety. I tried to get interested in my garden, in writing, in enjoying my time off and the warm weather. Megan and Annie were constantly on my mind.

One day, John caught me standing at the kitchen sink staring out the window. I said, "How could I have missed it? And what else have I missed?"

"Missed?"

"Are we so preoccupied with our next cappuccino that we don't notice when people are in pain? Suicidal? We're too busy to stop and do something?" I leaned heavily on the counter with my hands hanging over the sink.

"Sit down." John reached for a wineglass from the cupboard and poured a glass of merlot for me.

I sat down, feeling childish, but accepted the wine. John sat next to me and his earthy presence reassured me. We had found each other later in life, and there was so much joy in that. It seemed unfair that other people in our lives should be so miserable while we were so happy.

"I feel guilty," I said. "I've spent my whole life chasing happiness. Satisfaction. Meaning."

"You don't think you're allowed to feel joy in life? If other people are in pain? That's your Catholic guilt."

It annoyed me when he blamed things on my Catholic guilt. "It's not that. I know I couldn't have done anything to stop Megan, but I still feel like I could have done more to help her. Been more involved. Less worried about my own life."

"Honey, you are one of the best people I know. I wish you could take that in sometimes. You did more for Annie than you'll ever realize. If you weren't the kind of person you are, this could've been her instead of Megan. I don't know if anybody could have saved Megan. You did more than enough."

"What's enough?"

He said, "This is about Annie."

John is usually right in his assessments of my emotional state, even if I'm not always ready to hear it. It's frustrating when he sees things that I am blind to. "What do you mean?"

"She still needs you. It may not seem like it, but she does." The bright song of an oriole sounded just outside the kitchen window. "You should go see her."

When Annie was in the hospital with her knee surgery, the nurses and technicians kept referring to her by her legal name on their paperwork. They have you say your name dozens of times when they prepare you for surgery, because they are always verifying you are the right patient. This was very upsetting to Annie and her friends.

My only concern was with her wellbeing. I believed she wanted me there at the hospital, so I tried to explain things to the staff. After a while, her friends told me that Annie wanted me to leave, that I was making things worse. It was one of the most painful moments of my life. For so long, I had been the one she came to, crying, sad, or depressed. I had been the one taking care of her.

Now I wasn't sure what I was to her, and she wasn't around for me to find out. My tears this time came from an unreachable place that I didn't know existed.

"I miss her."

"I know you do, honey."

"I was hoping she was doing well on her own. Now this thing with Megan," I said. "I'm so scared."

John said, "Get her home for a visit. Or let's look at tickets for you to go out there."

About a month later, Annie did come home for a week. She didn't come to our house a couple of hours from Minneapolis but went to Minneapolis instead to see her friends. I wasn't surprised by this as she had never lived in our house in Wisconsin and knew no one there. I hadn't told her that I wanted her all to myself for a couple of days. Maybe I didn't realize it at the time, but what I wanted was to make French toast for her, huddle on the couch and watch episodes of *Star Trek: The Next Generation*. That was what we used to do after my divorce when one or both of us needed comfort.

What shocked me was that she was planning to stay at the house where Megan had died. I had no desire to go back to that house and revisit Megan's death. But I went anyway, and Annie met me out in the driveway. When she lived in Minneapolis, her hair had been really long, almost down to her waist, and had been long for years. Now it was cut in an edgy bob with purple highlights. I hugged her six-foot, slim body, checking to see if she was too thin. She had trouble eating well and keeping on weight.

I felt really distant from her at first. She was distracted, tired and hungry, concerned about having to move her stuff. It wasn't the reunion I had imagined. We had been very close before she moved, and she had depended on me a lot. Megan's death was not uppermost on her mind either, where I had been hoping to process it with her for both our benefits.

I said, "Isn't it hard for you to be here?"

"It's so different that it doesn't even seem like the same place." In the three months since Megan's death, the bedroom had been completely redone, a wall had been taken out, and the tiny loft room had been turned into a spacious, airy room with two full-sized windows. It must have been an effort to exorcise the horrible incident from the house. Megan would have had nothing to hang from in this newly configured room.

I stepped into the kitchen and smelled coffee. The first time I'd met Megan, we were at their other apartment, a dumpy Victorian in a scary neighborhood. Megan offered to make coffee for me and asked if I'd ever had it with butter. "It gives you an extra lift," she'd said with her sweet Virginia drawl.

Annie's voice brought me back to the bedroom. She asked if I'd take her to deliver some parts to a bike store. "But first I have to change my clothes," she said. I started to leave the room, but she stopped me. "It's okay if you stay in here. I'd kinda like you to see my boobs." She giggled, which was something Annie had done her whole life when she was nervous. It was the first time she had ever asked me to see her new body since hormones. "And I've gained some weight." She patted her stomach.

I had wound all my feelings into a tight coil and tried to make light of everything: my grief and denial about Megan, my fear that the same thing could happen to Annie, and the disappointment at the lack of connection with her. It all unwound at that moment. I was rooted again as her mother, connected to her as my child even as she stood there, grown up and vulnerable like a lot of other young people.

Annie said, "Are you okay? Don't, because then I'll cry."

"Okay, I'll try." I did feel like crying, I was happy to feel close again. And happy to see her able to find herself in this new body and expression. "You look great," I said. "Beautiful."

After that, she opened up more. I watched her dress, and she talked about finding clothes that fit and about her roommates' problems. She corrected me when I used the wrong term for something related to being non-binary or trans. It felt more natural. I drove her around to bike stores, and we stopped for lunch at a Vietnamese grocery, where we shopped a bit until our food was ready.

I brought the conversation to Megan. "Do you think I should call her mom? You know, since I'm closer to her age and I saw her not too long before it happened?" Every time I thought of Megan's parents, I panicked, as though hearing the news of her death for the first time.

"I don't know. They didn't want to have anything to do with her. Her mom was really bad."

"I can't imagine how they feel. I put myself in their place, imagining it was you."

Annie hugged me in the middle of the tea aisle. "You don't have to worry. I'm good. Really. Megan was messed up. Maybe even schizophrenic."

I got the impression that Annie had already moved on. In other conversations, we had discussed that there were trans girls of color being murdered in Louisiana, trans sex workers in San Francisco being raped. It was all part of a big picture that was beyond anything I could begin to take in and respond to.

Annie went on to tell me about her new therapist, how they had their sessions on Skype, and she really liked him. She had found a medical doctor at a different clinic and was even looking for a dentist. She had started the paperwork to have her name changed.

"I'm so impressed. You're doing all this on your own. You're growing up."

"Finally," she said, "at twenty-four. You should come visit me when I'm more settled."

When she left to go back to San Francisco, I was sad not to have more time with her alone, but I realized I needed to let her go. There would be other times. As John had guessed, my grief for Megan had been tangled up with the loss I felt when Annie left. I had been suffering from the tragedy of Megan's death but was also grieving the way any mother does when her child leaves home for the first time.

Annie called me a few weeks later, and she sounded upbeat. She told me about the park in San Francisco by the bridge, and about all the hummingbirds in her back yard. I knew she would have more problems, more challenges — not just being transgender but simply finding her way at a difficult time in most people's lives. But now I could imagine her there in my mind's eye, enjoying her life for the most part, and doing the work that all of us do to stay on course.

— Sharon LaCour —

Our Woods

Step out of the history that is holding you back.
Step into the new story you are willing to create.
~Oprah Winfrey

I've lived in the new house for a week. While the weather's mild, I take my coffee out to the back porch. It wasn't easy moving during a pandemic. It wasn't easy separating from my husband and uprooting the kids from the only home they ever knew. I'm hoping I picked a good place to be our new home, but it's too soon to tell.

Today, I hear a new noise in the woods, not drowned out by bird calls. Twigs snapping. Branches swishing back against movement.

My first thought, a hopeful one, is a deer. What if I have a deer family living in the woods behind my house? What if they are somehow emblematic of my new life? A peaceful animal to symbolize the gentleness of my new life?

Or could it be something dangerous, even terrifying? The devil, a hostile animal, a naked man. But no. This is my new home. My new life. There will be no monsters.

It's probably a coyote or even a raccoon. They love these parts.

What about a mountain lion? A cougar! There have been sightings!

It could be a groundskeeper. Who am I kidding with monsters? I moved to suburbia. This isn't the untamed wilderness. There are trails in these woods, maintained by the homeowners' association.

So, what's in my woods?

I make a plan. I put on long pants and boots and announce that I will now stomp into the woods and find the trail. I will look for signs of life in my woods. Animal droppings. Fur. Masticated carcasses. Satanic symbols. My daughter wants in. My son is busy showing all his toys to his grandfather, who has come to visit and check up on his heartbroken daughter.

My daughter and I go to the edge of the property line and keep going. Twigs snap. Birds get quiet, sensing a blundering predator. We walk straight back, not paying particularly good attention to landmarks. Without much ado, we find the trail and one of the most spectacular trees on earth. It is like a Pacific Northwest banyan tree with multiple trunks shooting out from the ground. My daughter immediately climbs it and declares, "This is the fairy tree!" She throws her triumphant arms in the air, and I snap a picture. She's in rainboots and a tutu and looks perfect among her trees.

We hear the sound of children. Having been in quarantine since March with no end in sight, my daughter practically salivates at the sound of their play. We follow the path and pop out on what I know to be the other side of the natural area. There are three boys on bikes on the street.

"Hi!" my daughter yells. "I'm new here!"

The boys, who might be a couple years older than her, look down their noses at the little blondie in the tutu and say nothing. My daughter cringes and says to me under her breath, "They don't want to play with me?"

"They're boys, honey. They're doing their own thing right now, but we will find other kids."

She's disappointed but doesn't let it bring her down. As we reenter the woods, she finds a clearing with some downed trees and declares it the "play area." She climbs the fallen tree trunks and jumps off them, sending up a puff of dust.

We keep going. Soon, I realize we're back on our side of the natural area, but we can't find the fairy tree. We can't find the non-path back to our house. Nothing is familiar. But, using my phone's GPS, I point us in the direction of our address, and we climb through the brush, snapping dry branches to make our way and trying not to get too snagged by blackberry bushes.

"Are we lost?" she asks me.

"Yes."

"We're lost?!"

"I see where our house is, but I'm not sure of the best way to get back."

So brave, so unwilling to accept our fate, she leads the way through the thick, unmaintained forest.

"I wish it was night," she says.

"Why?"

"So the stars could guide us home."

After a particularly hairy climb through a series of blackberry bushes and pokey twigs, we pop out into a back yard two doors down from our house.

"This is one way to meet the neighbors," I say, and we surreptitiously make our way back to our property line.

My dad and son are standing in the yard, looking for us. We've been gone far longer than anyone expected and are filthy. I'm dripping with sweat and have brambles in my shoes. My daughter looks exhilarated.

"There are so many secret play areas!" she tells her brother. He begins to weep with jealousy, and we promise to take him adventuring in the morning.

That night, my dad and I are sitting on the back porch, listening to the crickets and discussing my finances, when my daughter comes out with a sleeve of saltines. She eats a few and points out the stars, showing how we would have been able to follow them home from the forest. She stands and yawns, proclaiming she's ready to sleep. She kisses my dad on the cheek and comes to kiss me. Then she whispers in my ear, "I had so much fun with you in our woods today." She goes to bed.

The next day, she eats her breakfast and puts on her boots. She packs a backpack with a water bottle and snacks and coaxes her brother into the back yard. We mark the way with red ribbon and run through the woods, easily finding our way home following our ribbon trail. We come inside, filthy and full of fresh air, and both kids fall asleep within minutes, which is not their custom. I make a second cup of coffee and take it out to the porch, listening to the birds who resume their chatter now that the children have gone quiet.

No monsters in these woods. No beasts. We are in our new home, with our new woods to explore. We run; we climb; we imagine magic. No murderers or bears. No devils or deer. Just us three on our own new adventure in our woods.

—Laura Wheatman Hill—

Look Up

To one who has faith, no explanation is necessary.
To one without faith, no explanation is possible.
~Thomas Aquinas

Thirty-eight days had passed since my mom died. Although life continued, I wanted nothing to do with the living part of it. I'd lost weight, dropping to ninety-two pounds. And, to make matters worse, several of my siblings and I weren't getting along since our mother's death.

Just days before dying, Mom had said to me, "We're one heart. Half belongs to me; half belongs to you. When I cry, you cry. When I laugh, you laugh." She was right; we truly were one heart. We used to joke about finishing one another's sentences, so I felt certain that my suffering was causing her great pain.

And so it was after yet another fitful sleep, worrying about my mom's peace, that I found myself depressed, not wanting to rise from my bed. I wanted nothing to do with getting up and facing the world. Instead, I lay there feeling sorry for myself and ignoring a little voice within that was willing me to get up.

"Get up, get up, get up," the voice nagged me. Despite how bad I felt, I had to keep on living, if only to spite my siblings. The anger I felt toward them became like a swift kick in the butt as I made my way to the bathroom. *You'll never get the better of me,* I thought as I stepped into the shower.

I had anticipated that taking a shower would make me feel better, but I felt worse. I could only hope that my routine morning walk would stir some life into me.

I stepped outside, breathing in the coolness of that December morning, hoping it would awaken something inside me. It didn't, so I walked sluggishly with my head down, tears falling, as I continued mourning the loss of my mom. Memories of the fight I'd had with my siblings just the day before lingered on the surface. I was certain that I hated them, but somewhere during the night, I started feeling remorseful for the fight we'd had.

"I'm sorry, Mom." I found myself pleading to the heavens for her to understand why her children were fighting. I cried as I walked onward, and the more I cried, the more sorrow I felt.

"We're one heart," I could hear Mom saying to me. "When I cry, you cry." And there I was crying.

"I'm sorry that my tears are causing you pain," I said.

I felt defeated by my inability to stop crying, to drop to my knees in prayer and ask God to make everything okay.

I wanted Mom to have peace. I *needed* her to have peace. She deserved it. I wanted it just as much for myself, but I didn't know how to get that peace. If only I believed in prayer. If only I believed that God could hear me.

Suddenly, I grew tired of wondering what God could and couldn't do as I walked sluggishly in my coveralls and heavy, winter boots, feeling completely alone and far from peace. "Mom," I cried, "please let me know that you're at peace." As the words left my mouth, I remembered similar words I'd spoken in the few days just before her death. I'd asked her to send me a rainbow as a sign that she was okay.

"That's enough of that," she said, bringing laughter to both of us. Our joined heart told me that she was going to heaven to rest, not work. But there was no laughter as I walked that morning and no peace. There was only the sound of my own voice.

"I'm sorry, Mom, that your kids are fighting." I was crying so hard that I could barely see two steps in front of me.

"I'm sorry, Mom." I leaned my head forward. My eyes were closed as I tried to drown out the thoughts going through my head.

"Ahhhhh!" I screamed. I willed myself to continue walking. With my head still down in sorrow, I started my second lap around my yard, continuing to ignore my surroundings. I felt no desire or need to look anywhere else but down at the dead winter grass.

"I need to know that you're okay, Mom. Please," I begged. There was only silence.

My tears stopped as I found resolve. "Please, God… help me," I said, surprising myself. I wiped my running nose with the back of my glove.

"Look up," I heard a voice say to me. The voice was like the one I'd heard earlier that morning, which had willed me out of bed. I looked up and felt my knees buckle as I stumbled forward before catching myself from falling. My tears resumed, but now they were tears of joy. For there was a big, beautiful rainbow in the sky despite the fact that it hadn't rained at all.

My fears and doubts were released, and a feeling of happiness and peace washed over me. All the weight of the world was drained from me.

"Everything is okay. I'm happy and at peace," I felt my mom say.

I walked until the rainbow faded from the sky, and then I made my way back indoors. I found myself smiling, knowing that my mom was at peace. In that moment, my anger faded. I forgave my siblings, and then I thanked God for willing me to stop focusing on the dead, winter grass and instead look up and see a rainbow in the unlikeliest of places: a mid-December sky in Ohio.

— Cheryl L. Forshey —

Moving Forward in a Paused World

I truly believe that if you put your goals in writing,
speak them out loud, and work for them,
they will happen.
~Ciara

My phone chirped, alerting me to a text message from a friend. I read it and then handed my phone to my eighteen-year-old daughter, Julia. "Sarah sent another meme about the disaster that is 2020," I said.

She read it aloud. "I'm not adding this year to my age since I didn't use it."

"I'm on board with that," I said. "It goes with the one she sent yesterday comparing college kids gaining the Freshman-15 with all of us now gaining the COVID 19. But pounds gained during a global pandemic shouldn't count."

"You're right. They shouldn't. But, unfortunately, they still do."

"It feels like the whole world is on pause," I said. "Everything is closed, and we spend all day at home staring at screens. It's like time has stopped, and nothing we do right now matters in the long run."

Julia nodded. "I feel that way, too. I'm already accepted into college, so my grades don't matter. The restaurant where I work is closed, so I can't earn any money. I can't see my friends either." She shrugged. "It's easy to feel like this time doesn't matter. And if you're not an essential worker, it's fine to just binge-watch Netflix and eat snacks all day."

I chuckled. "I think that's what I've been doing."

The next morning, Sarah texted me another 2020 meme. This one said, "The worst purchase I've ever made was a 2020 planner."

I laughed and showed it to Julia. But, to my surprise, she didn't laugh. Instead, she stood up and said, "I'm going upstairs to get my 2020 planner. You need to grab yours, too."

It took me a few minutes to locate it because it had been weeks since I had any actual plans to keep track of.

When I went back downstairs, Julia was sitting at the kitchen table with her planner and a pen. "I'm done with this," she said. "We've been joking about how this year doesn't count and nothing we do matters, but it's not true." She pointed to the open page in her planner, which was covered in her own handwriting. "Last December, I made a list of goals for 2020. I just read it over, and I can still accomplish some of them." She looked at me almost defiantly. "I know you made a list, too, Mom."

I smiled. Julia and I are so alike, and she knows me well. Of course, I'd written a list of goals for the new year. Planning was part of our DNA.

I found my 2020 To-Do List, which was full of goals for getting healthy, de-cluttering my home, and being a better wife and mother.

Julia read my list and nodded. "The virus does make it seem like the world is on pause, but we can still move forward with a lot of our goals. And I think we'll both feel better if we do."

I knew she was right. When the pandemic first started, I'd spent hours each day watching the news. I felt anxious and scared all the time, and eventually, I realized that I needed to cut back on it. But instead of turning off the TV altogether, I binge-watched movies.

My viewing choices had changed, but my behavior hadn't. My only goal was to get through the day until life got back to normal. But Julia was showing me that, even now, I could live with purpose and accomplish things.

I nodded. "I'm in."

She laid our lists on the table, side by side. "I see that one of your 2020 goals was to spend a lot of time with me before I leave for college," she said. "One of my goals was to learn to cook before I move out." She smiled. "I think there's a significant amount of overlap there."

I laughed, feeling better than I had in months. "I'd love to teach you to cook."

Julia pointed out that we had both set a goal to get more exercise. "I wanted to join a gym," she said. "That's not going to happen obviously, but we can still work out together. I'll find some fitness apps on my phone."

"I'd be happy just going for a daily walk with you," I said. "Just like the cooking, it would work on two goals at once."

And there was overlap in other areas, too. I pointed to a goal on Julia's list. "Purge my room," it said.

"I won't have much space in my dorm room, so I want to get rid of clothes I don't wear," she said.

I nodded. "Cleaning out closets and drawers and finally getting this house organized has been a goal of mine for years. We can work on that one together, too."

I found that day's page in my planner and wrote down some tasks to do right away: Go for a walk. Clean out a drawer. Look for some recipes that would be suitable for a beginner cook.

It was the first entry I'd made in my planner in months, but as Julia and I checked off the tasks together, I felt my spirits lift. I'm sure Julia's presence was a factor, but it also felt good just to accomplish something again.

As the days went on, my house got a little cleaner, Julia grew into a proficient cook, and I even liked the number on my bathroom scale a little better.

Julia was right. Although the world was grieving and seemed to be on pause, what we did as individuals still mattered. Even during a pandemic, we could still take small steps each day to move forward on our goals. We could still help other people, improve our health, and build stronger relationships with those we love.

The year 2020 taught me that all time matters, and every step in the right direction counts. Working with Julia on our mutual goals taught me that progress adds up one daily walk and organized junk drawer at a time. We also learned that when we feel the least like doing something productive is when we need to do it the most — not to complete the task itself but to give purpose to our day and remind ourselves that we are capable of big things.

— Diane Stark —

The Rose

Roses do not bloom hurriedly; for beauty,
like any masterpiece, takes time to blossom.
~Matshona Dhliwayo

On my parents' thirty-seventh wedding anniversary, my dad gave my mother a coral rose on a gold chain. Accompanying the necklace was a simple card on which he wrote, "Even thorns have roses, too. Love, E."

It had been a stormy year in their marriage, my mother once told me. Dad's card had been an invitation to open her heart, the rose a peace offering. My mother accepted both.

The rose graced my mother's neckline often during the remaining twenty years of their marriage. After my father died, she continued to wear it, though less often. In her ninety-first year, when she was wheelchair-bound and spiraling into dementia, she moved to a nursing home near me in Connecticut.

I wanted to make her new surroundings as familiar and welcoming as possible, so I carted in the things I thought were important to her. My husband covered her walls with framed photos of the family, and I crowded the top of her dresser and night table with statuettes and plants that had been in her house "forever." And I brought along the elaborately carved wooden chest that held her sizeable collection of costume jewelry: dangling earrings, beads and baubles, handcrafted pins and a wide assortment of bangle bracelets. But she didn't want any of the jewelry.

"I don't need it anymore," she said. My mother always wore jewelry, like some women always wear lipstick. This indifference to the jewelry felt like yet another loss, another step in the slow fade that was erasing much of the mother I knew.

"Okay, Mom," I said. "I'll keep the jewelry box at my house. If you decide you want it, just let me know."

While we spoke, she was fingering the coral rose that hung around her neck. As I readied to leave, she lifted the necklace off and handed it to me.

"Keep it safe," she said. "I don't want it getting lost."

"Of course, I'll keep it safe, Mom."

And it is safe in my lockbox. Though I wear the other jewelry I am storing for her, I never wear the rose. There is time for that after she passes, when my wearing it will not feel like an intrusion on the intimacy of her relationship with my dad.

For the time being, the coral rose is theirs alone. But not so my dad's words. Though Mom's dementia has left her with a crazy quilt of memories missing whole patches, she remembers the rose and the sentiment that accompanied it, and she shares the words with me with a smile and a knowing nod. They're her shorthand for seeing the best in people and the positives in seemingly unredeemable situations.

They are words that buoyed me during the pandemic and kept me afloat at times when my heart felt like a sinking ship. The lockdown order came for her nursing home on Tuesday March 10, 2020. I had seen her the day before, never imagining it would be more than a year before I could sit with her again, see her whole face, and hold her hand.

I was terrified the confinement and isolation would send her plummeting deeper into dementia and set off an old pattern of depression, negativity and discontent.

It didn't.

My mother missed going outside but found great enjoyment in the garden view from her window. She entertained herself with her photo albums and find-the-word puzzle books. Soon, the staff, who had always been exceptional, found a way to address the residents' social needs even under the bleakest of circumstances. Hallway bingo, with residents spaced six feet apart, lacked the chumminess of a crowd around a table, but it was something. Piped-in music, though a poor second to live entertainment, added some cheer.

Throughout, my mother's attitude was optimistic, and her mood bordered on joyful. She spoke about what she missed but focused on what she had: her family (on the walls around her bed), her memories, her poetry books, her garden view. This new and consistent wealth of gratitude for what she has was nothing short of inspiring.

And, from time to time, she would smile and remind me, "You know, even thorns have roses, too."

One of the roses bloomed early in the pandemic, nestled amongst the thorns in a most unlikely place: a computer screen. During the first year-plus of the lockdown I was able to chat with my mother via Skype every day. A staff member would don a Tyvek gown, hairnet and mask, and bring an iPad to my mom's room.

At first, the sound of my voice and sight of me waving at her from a small screen confused and delighted her. She asked if I was "in there." But it did not take many days for her to feel comfortable with our new style of visit. She marveled at the "invention" of a picture phone and told me someone was "very smart" to have come up with it. And soon, these "on-the-screen visits" as we called them, became almost as satisfying as seeing each other in the flesh.

They gave me something I never had as an adult: a relaxed daily relationship with my mom. Ever since I married decades ago, I had lived very far from her and my dad. My life took me to Florida, Hawaii, Israel, Tennessee, and finally to Connecticut. I always spoke to my parents on Sundays, calling in the late morning while they lingered over the breakfast table with the Sunday paper and coffee. But I never lived close enough to drop in, take her to lunch, or go shopping with her. Until I moved back to the East Coast, spontaneous calls were all but impossible. Our time zones and schedules were too out of sync.

Once she moved to Connecticut, I did visit several times a week, but much of my time there was spent watering her plants, tracking down missing clothing, and following up with the nurses on changes to her care. After that I would drive home through city traffic.

With most of my usual activities suspended by the pandemic, I had ample time to pour a cup of tea, pick up my embroidery, and cozy up to some unrushed, uninterrupted screen time with my mom. We talked, reminisced, and shared our day-to-day activities. Those virtual visits brought us closer and showed me that dementia had not taken her away. It only wore down the thorns and made room for an exquisite, late-blooming rose.

—Lorri Danzig—

I Was There

*Please remember the real me when
I cannot remember you.*
~Julie White

I stared at the photos, the memories just a void.
I could not relive birthdays, anniversaries,
  or Christmas mornings gone by.
I scrolled and scrolled, begging to find
  just one single photo of this life that was mine.
The memories were silent as the truth became clear.
These photos didn't resonate because I hadn't been there.
I clicked through each image but could not remember...
My mind grasped to feel just one tiny flicker.
I found toothless smiles and first days of school.
Classroom parties and days by the pool.
I scanned each one, but the truth hit me hard.
This was my life, yet not mine at all.
Nothing flickered. My mind was still blank.
The photos were endless, of a life that I lived
  but could never get back.
I clicked and I cried through first days
  of preschool, middle school and more.
My mind felt numb. Why didn't I know?
Shouldn't I have experienced these events once before?
I grieved for the days that felt so quickly gone.

Of milestones not recorded and baby albums undone.
Because life threw me a curveball, I could not have evaded.
I wept for the years that felt all but lost…
    once lived, but then again, actually not.
As I made one final click, on the screen came a photo.
I felt sick, and my soul felt depleted.
It was frozen in time, just like I remembered.
It told of a family of five by a bed.
It was mine, at the hospital, by which my family stood.
My presence was here, not in the photos I saw.
You see, it was here that I was fighting to live.
I stared at that photo of my five-year-old son,
    who was content and happy just to be with his mom.
It was at that moment, with my head bowed low,
    that my soul felt crushed, and I wanted to know.
I wept for the memories that were taken from me.
I cried long and hard… for all the things that were not to be.
The grief over memories I thought I had missed
    were replaced with the ones that did actually exist.
And yet for so long, I shoved them away
    because these were the scenes I had to forget.
I buried them deep because this can't be my story.
And yet here it was… unearthed to find me.
The scars have all faded but forever remain,
    a stark reminder of how quickly life changed.
As I stared at this photo, I felt my heart shift.
Maybe this pain was meant as a gift?
This photo begged me to find a new, beautiful story.
It told of a family standing together, remaining strong,
    with the odds against them.
It was helping with homework and stories of school
    while the machines quietly hummed by my hospital bed.
It was snuggling my littles whenever I could
    while carefully dodging IV wires and tubes.
It was watching them cry every time they heard

"Visiting hours are over. Please come again."
This moment in time had become our new normal.
It wasn't sunny park days or family trips to the zoo.
But there was one thing I know I believe pulled us through.
There was always plenty of love in that hospital room.
I remember the ache, and the days tore at my soul.
The tears to my doctors as I begged to go home.
As the months wore on, I came to believe
    that this was my life, and I was less of a mom.
I fought through the voices that told me this lie,
    but at the end of the day, this lie was all mine.
I retraced the years I thought I had lost.
It was then that I realized all these moments were mine.
I looked at that photo of my boy and I smiled.
It was true I had been there.
I was there this whole time.

— Ingar Lammers —

Chapter 2

Count Your Blessings

Worst Day Ever

Gratitude makes sense of our past, brings peace
for today, and creates a vision for tomorrow.
~Melody Beattie

It was the worst day ever. In fact, that's what we named it, all caps: WORST DAY EVER. The exact date was March 19, 2007, and I'll never forget it.

The day began as usual, with my husband, Alan, entering his office in our home to catch up on paperwork and participate in conference calls. He had worked his way up the corporate ladder and now managed multiple stores for a national restaurant chain. From my spot in the kitchen, I could hear him speaking on the phone to his boss. Suddenly, I overheard words that seemed unusual, some downright alarming. They were words like "turn in my laptop" and "severance pay."

When he exited his office moments later, my fears were confirmed. Alan's position had been eliminated. Downsizing, they said. Nothing personal; thanks for everything; you're no longer needed. I hugged my sweet husband as my heart sank, and my mind raced. What were we going to do? Would we lose our house if we couldn't afford to pay our mortgage?

"We'll be fine," he said.

"I know," I responded.

But, frankly, neither one of us was very convincing.

I wanted to crawl back in bed and pull the covers over my head, but I had to get to my own job. So, I quickly showered, dressed, and made my way to work. I was a few hours into my shift when I received a call from the surgeon's office. I had been noticing some strange lumps in my neck and underarms, and he'd been in the process of performing several tests to figure out the cause. The surgeon had removed one of the lumps from under my arm and was calling with the biopsy results.

"It's lymphoma. You have cancer," he stated, way too matter-of-factly. I distinctly remember my precise response: "What?" I must have misheard. It sounded like he said I had cancer, but that was completely ridiculous. I was a healthy, salad-eating, forty-two-year-old runner.

Cancer was out of the question. Wasn't it? The surgeon repeated those terrible words. It was true: Cancer was in my body. *My* body. He went on discussing future treatment plans and appointments, I think. I really wasn't listening anymore.

As I drove home, I thought about how wonderful things had been up until this day. Alan and I had enjoyed a happy life in a lovely suburban home in Orlando, Florida. We loved our jobs and the traveling and fancy dinners they afforded us. *It was all too good to last,* I thought. *Now it's time to pay back for all those amazing years.* I imagined hospital beds, chemo bags, my bald head, and worse. I prepared myself for a future of coping, or no future at all.

Alan scooped me into his arms when I arrived home, and I cried as he held me tight. "Someday in the future, we're going to write about today," he whispered in my ear, "and we'll call it Worst Day Ever."

We both got right to work. Alan began calling everyone he could think of with possible connections in the restaurant industry. He tirelessly applied and interviewed for dozens of positions. We were able to find a brilliant oncologist who immediately began to perform intensive scans and other tests to determine the stage and severity of my cancer. Time dragged on. Our anxiety was high, but we kept our heads up and always looked forward.

It eventually paid off.

Within several months, Alan was offered a new position at a thriving restaurant chain, with excellent pay and terrific benefits. My oncologist completed her tests, and the results were more than encouraging. She explained that my cancer was "indolent," a word completely foreign to me. "It's lazy," she replied, "not aggressive like other forms. This is manageable. You will most likely survive this." After I stopped crying, I gave her an enormous hug.

As the one-year anniversary of Worst Day Ever approached, I asked Alan how he'd like to commemorate it. I didn't really like remembering such an awful day, but I had another idea. "Let's celebrate it!" I suggested. "Let's take back control of March 19th, celebrate that we prevailed, and have a blast!" That's exactly what we did. We purchased tickets to Las Vegas that very afternoon and spent the day of March 19, 2008, reveling in our survival. Take that, Worst Day Ever.

In fact, Alan and I celebrate March 19th every year. In addition to Las Vegas, we've been to Savannah, Destin, and even Dublin, Ireland on the ten-year anniversary! Each year, we raise a glass and toast that awful day and all the days since, which we survived solely because of a bounty of blessings. And sure, there've been plenty of bad days mixed in, like when I finally did have to start chemo, and recently when Alan once again found himself without a position due to downsizing and COVID quarantines. Guess what? We prevailed. The only difference was that, this time, we absolutely knew we could. We survived March 19, 2007, didn't we?

And the greatest blessing of all? Worst Day Ever itself. It stripped away all the trivial stuff and shone a bright spotlight on all the important things, like faith, family, perseverance, love, and health. Alan and I were blessed with an abundance of these things. We'll never, ever take them for granted again. Worst Day Ever taught us how to cherish each one, on a much deeper, more profound level. Aren't we lucky?

— Joan Donnelly-Emery —

12

The Value in a Penny

One penny may seem to you a very insignificant thing,
but it is the small seed from which fortunes spring.
~Orison Swett Marden

I rummaged under couch pillows and ransacked my closet, picking through coat pockets and madly shaking all my old purses and wallets. I was looking for pennies, nickels, quarters — anything that would help me make it to the end of the week. At this point in my life, I no longer believed in luck, but I still hoped that God would have mercy on me and at least lighten my load. It sure was feeling heavy — almost unbearable.

A clueless girl in her twenties, I was in the midst of a separation, with an infant son and a five-year-old daughter. I was trying to give her some normalcy as her parents prepared for divorce.

Life had flipped on us. One year, I was having baby showers and taking vacations in the mountains of Tennessee; the next, I was scrounging around my small, two-bedroom apartment collecting loose change to buy food and gas. At the snap of a finger, I found myself dumped from middle-class smack dab into the bottom bracket of poverty, and it was humbling.

I'll never forget the jubilation of finding one penny during my hunt, then two, then fifteen, and then twenty-four, twenty-five, twenty-six. Every time I found one, it was as if I had won the lottery. Looking back now, I see that it was somewhat ironic because I had scoffed at pennies at one point in my life. They had so little value to me. If it wasn't silver coins or crisp dollars, I was uninterested in collecting or keeping them. I would casually throw them in those red penny trays that read, "Give a penny or take a penny."

My mantra was, "Here. You can have them all." On the off chance that there was no penny tray and I had to keep them, they would remain forever in the change portion of my wallet, and I shuffled them around in search of nickels, dimes, and quarters to pay cashiers.

I sat in my bedroom that night and sorted all the change from my hour-long quest. I took paper coin rolls and got to work shoving my thumb in one end and stuffing pennies in the other end. My daughter wanted to help. Her naive eyes saw it as something fun to do while sitting in the middle of the floor with Mama.

If she only knew how tough times really were. It made me wonder if my daddy ever felt the same when I used to help him make those rolls of pennies back when I was little.

I smiled and made jokes with her while we packed our pennies. Her brother joyfully bounced up and down in his bouncer. They had no idea how many nights I would cry with my face buried in the pillows, wondering how I would keep a roof over their heads, lights on in the house, and food on the table.

I remember those days like they were yesterday.

I remember the shame I felt walking into the neighborhood convenience store to pay for my gas in rolls of coins, feeling as if people holding debit cards and dollars were judging me. I remember the embarrassment of having to pay for seven dollars' worth of groceries in change; the impatient shoppers behind me in line had no idea I was deathly afraid that the total and tax would be one cent over, and I would have to suffer the humiliation of putting something back.

I remember those days, but I don't remember them with sadness. I remember them intentionally because I promised myself and God that if I were ever to escape the pains of poverty that I would never forget the value of a penny.

I've kept that promise, too.

My daughter and I were walking just the other day, and I found two pennies lying useless and unloved in a parking lot. From the dirt and scuff marks on them, I could tell that they had been trampled a hundred times before I rescued them. I stuffed them in my tennis shoes because my workout pants didn't have pockets. As I slid them in the corners of my shoe, I whispered, "Thank you for the increase." That's been my ritual whenever I find coins on sidewalks and in parking lots since I made my promise.

I never thought I'd see the day I'd be so grateful to find pennies, but those scavenger hunts in my apartment taught me two things I will never forget: Tough times mold resilience, and one can always find immense value in little things if we are brave enough, bold enough, and humble enough to look.

—Lexcee Reel—

13

Fire on the Mountain

Hope is important because it can make the present moment
less difficult to bear. If we believe that tomorrow
will be better, we can bear a hardship today.
~Thich Nhat Hanh

The black smoke billowed like storm clouds and the ash fell gently around me at our home in Los Alamos, New Mexico. Although it was only 2:00 P.M., the streetlight in front of our house flickered on and off. The firefighters had been battling the Cerro Grande wildfire for nearly a week when our mountain community was told to evacuate immediately.

This would be no small feat. Approximately 18,000 of us had to get off the plateau that May afternoon. There were only three roads out, and one was already cut off.

I was home alone at the time of the evacuation, so it was up to me to save my family's most valued possessions. I scrambled to pack the car, mindful, even in my panic, of the paradox. I abandoned my computer (too big) and seven years of tax paperwork (who cares?) to make room for family photos, a zither that had belonged to my husband's Polish grandmother, and my first-ever book contract with Random House, which had just arrived in the mail. Then I made a beeline for our teenage son's room.

Jordan was away at school—a cadet at New Mexico Military

Institute. I rescued his treasured collection of *Star Wars* cards and the shadow box hanging on the wall near his bed that contained his grandfather's Bronze Star and other World War II medals. I cast a regretful glance at his pinewood derby trophies and his Matchbox cars. These would have to be left behind.

Our daughter Bethany was serving in the Army at the time, stationed at Fort Gordon in Georgia. What would she want me to save? I made a frantic search for her beloved Lamb Chop doll and carefully removed the framed watercolor painting for which she'd won a blue ribbon at the county fair when she was in high school.

When I'd crammed everything I could into the car, I called my out-of-town husband to assure him that I was leaving, and I was all right.

Glancing again at the pillars of billowing black smoke, I wondered what would become of the house finches nesting on the outside lip of our kitchen exhaust fan. And what about the chipmunk we'd dubbed Chubbs, who lived in a hole underneath the garden shed? I quickly filled all the birdbaths with water. I emptied the refrigerator of fruits and vegetables, tossing them in a pile in the back yard, which had already become a sanctuary for soot-covered robins and squawking, frightened Steller's jays. Perhaps the deer and raccoons would take advantage of the food as they fled to safety.

Then I coaxed our aging Scottie into the front seat of the car. Although deaf and nearly blind, Wimsey had been nervously sensing the imminent danger for days and was eager to leave.

I paused in the driveway to take one last long look at the modest house we've called home for so many years. It wasn't fancy, but it was ours. I swallowed hard and glanced at my newly planted pansies, their sad faces drooping in the parched breeze. *Life is more than possessions,* I reminded myself.

Then I joined the long line of evacuees slowly snaking our way down the steep Main Hill Road. I knew we would survive the destruction of our home if it came to that. But later, reunited with my husband in a motel in Albuquerque, I recognized the incinerated house of a neighbor on the evening news and burst into tears. Never before had I felt so vulnerable, so miserable. I kept repeating a Bible verse from

Joshua 1:9: "Be strong and courageous... for the Lord your God is with you wherever you go."

The next morning, longing for coffee and comfort, Bill and I staggered wearily into a donut shop. We ran into other Los Alamos evacuees there. "My place is gone," one man wept. "Everything. We lived in that house for nearly fifty years." Bill squeezed my hand. Was our house gone, too? The fire on the mountain was still blazing out of control. Were we homeless? How would we be able to start up our home business again? What would we do? Where would we go?

A phone call from our son restored my perspective. Having completed his final exams for the semester, Jordan was anxious to leave school. "I've been watching the fire news on television," he told us. "Can you and Dad come get me? I want to come home. Sunday is Mother's Day," he reminded me.

"Honey, we can't go home," I replied with a ragged sigh. "We don't know if we even have a home."

"Is Wimsey with you?" Jordan asked. I assured him that the dog was with us — safe and sound.

"Then the three of you come get me," he said. "And when you get here, we'll all be together. When we're together, that's home."

For a moment, I was speechless. I knew in that moment, no matter what happened, no matter what the fire consumed, I was blessed.

More than a week later, we were allowed to return to our home. To our relief, our house was intact, having suffered nothing more than minor smoke damage. However, more than 400 families — many of them our friends and neighbors — lost all they owned in the Cerro Grande blaze of 2000. Homes where we'd taken our children tricking-or-treating and Christmas caroling were now smoldering black piles of debris. The forest fire had been so intense in some areas that even the kitchen appliances had burned to ash.

The blackened slopes surrounding the plateau looked like gigantic charcoal briquettes. How could anything wild ever survive there again? But even as we donned our rubber gloves to tackle the task of sponging everything clean and hosing off the ash that covered the outside of the house, we heard the faint cheeping of the finches in the exhaust fan. A downy woodpecker showed up at one of the bird feeders, and Chubbs darted across the patio to drink from the birdbath.

Later that evening, a doe and her yearling showed up on the edge of our property. My husband pointed, whispering, "Hush." I knew the deer would eat all the tender new growth on our apple trees, but I didn't care. They'd survived. We'd survived, too. With a prayer of thanksgiving, we realized all too well that there really is no place like home.

— Shirley Redmond —

14

Be Like Dad

Be the reason someone smiles. Be the reason someone
feels loved and believes in the goodness in people.
~Roy T. Bennett, The Light in the Heart

I was in my home office on a cold and dreary Sunday in May 2020 when I glanced out the window and saw my dad's car parked in our driveway. He was walking from our front door to his car, about to drive away. Why would he drive all the way to my house, only to turn around and leave? Had the doorbell stopped working? Was something wrong?

I raced downstairs, flung open the door and yelled out "Dad!" just before he made it out of the driveway. He looked up, startled, and stopped the car.

"What are you doing?" I exclaimed.

My dad lives forty-five minutes away, and I hadn't seen him in person since COVID-19 had been declared a pandemic two months earlier. We were all following the health-department guidelines to self-isolate and not leave the house unless absolutely necessary, so it was strange that he would just show up.

My dad smiled sheepishly and pointed beside the door, where I could see what looked like a plant wrapped up in wrapping paper.

"Open it," he said.

I opened it to find a bright, cheery yellow begonia plant. It occurred to me that it was Mother's Day, and I had seen many women posting pictures on social media of the lovely flowers they had received from their kids and spouses.

"But… but I'm not a mother," I said, bewildered.

My dad smiled. "Well, there are some special people out there who aren't mothers, and I think they should get flowers, too." With that, he winked and drove off.

Later that day, I called to thank him and let him know how touched I was that he had driven an hour and a half round trip just to leave begonias on my doorstep.

"I'm sad that I couldn't hug you," I said.

"Me, too," he agreed.

We got to talking about the pandemic and how difficult it was to go so long without hugs or visits with family. That's when he let me in on his little secret. It turns out I wasn't the only recipient of a random act of kindness from him. He had decided, as a way of coping with the social isolation, that he would turn his attention away from the loneliness he was feeling and instead challenge himself to do one act of kindness per day. It made him so happy to see the smiles on people's faces or, if it was an anonymous act, just to know that he had brightened someone's day.

Intrigued, I pressed him for more information. "What else have you done?" I asked. It took some coaxing, as my dad is not one to brag, but finally he told me more.

It had started a couple of weeks before when a friend of his was having a rough day and called him to talk about it. He knew she loved ice cream, so after they hung up, he went straight to the grocery store, bought a huge tub of ice cream, drove to her house (another forty-five-minute drive for him) and left it on her doorstep. That time, he called from the driveway to tell her to look outside because he didn't want the ice cream to melt before she found it.

"Ange," he said, "she just beamed when she saw it. I don't think leaving her a million dollars would have made her happier."

On another occasion, a customer at the hardware store where he worked was disappointed to learn that a part he needed was backordered for several months. Coincidentally, it was a part that my father had also ordered a while back. The next day, my dad's part arrived.

Without hesitation, he looked up the customer's address, drove to his house and gave the man his own part so that he wouldn't have to wait.

After listening to story after story like this, I was inspired. My dad was making a difference in people's lives, and it was making him so happy. It made me want to start performing acts of kindness, too. After I got off the phone with him, I immediately went online and ordered some supplies to make up gift bags to use for my own acts of kindness. Over the next several months, I anonymously dropped off gift bags on people's porches when I knew someone was struggling, had gone out of their way to help others, or just because I liked them and wanted to brighten their day.

Sometimes, if they happened to be connected with me through social media, I would see a post about how this surprise had made their day. My dad was right: It felt amazing.

Ten months into the pandemic, in January 2021, Dad and I were texting back and forth about the crazy year that was 2020. I asked him if there were any insights or lessons that he got from 2020 that he would take with him into 2021. Here's what he texted back.

"The main insight from 2020 for me is this: You don't have to do anything earth-shattering to make a difference. You don't have to speak to a crowd of hundreds or thousands. Each and every day, I have the privilege of meeting people. Some days, a lot of people. I already knew about the importance of being present in the moment, but 2020 caused me to reflect on how fleeting and fragile life is. So, I try to be present with each person I am spending time with, even if it's a brief encounter. I want them to feel that there is nothing more important to me than being there with them in that moment. I watched the movie about Mr. Rogers' life, and I know that's what Mr. Rogers did. My goal is to be more like Mr. Rogers."

Funny, my goal is similar. I also want to be more like a kind man who goes out of his way to make people feel special.

I want to be more like my dad.

— Angela Rolleman —

15

Bald Is Beautiful

I am not this hair, I am not this skin,
I am the soul that lives within.
~Rumi

I am bald. Sure, it is one thing to say it, proclaim the reality for all the world to hear, but it is yet another to have family and friends sit across the table from me and pretend that I am as I always was. Unchanged.

The lack of hair makes it abundantly clear that I am different, either sick or having joined the cast of *Star Trek*. I had somehow forgotten how hair enhances a person's appearance, especially if that person is a woman. Yeah, I look weird. Even my grown kids were a bit shocked when I appeared in the kitchen during a recent visit without a head covering. I got a sympathetic look and a hug. I understand.

To be perfectly honest, I had held onto the tufts of hair that chemo hadn't claimed. I was adamant that some hair was better than none. I now understand why balding men resort to comb-overs. I tried that. I also used hair thickeners and spiking gel. But, after a while, as I lost more and more, I only looked ridiculous and a little scary. I avoided mirrors. Yes, it was time to shave it all off.

So, last week on my birthday, my buddy, who always knows what I need, showed up with cake and beer and a pair of shears. We laughed throughout the afternoon as we alternated sips of brew with bites of chocolate ganache. And then it was time. I sat on a chair outside as the trimmer buzzed to life. She made jokes to distract me but made quick work of the remaining fuzz. The hair floated through the gentle breeze as I quietly made a wish that the birds would find it and use it to pad a nest. It was a lovely thought.

Within moments, the deed was done. I expected that I would be emotional, crying about this, my final concession to the disease that has altered my life and my appearance. But instead, I felt an overwhelming sense of relief. It felt good to have a smooth scalp, cooler, cleaner. And when I looked at myself in the mirror, I laughed. My dear friend, who always has her camera at the ready, snapped my picture. But it wasn't until she sent it along, and I had a chance to study the image, that I saw it on my face — the look of pure joy over being alive to celebrate another day. It is hard to fake happiness. And so, perhaps appropriately, appreciating the present is the best gift I got for my birthday. Truly.

I have faith that I will enjoy many tomorrows, that ultimately my hair will grow back. In the meantime, I have ordered another wig and two soft caps. Happy birthday to me.

— Paula W. Millet —

16

Fortitude & Gratitude

Start each day with a positive
thought and a grateful heart.
~Roy T. Bennett, The Light in the Heart

The bitter chill of a fierce winter greets me as I exit onto 14th Street SW and the Washington Monument appears in the distance. I start my trek back to the Smithsonian Metro and take a moment to look at how empty the capital is, so eerily calm. Once upon a time there were food trucks aplenty lining the National Mall and football games being played on the lawn, as well as people of all different faiths and races watching the world go by and taking in this majestic landscape.

Ten minutes later, I arrive at Union Station, which is more desolate than ever. The public-address system tells me what track my commuter rail is on, but I fear it is being played for an audience of one. I silently begin to weep, and then my tears start to break down my emotional dam. I am at a funeral, and the eulogy I am hearing is for the loss of life as it used to be. This takes place every day. To be quite honest, I don't know if I will see a rebirth of it.

As of this writing, it has been almost one year since the pandemic began. For me, everything changed on March 8, 2020. I was in my office at 2:00 P.M. when one of my acting supervisors announced that we were to immediately vacate the building and await further instructions. For two hours, I sat on a bench on Constitution Avenue, my heart racing, while they figured out what we were to do.

I started hearing terms such as "indefinite telework" and "contingency plans." I didn't have any real experience working from home. The one day I did, my cat enjoyed my laptop so much that I had to forcefully remove him, and a few keys came off. Needless to say, he wasn't happy, and neither was my boss.

I told my chief I'd do whatever he needed me to do to keep our office going, including going into work. I held out hope that this would last a few weeks, and it would be just a blip on the radar. This, of course, is when everything changed. Conventions got canceled. Professional sports soon followed. I started to get really frightened. I watched the news like a sponge trying to learn every detail. The number of infections kept increasing: 25,000 dead. We soon passed 100,000. It was like watching a disaster movie.

As a person with Asperger's, this pandemic has wreaked havoc on me because my life is all about routines, sometimes to the extreme. I have always been a social person, even though I stutter. Now, I wasn't allowed to socialize. I had no problem wearing a mask every time I went out. It just became part of my day.

But I couldn't stand being deprived of handshakes and hugs. My depression and hopelessness started to crush me. As a suicide-attempt survivor, I know when something is wrong and I need to reach out for help. I'll be on medications and in treatment for the rest of my life. However, there are just some things that can't be controlled. The late reggae singer Bob Marley said, "You never know how strong you are until being strong is the only choice you have." How true that is, and it was especially meant for times like these.

In many ways, coronavirus has forced me to count my blessings. For starters, I have a job. I work in a city that means a great deal to me personally, where I feel safe and no one judges me because of my disabilities. My friends and allies in the stuttering community have continually helped me get through several rough patches I have had.

Perhaps the most important thing of all is that I've reconnected with my family. We haven't always had an easy relationship, and at times we have been estranged. However, sometimes it takes something tragic to forge new bonds.

Fortitude and gratitude… Never in my wildest dreams could I have imagined that a virus would make me thankful, but it has made me see life with a new perspective.

—Steven M. Kaufman—

That Silver Linings Playbook

You're not obligated to win. You're obligated to keep
trying to do the best you can every day.
~Marian Wright Edelman

A s a busy journalist and a married mom of two young, rambunctious kiddos, I always lived on the go. It felt like a treadmill that never completely stopped, only slowing down occasionally. I never pictured myself being holed up indefinitely in my home with my entire immediate family in order to dodge a deadly virus. Sounds like a Will Smith movie made real, right?

One minute I was working on my podcast, shuttling my kids to and from school every day and planning the big PTA fundraiser, and the next, the four people I live with were all in my home with me. All. Day. It was weird and jarring. The never-ending family slumber party was fun that first weekend, but then Monday rolled around. That's when I thought, *Wait a minute. I have work to do. How am I supposed to get that done, homeschool, and manage my regular household duties, all while disinfecting everything like a madwoman?*

I considered hiding out in our home office; yes, the one that, ironically, I had pushed myself to set up the year before despite any indication whatsoever that it would be used. I installed a funky glass desk, fluffy rug and even funkier drapes — the works. Later, the laser printer, file cabinets and bookshelves sealed the deal on my pristine yet rarely used — until now — office.

Unfortunately, my husband beat me to it. That first week, he'd close the French doors and disappear into a vortex of Zoom meetings and conference calls. But little did I know that this office space would become a little "Santa's workshop" of sorts, a space where my wifely fantasies would finally come true. In the evenings, during what was once his normal commute time and on his lunch breaks, he started tinkering with stuff.

Each day, I encountered something different: twelve framed art pieces and ledges displaying my journalism awards were finally hung; the home-office desktop was decluttered; patio accessories were ordered; a security system complete with cameras and lighting was installed. He even set up the Facebook Portal and Alexa thingies that had been still in their boxes for an embarrassingly long time. Was this the same dude I had to beg for six weeks to hang a single curtain rod in said office?

Let's just say it's amazing what one can accomplish with the absence of any live sports being broadcast. Now, work begins when you flip open your laptop; meetings become detailed e-mails; dressing up is cut out altogether; and, for the win, a 66-mile, round-trip daily commute to the office vanishes. Poof! Bosses of America, are you listening? Working remotely can work. This was like being in the Twilight Zone, only it's real.

It was like one of those science-fiction flicks where someone knocks you unconscious, takes over your body and makes you do things you don't remember. Perhaps this meme summed it up best: "The virus has done what no woman was able to do: cancel all sports, shut down all bars and keep men at home."

Okay, all joking aside. As a Black woman and New Orleans native, with disproportionate death rates in our community, I take this very seriously. I know that I was privileged to be able to work from home when so many others were forced to work on the frontlines whether they wanted to or not. I did struggle with insomnia and anxiety, worrying about the deep suffering my fellow Americans and those around the world were and are enduring.

During this time of uncertainty, I leaned on the lessons I learned during my family's heartbreaking ordeal in the aftermath of Hurricane Katrina fifteen years ago. In times like these, we must commit to searching for the silver lining; it's the only way to stay sane and maintain a sense of optimism, hope and peace in a world that way too often feels cold, cruel and blatantly unfair.

We pulled out that silver linings playbook for the pandemic. My family made it a point to sit down to dinner together every night. We also found fun things to do together, excursions and activities that got us out of the house safely. There was that delightful day trip one Saturday when we checked out, exclusively from the car of course, the gorgeous mountain views that we've often taken for granted. There were family movie nights, long neighborhood walks, an indoor Easter egg hunt, and even a fun night of impromptu family yoga. Special moments with friends included Zoom game nights, hours-long catch-up phone calls and consistent texts and e-mails, just checking on each other.

The pandemic reminded us again that life is fragile and fleeting, but it also reinforced that we're only as strong as the relationships that we've built up and nurtured before the inevitable storms of life roll in. Those relationships, in all of their beautiful complexity, are the best silver lining that life has to offer.

— Chandra Thomas Whitfield —

It Started with a Dollar

Thankfulness is the beginning of gratitude. Gratitude is the completion of thankfulness. Thankfulness may consist merely of words. Gratitude is shown in acts.
~Henri Frederic Amiel

"Hi, Donna. I'm Joe, the new regional director for Europe, and I am starting this year's scholarship fund drive a little earlier than usual. I'm traveling around the region, visiting all our European offices and getting to know the faculty and staff, so I thought I would solicit donations at the same time. I'm looking forward to working with you and hope you will contribute to the university scholarship fund. It only takes one dollar to get started."

I stood there, stunned. I had just begun my new job and life in Aviano, Italy, and I was really short of funds after my recent divorce. I couldn't wait until my first paycheck hit my empty bank account. But I wanted to please the regional boss who had just walked into our campus office. I did not even have one dollar bill, but I managed to find some loose change at the bottom of my purse.

Perhaps noticing my embarrassment, my new boss didn't miss a beat. "It can all be done through payroll deductions," he clarified. Then he went on to explain how I could commit to having one dollar per paycheck deducted for bursaries and scholarships for university students in need.

It was a good cause, so I signed up, grateful that I could still afford to do a little for others. It made me feel good to help, better than I had felt in ages. I had been the lucky recipient of grants, bursaries and scholarships during my own university years and had always vowed to pay it forward. Now, I had the perfect opportunity to do just that.

I couldn't imagine that giving a dollar per pay period would even cover the basic cost of the paperwork it generated. However, it was an affordable amount that allowed me to give at a time when I was penniless, and I mentally resolved to increase the scholarship payment as soon as I could.

Time passed, and my situation improved, so I was able to give more to the university bursary funds and join other charitable organizations. I marveled how each time I became more involved in helping others, my feelings of self-esteem and contentment increased. The more I gave to others, the more I was satisfied and noted my own blessings.

Giving to others became my good-luck charm. I noticed that every time I gave a little extra, I got back more. Giving made me happy and going around with a positive attitude seemed to make even more fantastic things happen. It was an endless happiness cycle. Give a little, get more back, count all the blessings.

It wasn't long before another happy occurrence came along in my life: the man I would later marry. We were able to buy a small house in Italy, all while increasing our commitments to help others through charities. All my dreams were coming true.

We met many wonderful people through our charitable giving. They were as dedicated to giving as we were, and we formed a community of benevolent donors in our area, committed to making life better for students and others. Many of these students were going to change the world.

Today, thirty years later, we are more devoted than ever to university endowments and other philanthropic causes. Since we have no children of our own, we have earmarked all our earthly possessions to charity.

It started with a dollar but has multiplied into something much greater than that. Helping others through their tough times will definitely get you through your own.

—Donna L. Roberts—

19

How's It Going? What's New?

*The strongest force in the universe is a human being
living consistently with his identity.*
~Tony Robbins

Today, I talked to one of my favorite people on planet Earth: my sister, Katie.

For the past several months, I've been avoiding phone calls, Zoom meetings and FaceTime. But, today, I talked to Katie. And she asked me, "What's new? How's everything going?"

I gave her some highlights: this project or that goal or this challenge or that excitement.

I wonder if we will ever give real answers to questions from the people who love us most. I'm making a more conscious effort to give real answers. Otherwise, what's the point of communicating?

So, here's how I am doing. Here is what's new.

I am feeling the invigorating sensation of nine-degree ocean water on my face as I swim in the winter in Uruguay.

I am building my own compost bin with worms, dirt, food scraps and other things. I have no idea how to do it, but I want to learn. I want to have my hands in the dirt as much as I have them on a screen.

I am embracing "I don't know" as a complete sentence. I am embracing "No" as a complete sentence.

I am buying food from a local farmer named Diego who loves the fruits of his labor, not a supermarket chain owned by an American hedge fund that couldn't care less.

I am moving my body several times a day and getting strong. Life is so much better when you're strong.

I am making a conscious effort to eat the rainbow.

I am missing my friends and family. I'm grateful to have friends and family to miss.

I am trusting that this is exactly where I need to be. I try and remind myself of that every day.

I am inspired and impressed with Uruguay — its people, nature and charm. More so every day.

I am connecting deeply with a special human, and a furry being, too.

I am looking up to the sky's clarity when the world at my feet feels foggy.

I've replaced purchasing single-use plastic with refilling glass jars, valuing the sanctity of Earth more than my own convenience.

I've been gone for five months now. Some days, time feels like an illusion. Other days, it feels real.

I'm excited. I'm frustrated. I'm at peace. I'm irritable. I'm focused. I'm lost. I'm connecting with the land. I'm masking isolation with social media "connecting." I'm meditating and empowering my mind. I'm falling victim to emotional shortcomings.

But, every day, I am trying to fall in love.

Not with what I wrote above.

But with the person who wrote it.

And, for the first time in a long time,

That feels like enough.

That's how I am doing.

That's what's new.

— Brian Rashid —

20

Puzzled

This struggle is real. The juggle is real.
That's why everyone should hire working mothers.
They are put in crazy situations all the time
and are forced to problem-solve.
~Sara Blakely, founder of Spanx

"Want to work a puzzle, Mommy?" I looked down at two-year-old Maeve, who was expecting a yes, and wished I could drop to my knees and play.

"After Zoom math for Clay," I said. "Okay?"

She frowned. Puzzles had become our thing during the pandemic. I swooned the first time she opted for solving a 24-piece jigsaw over watching *Wild Kratts* with her siblings, Clay and Ruby.

But when remote second grade and kindergarten started in the fall, a part of me wished Maeve loved watching the tube. Due to the coronavirus, she wasn't in preschool, and she wasn't interested in sitting in front of a screen.

I started thinking of our situation — with two children in remote school and one in diapers — as a new puzzle I could solve. There had to be a way to make all the pieces fit.

On the first day, the campus-selected online platform froze. All day, we refreshed, waited, and signed into ten different Zoom sessions.

Ruby, a kindergartner, spun her swiveling chair around and around, knocking over her iPad, which pulled her headphones off and slung them to the floor. When I steadied her chair and replaced her head-phones, giving my nod of apology to her teacher, I saw my daughter's face reflected on the screen below me: fish lips.

Clay, a second grader and perfectionist, pouted. On a mandatory survey asking about his favorite part of the day, he wrote, "Nuthing." I almost made him start over but reconsidered. He was being honest.

"'Nothing' is spelled with an 'o,'" I said.

"I don't like second grade," he said, looking at me through teary eyes.

Mid-week, I bought a bulk pack of Nutella sticks and replaced one veggie snack with a sugary one. They were elated. I played Taylor Swift on my phone after a morning walk.

"Dance party?" I asked with more excitement in my voice than I felt. The girls jumped right in. Clay wasn't up for dancing, but he laughed with his sisters and at me. Dancing and laughing. Those puzzle pieces fit.

Of course, mid-day levity didn't fix everything. Maeve was all about a hairbrush microphone, but she still wanted my full attention. The prior year, when she was in preschool, she'd been so much more independent. On her last day, she bounced into the building holding hands with Ruby. Now, months into the pandemic, she bawled if I passed her off to my husband at bath time.

During the first weeks of school, I wanted to be physically accessible to my big kids. Okay, I also wanted to eavesdrop. I was curious about what they were learning and how they'd behave in video conferences. So, Maeve and I stationed ourselves in the makeshift classroom with Ruby and Clay. But I struggled to keep her quiet. I offered markers and paper, stickers, and even a tablet with some toddler-appropriate apps installed. Then I put a finger across my lips to remind her to use a whisper voice.

She was not amused. She screamed. She threw glue sticks and knocked over a decorative bowl of silver bells she used to love sorting. She pushed over Ruby's tablet during a Zoom class. Finally, she crawled under the desk and refused to come out. This part of the puzzle had me stumped.

"I don't know how we're going to do this all year," I said to my husband Paul after the fourth day.

"Give it time," Paul said. "Eventually, Clay and Ruby will be able to do more independently."

Maybe, I thought, filling water bottles for the next morning, *but Maeve will still be throwing loud, on-screen fits when I have to drag her away from the action.*

I realized I had an easier go of the pandemic than many parents who worked regular business hours. (I could get my freelancing done before the kids woke and after bedtime.) But I still wondered how my kids could thrive in the absence of basics like social connections and one-on-one attention. Would anyone learn? Would my kids come out on the other side of the pandemic even liking school? Would I give short shrift to Maeve?

I spent a weekend re-preparing our remote classroom in a spare room. I ordered a pocket calendar. I moved a white board upstairs, wrote schedules in bold colors, and even added little clouds around the times for scheduled Zoom classes.

Then, we got a note from the school over the weekend advising parents to leave the room once kids were logged on.

It seemed so obvious the moment I read it: Teachers didn't want parents "helping" keep kids on task during remote school any more than they wanted or needed that kind of assistance in the classroom. If Ruby flailed in her chair, her teacher would ask her to sit up. And if she didn't listen, then her teacher and I could plan a solution together.

With the refreshed space set up in our home and the new guidance from teachers, I felt our puzzle had at least its edge pieces in place.

Within a month or so, Clay and Ruby began to settle into their routine. Clay checked Zooms off the white board, and Ruby learned to navigate parts of her Bitmoji classroom. They still needed heavy support between Zoom calls to find assignments and, in some cases, to read directions. But I spent a couple of mornings downstairs with Maeve, lingering over breakfast because we could.

"Should we work the taxicab puzzle or the jungle puzzle today?" I asked her on a Friday morning that seemed to be humming, my coffee resting on the counter and the older kids quietly schooling upstairs. I watched Maeve study both boxes, deep in thought.

For a moment, the pieces of our bigger puzzle seemed to be clicking into place. Maybe the relative order wouldn't last, I realized, but maybe it would. If the pandemic taught me one thing, it's that the best we could do was maximize and celebrate what works, and just get through the pieces that don't.

Maeve probably wouldn't be a three-year-old who could write her name. But my goals for 2020 had changed for all my kids: safety, connection and knowing they were loved. And, on a good day, mastering a new skill or two.

"Jungle," Maeve said. "Can we bring it upstairs?"

"We can, but we have to be quiet," I told her. She put her finger across her lips. She still preferred being where the action was, even if she wasn't exactly in it. We spread the puzzle pieces on the floor right outside the classroom door. *At least she's not screaming under the desk,* I thought. Those days, I was learning to measure progress in baby steps.

— Nikki Campo —

Find Your Inner Strength

21

Becoming a Butterfly

We delight in the beauty of the butterfly,
but rarely admit the changes it has gone
through to achieve that beauty.
~Maya Angelou

The Butterfly Egg: *The egg phase typically lasts three to seven days but can vary among the species of butterflies. Some may undergo diapause, a period of suspended development, during the winter, which can extend this phase.*

I was fifteen years old and pregnant in the summer of 1998. I told my mom and was sure my announcement would cause all hell to break loose. However, "I'm not mad at you, just disappointed," she said. So, that was not as bad as expected but I eventually had to tell my dad, who lived in another state since my parents' divorce.

Unlike my mother, he announced he was "PISSED." That was painful to hear because I never wanted to disappoint him. The distance between us offered mild relief from the sting of his response.

Fortunately, my pregnancy went smoothly. My days were the same: attend high school; return home. However, on the night of April 13, 1999, my little one decided he was ready to make his debut. Just as quickly as my water broke, so did my life break in new, unexpected ways I could have never imagined.

The Butterfly Caterpillar: When the butterfly egg hatches, a tiny caterpillar appears. Its first meal is the eggshell from which it hatched. It will spend this phase constantly eating to increase its body mass before moving onto the next phase of the life cycle. It will molt multiple times as it outgrows its exoskeleton.

I was sixteen and the mother of a beautiful baby boy whom I was determined to offer more than I ever received. I was responsible for keeping up with schoolwork, taking care of an infant, and working part-time to pay our expenses. My mom required us to pay rent. The father of my son worked, but things between us were starting to feel "off."

After a few months my mom was fed up with the father of my son. On a regular basis, she said hurtful things to me, like, "He's going to cheat on you like your dad cheated on me," or, "You're going to end up just like me." My mom always blamed her children for why she never finished high school. She had my sister at eighteen, and me when she was nineteen. She worked two, sometimes three, jobs at once to provide for us after she and my dad divorced.

One day, I became so affected by her hurtful words that we ended up getting into a physical fight. This happened as I held my son. That was it. I left, never to return. That was my first round of molting an exoskeleton that no longer fit.

For a short time, I moved into an apartment with my son and his father. It was in a high crime, drug-ridden area. It was scary, but it was also home. Soon after, he was arrested for selling drugs. The landlord changed the locks and all our belongings were trapped until he was out of jail. Our next move was into his parents' home after they each left to be with new lovers.

After his grandmother, who owned the home, angrily discovered we were living there, I could feel my next molting phase coming on.

Meanwhile, my world was about to collapse. First, my son's father confessed he was not ready to be a father. Next, he admitted to cheating on me throughout our entire relationship. On cue, the symphony of my mother's words began to play. His grandmother joined in by turning off the water and electricity. We were homeless. Time to molt again.

The Butterfly Chrysalis: The caterpillar is ready to pupate or form a chrysalis, also known as a cocoon. The caterpillar has spun itself in silk and will likely hang upside down from its silk pad. This phase can last one to two weeks but some pupa may diapause beginning in the fall throughout winter until spring when it emerges as a butterfly.

I was alone, with a one-year-old and nowhere to go. I refused to go back to my mom and hear, "I told you so." Thankfully, I was involved with the teen parenting program at my high school and was able to confide in a teacher. In that moment, I knew God was looking out for us.

The program set me up with a non-profit organization that provided transitional housing and supportive services to women with children experiencing homelessness. After an interview that felt like a friendly interrogation, we were accepted into the program! We had a home of our own and a new support system. However, the hard work was only beginning. I was in my last year of high school and had a class to retake in addition to my regular workload. I also worked and had the distraction of my son's father trying to get back into our lives. It was time to put my head down and work harder than I ever did before to change our lives for the better.

The Butterfly: Did you know when the butterfly emerges from its chrysalis, its wings are crumpled? It then hangs with its wings down, starts pumping them to get the fluid from their body to straighten the wings out. It then must wait several hours for the wings to harden and dry before it can fly away.

My wings were crumpled, but with my newfound support and the belief that I could succeed, I was able to pump my wings and graduate from high school on time.

I was accepted to three different colleges! I met the love of my life and enrolled in a college close to home. Twenty years later, I am happily married with four children, two degrees, an amazing career, and all is well with my soul.

—Lakeyshia N. Crummel—

22

Already Enough

It is never too late to be what you might have been.
~George Eliot

I spent my Friday working as I do every day. I volunteered for more and more projects so I wouldn't have time to think about the fact that results would be posted at 6:00 P.M. Then I would know whether they found me worthy of a California license or not. At 4:00 P.M., I closed my laptop and tried hard to concentrate and meditate. When that proved futile, I leashed my dog and walked out of the house. I needed air.

I walked alongside a farm field nearby, trying to breathe and contain my anxiety. I focused on the beauty of California's blue skies. I thought of all the reasons why it would be a tragedy not to pass the test. I'd prove to myself I was a failure. I'd show myself I didn't have what it takes, and it was a waste of time, energy and money to embark on this project.

Why did I decide to take this stupid test anyway? I needed this to go well. I had to do it right. I had to be on the passing list, or I was a loser.

Then I thought of myself almost two decades ago, fresh out of law school in Argentina and ready to take over the world. If I wasn't afraid then, why now? I thought of all the obstacles I had tackled since I moved to the United States. Language barriers, prejudice and racism were among the top ones. Still, I built a family with a partner who thinks I am about the most perfect creature walking the face of the planet and even survived — against all the odds — an accident that resulted in a spine fusion that forever reduced my mobility and took years of my life in rehabilitation. So what was I so worried about?

I had dared to try, and that is the real triumph. I opened those books after having been a lawyer for about twenty years. I dared to try after working hard to master a language I was not brought up speaking. The test came after studying so hard that, once it was over, I slept for sixteen hours straight. I studied while my three children slept or were in school. I still cooked dinner every night and went back to the books afterward. I put up with a pandemic that resulted in bar-exam delays, change-of-exam formats, change of the scoring system, and a million glitchy test tries that left exam takers confused and scared.

So, while wrestling with what failing would mean, I realized that I was so far from being a failure. If I passed this test, I wouldn't be *better*. I would be the same me. A new door was going to open, but the person walking through it would be the same determined woman. "I *am* enough," I said out loud and walked the dog back home.

By 6:00 P.M., there was pizza on the table, and the kids were arguing about what movie they'd watch. I went upstairs to check my computer for news. When I saw "Pass" in my applicant status, I let out happy screams that made my children and husband run upstairs. All of a sudden, we were a pile of humans on the bed, and I was a crying mess. My five-year-old was slightly scared by the commotion as my fourteen-year-old tried to explain to him what was going on. Then I saw my twelve-year-old daughter looking at me and smiling. I love that she will remember this when she is a grown woman. *I am enough and was enough before this, too,* I thought. But, of course, victory is sweet, and I found myself crying tears of joy in my family's arms.

That night, my dinner was my most expensive bottle of California wine and cake with buttercream frosting. I ate and laughed. I celebrated that a lady in her forties had passed the California bar. She passed after raising three kids, learning a new language, rehabbing after a freak accident, moving thousands of miles, navigating a pandemic, and helping with online school.

What is coming my way now? I don't know, but I did this, and I will do so much more. I am just getting started.

— Maria Victoria Espinosa —

23

From Tragedy to Triumph

I'm grounded in joy; I'm not grounded
in the trauma anymore.
~Tarana Burke

I thought I was living a good life. I was working as a clinical psychologist with a thriving private practice. Referrals for our services were steadily increasing and I was hiring additional clinicians and administrative staff to meet the demand. In addition, as an expert in mental health, in particular in the African Canadian community, there were requests from institutions and organizations for teaching and keynote speaking as well as radio and television appearances. I was building the career of my dreams.

I was also married to a great man who was cultivating his career as a police officer, with several promotions and opportunities for growth. We owned a beautiful 3,000-square foot home, drove nice cars, and seemed to live a "perfect" life. We focused on our families and we hosted all the holidays. Our house was the meeting place for our family and friends.

On the surface it looked like we had it all. So, what was next? Starting a family. Easy, right? When things didn't go as planned, I just said I would take control of this, too, confident it would work out.

However, everything unraveled right before my eyes. We were in and out of fertility clinics for seven years and six cycles of IVF with no success. As a result of the treatment and the stress, I gained a significant amount of weight, lost self-confidence and at times questioned my womanhood. In the meantime, my husband's brothers and friends were getting married and having children. This took an emotional and spiritual toll on both of us.

I decided to lean on my Christian faith and prayed that God would grant me the desires of my heart. I thought my husband was on the same page, but I woke up one day and learned that my "perfect" husband had been cheating on me for years. I tried to rebuild our marriage, but then I learned that my husband had purposely gotten another woman pregnant so that he could have a child. He wanted me to stay in the marriage and "co-parent" with him.

In that moment my world was shattered. I was at a loss for words and confused as to why this would happen to me. I was a good person, I always put other's needs ahead of my own. My initial thoughts were to stay in my marriage and adjust my sail to please my husband.

As time went on, in the midst of the confusion, insecurities and disconnect, I heard a quiet voice in my heart saying, "There is no way God wants you to live in this life of mediocrity. This is not God's best for your life."

I didn't know what was ahead, but I knew that it would be better than what I would be settling for. In that moment, I left. Fear, doubt, uncertainty followed me but resilience, faith and courage walked alongside me. So, I made the difficult decision to end my marriage. In the midst of my despair, I packed my belongings and moved in with my parents. One month later, I purchased a home for more than a million dollars and I moved into it three months later. I also decided to focus on my own healing, and I lost close to seventy pounds. Professionally, I partnered with my friend and colleague and we opened a psychological clinic. I also went on my first solo trip, on a yacht in the British Virgin Islands, and enjoyed Carnival in Trinidad.

My personal healing journey included challenging personal mindsets which were deeply rooted in my ethnicity as an African, Canadian, Caribbean, Christian woman. These mindsets created core beliefs that created the foundation of how I viewed myself, others and the world.

I was ultimately walking in the world wearing foggy glasses and I had to embark on a painful, yet necessary journey of self-love so that I could truly understand who I was.

Once I opened myself to embark on this journey, things happen in my life that can only be explained by God and His divine timing.

In early 2020, I received an e-mail from my first boyfriend — my first love. We first met at fifteen and dated throughout high school and early university. Once our relationship ended, we went our separate ways and I never thought I would see or hear from him again.

The e-mail began by saying, "Hi Natasha, I hope you are well. It has been over twenty years since we have seen each other but I hope that you are doing well." Once I recovered from the shock, I responded to the e-mail, which turned into a dinner date one week later, then turned into the rekindling of our relationship. We have been inseparable ever since. In him, I have found a love that I have never felt with anyone else before. In our pains and tragedies, our paths have travelled back to each other. We have decided not to waste this second chance that God has given us, and we have chosen to love each other, for the rest of our lives.

This life journey so far has taught me that healing is a continued process, but you have to be brave enough to take the first step. I can have the life that I want with no questions asked and no compromises.

— Natasha Williams —

24

What Does Love Look Like?

Being deeply loved by someone gives you strength,
while loving someone deeply gives you courage.
~Lao Tzu

A t first, I couldn't hear his tender words through the fog of anesthesia. I would only learn of them later when I asked for details.

When I awoke in the ICU after surgery, he sat in the only chair of the small room. The nurses busied themselves around me. Sensations from the PICC line, the blood-pressure cuff, the drainage tubes, and the pain stole my breath. I couldn't speak.

The breathing tube wouldn't be removed for another few hours. I mimed the act of writing with my right hand, causing excitement through the room.

"This is a good sign," said a nurse. She grabbed a sheet of paper and a pen for me.

They let me take my time as I wrote a single question: "What happened?"

As the facts were repeated to me over several days, the words started to hold together in hazy patterns. Still, when I heard the words "brain aneurysm" and "emergency surgery," they made little sense to me. I was a thirty-nine-year-old woman. I was supposed to be at work. I was fine yesterday — wasn't I?

My eyes darted to my husband for answers.

But instead of speaking over the nurses, he continued to let the staff stay within my line of sight and answer me. Each time, a nurse would patiently relay what she thought I could grasp. My mind was like a sieve, though, unable to hold answers.

Or maybe I just couldn't believe the story. Shock, surely, is a byproduct of brain trauma. But I wouldn't know that until I recovered and read literature on my condition months later.

That would be my recovery road. But, first, I needed to get there.

Luckily, I had one solid person in my life to help me: Brian. I knew he was in my ICU room, even when the equipment blocked my view of him. And in the first moments where consciousness started to appear, his presence mattered. To have him close meant I wasn't alone.

During our first exchange, the nurse prompted me for more. With the pen poised above the paper, my body knew what should be done, but my mind stayed one step behind as I struggled to formulate additional questions.

How my trauma-ravaged mind managed to turn its confusion into words, I'm unsure. But over the course of the next half-hour, a litany of them spilled onto the page.

"What is this?"

She explained the protruding medical equipment to me in the most basic of terms.

"Can I move this thing in my mouth from the right to the left?"

The answer was no.

"I feel tube," I wrote to her. "Chokey," I pleaded. "I feel chokey," I wrote again.

She understood and patted my hand. The tube would be removed at some point but not yet.

Had Brian not saved the sheet of paper on which I wrote, I might have found it hard to believe that I was so coherent.

Inside the room, Brian spoke most convincingly. "You're going to be okay. You're doing great."

Each time, the soft encouragement reached my ears like a song. How I wanted to touch him, better yet to be held by him. But instead, it was only the warmth from a blanket and the occasional brush from a nurse's hand that touched my skin, for he wasn't allowed to get close. Not yet.

Such is the way in recovery: close and far away.

Having him there, however, brought comfort, especially in an environment where so much was discomforting. The sounds around me were alien—mechanical beeps and wheezing of equipment that I couldn't name. Bags labeled with chemical solutions dripped steadily; hoses and tubes stretched taut across the bed. All spoke to the ways I had cheated death.

And, through it all, I endured—and he did, too. I saw it in his eyes. He was present when the nurses worked, humanizing each exchange. His hawk-eye focus helped him memorize the numbers displayed behind me on computer monitors, numbers that ultimately decided courses of medical action that could have, at any time, gone awry. I never knew how dangerous those ICU days were until I left them behind.

Even with all his focus on the external, however, his gaze slid always to me. His focus lit my way.

"She's a very lucky lady." The charge nurse nodded before motioning to him that it was now okay to touch me.

"And tough," he added. He rose from the chair and extended his hand to cup mine, cradling it like porcelain and finally staying close.

"I'll give you two a moment."

I looked to him and wanted to cry, but tears wouldn't come. Maybe it was survivalism. Maybe it was confusion. Or maybe it was just weakness. There was no space to identify feelings of my own. So I focused on him.

"You've made it past the hardest part."

Had I? How could he know—how could anyone know? I suspected the entire hospital stay would be hard. So, too, would be the recovery at home.

"I'll be here with you. I'm not going anywhere." His sincerity cemented the promise.

He sounded like the embodiment of comfort. No one recovers

alone, not from something like this. I had him and knowing that made all the difference.

Slowly, my anxiety eased. Caring for me was his heroism.

He was forgoing sleep, his life screeching to a halt because of this. But he never wore a face of agony or pity. He chose strength, and, because of that, I would, too. This—him—was what I needed, then, now and forever.

I could see into the future, and the future held better days with him at my side.

"I'm here." He squeezed my hand as he leaned in to plant a kiss atop my forehead. His lips were as gentle as his movements, his very presence my reassurance.

I asked myself, *What does love look like?*

The answer was easy: *It looks like him.*

—Audrey Wick—

25

The Health Benefits of Egg Yolks

Dismantle your wounds so you stop
living your life by them.
~Nikki Rowe

"Hey, honey!" I greeted my fiancé as he climbed back into the driver's seat of the car where I'd been waiting. "I was just reading about egg yolks and that they aren't as bad for us as some people think. Mom called, and I told her maybe she should lay off of Dad for his egg intake!"

"You were talking to your mom the whole time I was gone?" he asked with disdain as we began our twenty-mile journey home.

"Yeah, I was telling her about this book I'm reading. There's a large part about eggs, and they talk about all the nutrition that is in the yolk." I ignored his all-too-familiar attempt to shame me for talking to my mom and further distance me from my family. Instead, I spoke excitedly, hoping to spark a conversation and change the previously sour mood of the day.

"YOU'RE STUPID! YOU'RE IGNORANT! EGG YOLKS ARE NOT HEALTHY!" Rage filled my fiancé's voice as he continued to yell and belittle me for my comment about eggs.

I remember a silent resolve filling my mind and my heart as he carried on beside me. I removed my engagement ring from my finger and placed it in the center console.

"I am not stupid. I will not and cannot live this way anymore. I refuse to spend forever like this," I stated as a flood of emotions rocked me to my core.

Our entire relationship had been a mess. Oddly enough, it was a conversation about egg yolks, of all things, that was the proverbial two-by-four that God used to strike me over the head and bring me to my senses.

Within a matter of seconds, his demeanor changed as he pulled the car to a stop on the side of the road. I could see the confusion in his eyes at my sudden bravery, and he must have read the sincerity on my face as he began to grovel.

"I didn't mean it! You aren't stupid or ignorant! I don't even know what ignorant means!" He back-pedaled quickly as tears filled his eyes. He brought his hands to his face, trying to push down his anger as he made a frantic attempt to regain his control over me.

My resolve was intact. We'd been here before. While he was verbally and emotionally abusive, I was the one who had made the mistake of agreeing to marry him — not once but twice. The first time we were engaged, I ended it for the same reasons I did the second time. But the second time would stick, as I finally came to my senses.

More groveling ensued as I stood my ground, something neither he nor I was accustomed to. We were charting new territory as he drove us back to his house. Silence soon took over as we both tried to come to terms with what had happened.

I remember the tears streaming down my cheeks and the tumult of emotions within as I experienced sadness for the relationship lost, as well as gladness for my freedom gained. It felt as though I was being unchained from my prison cell, although I had been denying that the chains existed. The ironic thing was that, while he had built and kept me locked in that cell, I was the one who had entered it of my own free will — and I was the only one who could set myself free.

Difficult weeks followed the breakup. But with each day, I found more and more of my old self and began to grow from my experience rather than let it hold me down. He met and married another woman within a year of our breakup. I waited years for the right one, not really believing that he existed.

He did. With almost two years as his wife, and a nine-month-old daughter by our side, he still does and will forever be my Mr. Right. I am so incredibly thankful for the health benefits of egg yolks.

—Whitni Kostboth—

26

Growing into Confidence

In a world where deep down everyone just wants to fit in,
I wish we could realize that it takes true confidence to have
enough love for ourselves, a belief that we are enough.
~Justin Baldoni

I've played a lot of traditional roles throughout my nineteen years. I've been the angsty tween, the hard-working high-school student, the sleep-through-my-classes university student. But the one role I could never quite fit into was that of a stereotypically "masculine" man.

Growing up, I was raised in a female-dominated environment. I have three sisters with whom I'm close and an extremely involved mother. My father plays a very active role in my life, but we're outnumbered by my family's female power.

My mother and sisters undoubtedly provided me with numerous qualities for which I'm extremely grateful. They taught me to express my feelings, show compassion, and stay loyal to the people I care about. And, yes, there were a few interests and mannerisms I picked up from them that I'm not sure I would've otherwise. For example, my hand often gravitates to my hip in the most Jewish-motherly way possible and there were a solid five years when I could've told you exactly what happened on that week's *America's Next Top Model* episode.

I never saw anything wrong with the way I walked, talked, or naturally gravitated to girls for friends since they're who I felt most comfortable with — until I started grade school.

As a kid, my physical attributes never seemed to properly align with my age. I was below average in height for my entire childhood, which, coupled with my disinterest in most sports and my high-pitched voice, made me stand out among my male peers at school.

Most of the guys I went to school with shared some common traits. They all played sports together, had more male friends than female ones, and didn't discuss their feelings. I'd later learn these traits fit into an idea called "masculinity," a term often used to tie strength to men. I didn't possess many of these qualities — or at least not to the extent that my classmates did — so I was associated by others with "femininity," a term often and unfortunately used to tie weakness to women.

The boys in my classes didn't approve of my breaking this social taboo, and their disapproval was often expressed in a method I similarly wasn't overly familiar with: aggression.

I was called "gay" as an insult for the first time at age six. I remember it more clearly than most of my childhood birthdays. I didn't know what the word meant, but I could tell by the disgust dripping from the boy's tone that I was meant to feel offended.

Around this time, I started playing tennis. My proficiency for the sport quickly came to surpass most other six-year-olds thanks to a combination of natural skill and a good work ethic.

I joined a high-performance program at the age of nine. I was the youngest and smallest player by a wide margin, but I was also the fastest and most strategic. There was a strength in that — not necessarily a physical one but a power in excelling at a sport despite having none of the usual qualities used to do so.

My tennis skills also protected me somewhat from my elementary-school bullies. I was still short, squeaky, and predominantly friends with girls. But I was also playing a sport at a high level, something that people who were considered "weak" or "feminine" were apparently not typically capable of doing.

Tennis became my shield against accusations of weakness. The insults they launched continually bounced off my against-all-odds athleticism. So, people eventually stopped firing them.

With a newfound confidence coming into middle school, I made more friends, got a girlfriend, and found a second family in the kids I trained with. I still had various underlying insecurities about my lack of growth and stereotypically feminine features. Even so, if no one was calling me out on them, I saw no reason to change.

But then some cracks in my love of tennis began to manifest. To play tennis at a professional level, it's essentially required to compete in tournaments in order to attain a provincial or national ranking.

Tournaments always confused me. I trained with a group of other players, but when it comes down to it, tennis is a one-on-one sport. I didn't like having to turn against my friends the second we became "competitors." I didn't like seeing them lose as much as I didn't like seeing myself not win. Still, I never voiced these concerns out of fear my compassion would appear cowardly.

Though I settled into the practices of playing a sport I no longer loved, high school proved to be an even larger struggle.

Still missing a growth spurt, I stuck out more than ever. A quick scroll through my ex-middle-school-girlfriend's ASKfm account gave me a pretty clear indication of how my ninth-grade peers perceived me. One "question" read: "the only guy you ever [hooked up] with is [J]osh [G]ranovsky and he doesn't really count because he's... kind of a girl."

I didn't have an account of my own, so her page became a sounding board for doubts of my heterosexuality and degradations of my "masculinity" in any other ways their adolescent brains could muster.

My only method of defense against these comments, since I had no way to respond, was to throw myself further into tennis. I upped my training to six times a week, sometimes starting at 6:30 A.M. and ending at 10:30 P.M. My ranking rose to a peak of 49 in Ontario and 200 in Canada. I posted about my strict regimen on social media, revelling in the shock of my classmates' comments about my "hidden manhood."

As my commitment to tennis expanded, so did my hate for it. I still didn't like battling my friends on court, but now I also resented missing out on after-school activities or having to leave school early to accommodate training.

Then, toward the end of tenth grade, my prayers were answered. I grew a full foot, and my voice dropped an octave or two. I found the confidence to join a new friend group, gain a serious girlfriend, and, eventually, quit tennis. That year, I dropped my weekly training to four days, which soon wilted to two, and ultimately to none.

Finally, without constant commenting about my femininity from those around me, I became more assured of my self-worth.

My social and mental stability meant I no longer needed tennis to shield me from people who thought I was "girlish."

While I'm happy to not be the anxious, five-foot-tall kid I was when I entered high school, I wish I hadn't needed to grow a foot to gain confidence. I wish I didn't have to stick with a sport I hated just to feel strong. I wish I didn't need to wait almost two decades to truly realize I could be a man just as I am, no matter what society historically defined one as.

Now, at nineteen years old and six feet tall, I can't remember the last time someone questioned my masculinity. More importantly, I can't remember the last time I questioned my masculinity.

I like to think it has less to do with my proportional stature and more to do with learning to define my masculinity based on what makes me feel like a man, not what everyone else thinks a man should be.

In an ideal world, sharing my story would contribute to the growing movement of dismantling what is now known as "toxic masculinity." But I'll still be more than satisfied if I can get just one boy to read this, realize he doesn't have to fit into any male stereotypes, and maybe even quit tennis.

—Josh Granovsky—

27

First, You Weep

Stand in your light and shine brightly
because that is how you defeat darkness.
~Leslie Esperanza Espaillat

I lay on the table poised only a few feet from the circular dome where the CT scan would be performed. The technician wrapped a wide Velcro belt around me, a concession made so that I wouldn't fall off.

I had already drunk the vile container of barium. It had a bit of a milky coconut flavor to it, and I made a mental note to avoid piña coladas for the next few months. The IV was inserted. I was warned that I would experience abdominal pressure and a warm sensation in my throat.

As I stared at the ceiling, I prayed. And I wondered how many prayers had been said in this very same space, people pleading with God for a positive outcome, a few more years of life. I thought perhaps that made this a sacred place, a temple of sorts, where the sick and the desperate come to receive a sentence or a dispensation.

It was over in a matter of minutes, a simple procedure of holding and releasing my breath as pictures of every vein and artery, every organ inside my body, were photographed, recorded for posterity.

And then I waited.

Over the previous six months, I had displayed a variety of ambiguous symptoms and gotten no answers. I was beginning to think it was all in my head. Finally, my doctor ordered this test with expedited results. Of course, the receptionist was quick to point out that without preapproval from my insurance company, I could be responsible for the charges, and she made me sign the form for good measure. Surely, my life was worth it. I vowed to buy fewer shoes, just in case.

I sat in the reception area and read a frivolous women's magazine, the kind that shows pencil-thin models in outrageous-looking clothes with outrageous price tags. I read about techniques for applying summer-proof eye make-up, and how to pack for a week's vacation in a carry-on.

Across from me sat a woman who worked her prayer beads, her lips moving fast as she spoke to her god. The idea that we all turn to The Great One when we are in trouble unites us, binds us as children of The Almighty, seeking solace and comfort from His promises. Well, except for the atheists, of course. I guess they ponder what they are going to have for dinner when they lie on the table, Velcroed on for good measure. I'm glad I have my faith.

I was told to return to my doctor's office. You know they know something you don't when they treat you a little more politely and don't make you wait. I was ushered into an exam room where I sat and read the rest of the pointless magazine.

The doctor came in and mustered a weak smile. "This is the conversation we never want to have with our patients," he said. My heart began to race as the little voice inside of my head whispered, "Uh-oh." I braced myself.

"You have ovarian cancer that has metastasized," he said all at once, his words dancing along the sterile walls.

I think they call this "dropping the bomb," the most efficient way to deliver bad news.

I felt dizzy as my mind struggled to process the implications.

"Prognosis?" I managed to ask.

"It's at a Stage 4, in the peritoneum and lower stomach. There is fluid on your lung, which explains the breathing problems. And the distended abdomen is the growth of the tumor, along with accumulated malignant fluid. Ascites."

I thought back to last summer. I had had a flat stomach for a full two months, the result of dieting and exercise. I thought I looked damn good for an old broad. And I did until cancer took up residence and started messing with my body and my life.

The rest of the conversation was a blur. He spoke of the need to eat well, exercise and get lots of rest. I wondered if he considered chocolate a food group like I did. He mentioned a vegan diet. I tried not to laugh. I mentioned my inability to sleep, the discomfort and pain.

"The oncologist will address that. I will refer you, of course. But don't worry if it takes a few weeks."

I thought of that statement. Easy for him to say. He didn't have some alien being growing inside him, wrapping its insidious tendrils around internal organs. I wondered if he was writing me off, dismissing me. Had I already been handed a death sentence?

He hugged me goodbye and told me to go home and tell my family. That part was hard. You want to be strong and brave for everybody else, reassure them that everything is going to be alright, and that Momma will be there to hold the world together as she always has. I had to dig deep into my acting days for that performance. I called a few close friends. They rallied around me, pouring out their love and support.

I thought of a million things in the next few days. I wondered who would want my extensive collection of accessories. I contemplated my funeral and considered making gumbo to freeze to serve at the after-party. I regretted never having seen Paris. I prayed that God would give me the strength and courage to fight without being in too much pain. And if the inevitable happened, I hoped to be worthy to be welcomed into heaven.

I have done breast self-exams since I was sixteen and had regular mammograms. I have sported pink ribbons and celebrated during the month of October. But nobody warned me of ovarian cancer. And, without a family history, I had no idea I was at risk. Now, I was arm-wrestling it for my life. But I can be a badass when pushed into a corner, and I knew I would come out punching.

The irony wasn't lost on me. More than any other part of my anatomy, my ovaries are what made me a woman. Indeed, they were firmly in charge of my libido, my hormonal mood swings, and my

PMS (which my husband once dubbed Paula Millet Syndrome). Every month, they released an egg. Three of them were fertilized. My three sons. They created life. And now, they threatened to rob me of mine. Life can be a beach, but it can also be a bitch.

I wrote these words almost four years ago when I was filled with so much fear and anxiety about what was to come. Since then, I have strapped on my battle armor three more times and arm-wrestled the Grim Reaper through numerous surgeries and ongoing chemotherapies. So far, I am winning. In the process, I have discovered an untapped strength, while learning who and what is important. I haven't taken up bull riding, but I have learned to make every moment count and to call myself a survivor because that's exactly what I am.

— Paula W. Millet —

28

Patience and Crutches

You can't just sit there and wait for people to give you
that golden dream. You've got to get out there
and make it happen for yourself.
~Diana Ross

In December 2012, I broke free of an abusive relationship and decided to get away — far, far away. I organized a trip to Kenya and Tanzania and made plans to climb Mount Kilimanjaro. I was going to reboot my life, and a vacation in East Africa was going to be the catalyst. From there, I would decide my next move: a new job, a new location.

I organized my savings and downsized my life. I gave notice at my job and ended my apartment lease.

The same week that I sold my car and moved to a rented bedroom, all my well-laid plans fell apart. At a friendly soccer game, I tore my calf muscle. Initially, I thought I just strained or pulled the muscle, but I could not walk. Even if I tried to bear the pain and force myself, I could not manipulate my muscle to function.

The next morning, my leg was so swollen that I called a taxi and went straight to the doctor. He concluded that I had torn the muscle and would require crutches to assist with mobility for the next few weeks. I would need physical therapy to walk normally again. I would have to be patient and rest; there was no other treatment.

Climbing Mount Kilimanjaro was definitely out.

Flying anywhere alone was not an option.

Not only were all my exciting plans canceled, but I had already quit my job, terminated my housing, and sold my car. I hobbled to the rooming house on crutches and barely made it to the shared couch before I broke down in tears. It was hard enough going through a breakup and ending a toxic relationship; adding a physical injury was just too much. I was trying so hard to be positive and focus on my future, but everything was falling apart, including my body.

I still wanted to move, to be away from my ex and get a fresh start, but that seemed completely impossible if I was hobbling about on crutches.

Thankfully, some wonderful friends offered to help. Normally, I am not the sort of person to accept handouts, but being temporarily crippled, jobless and homeless, I wasn't in a position to refuse anything. Hanani, a friend who lived two hours away, offered her home, and another friend shared her car. Soon, I had moved my few remaining possessions to Hanani's house and was settled in a comfortable room in her basement.

Hanani is from Uganda, and her home was as warm and sunny as the Pearl of Africa. I couldn't mope around her jolly house with little Umi dancing around on my crutches and her son Sulieman telling jokes all the time. Hanani and her kids helped me keep my spirits high, and staying with her cheerful family helped me through the most difficult December I'd ever known. Hanani even took me out dancing on New Year's — on crutches!

She also insisted on practicing Swahili with me, prepared excellent Kenyan and Ugandan dishes, and taught me a great deal about East African culture. While I wasn't actually in Kenya or Tanzania, I was still getting a taste of the region because of Hanani.

Soon, I started physical therapy and practiced walking every day. Umi designated herself as my walking coach. I would walk unevenly down the hallway, and she would mimic me, showing how I put too much weight on one side or dragged my leg. In time, she proudly announced my steps were improving, and I could almost walk as well as she did!

When I could walk normally again and my ultrasound came back clear, I knew it was time to go. But this time I wasn't feeling desperate. Staying with Hanani had helped me through the roughest time of my breakup and leg injury.

I decided to move to Toronto, Ontario. I rented a room and found a job straightaway. I made new friends easily and attended events. One day, I saw a group of people playing soccer at the park across the street from my apartment and asked to join in. It wasn't until the end of the game that I realized it was the first time I had played soccer since tearing my leg muscle. I wasn't in pain, and I was running again.

My body is stronger than I give it credit for; it just takes time to heal. Like the doctor said: rest and patience.

Two years later, I took a two-week vacation and visited East Africa: Uganda, Kenya, and Tanzania. I stayed with Hanani's family in Uganda, who are as welcoming as she is, and I spoke to them in the Swahili that Hanani had taught me. Then I went to Kenya and Tanzania.

And I stayed in Tanzania.

I got a job, found an apartment, and made new friends. I wasn't afraid to move or start over because I had done it before, and I knew I could do it again. It just takes patience. It's been five years now, and I still live in Tanzania. Next year, Hanani is coming to visit me, and I am going to prepare Tanzanian dishes and speak to her in Swahili. I will take her out dancing—this time, no crutches!

— Ree Pashley —

29

Golden Noose

Know your worth, hold your own power, be you.
~Morgan Harper Nichols

Noose (noose) n. 1. A loop formed by a rope or cord, as in a lasso. 2. A snare or trap.

Somebody once told me that memories only have as much power over you as you allow them to have. I have a memory of my long hair. Long, blond, wavy and silky hair grazing just under my bra line. These tresses (for lack of a better word) then were a silky noose. A noose made from many strands of human DNA. A soft noose harsh against my neck.

Every time he caressed my hair, I felt like he tightened the noose more firmly around my neck. Every time he told me how beautiful my hair was, all I could think was how little hair had to do with who I was.

My solace was found in tying my hair back and confining it in a beautifully packaged and altogether different kind of noose. This gave me room to breathe, but only for moments. He caught on and began pulling the hair ribbons out of my hair in the car just as we arrived to whatever outing we had to attend.

At times, I felt as if it didn't matter what I was wearing as long as he could show that he was in possession of such shiny golden hair.

Sometimes, when he lightly touched my hair, I was reminded of being a little blond girl in Italy where old, wrinkled Italian men and women would marvel over the lightness of my strands and pinch my cheeks. I remember the flesh on my face being tugged and how I would try not to cry out because my mother once told me it was rude to express pain when all these men and women were only admiring my beauty.

I believed that long hair looked elegant pulled back and piled up on the head, especially for a night out when I dressed in my best clothes and put on make-up. I would do so thinking how graceful my neck seemed when it was exposed. He liked my hair up in order to show off the gold necklace his mother gave me, which he always made me put on even when I sometimes tried to leave the house without it. The cold yellow and white gold (similar to the color of my hair) served another purpose in my mind. It was yet another kind of noose — a collar — to remind me that I was caught in a horrible relationship, one where even his mother was a part of the torment that coiled around me.

Once, when we had a "difference of opinion" and he was out of town for the weekend, I tore out to the supermarket to buy hair dye. Red hair dye. Only it wasn't quite red, more like a violet-red, or as the Italians would call it, *melanzana* — eggplant. Rebellion caused me to keep that eggplant rinse on my hair an hour longer than the time the box said to, caring only that I was destroying the shiny gold, hoping to color away the caresses and compliments.

Maybe by having the power to change the color of my hair, I could also change the tone of the relationship. I knew he would be devastated when he saw my new eggplant strands fluttering in the wind instead of the golden ones. For whatever reason, he liked the new color instead. That information only armed me for the future, when the purple-red eventually faded and I went to a professional for more color. I sun-glitzed the *melanzana* away.

When we spent three glorious/horrible months in England, I needed a trim. He went with me to make sure I got a perm. Was I weak-minded to allow a man to dictate what and how my hair should be? I looked at it differently. As long as I could avoid any possible ill treatment, I was willing to try anything (within reason) to keep the noose as loose as it could reasonably remain despite the circumstances.

After his initial passionate embrace of the blond ringlets with which he managed to entangle his fingers, he tugged the roots seemingly out of my scalp, dropping me to the floor. He became unreasonable again, blaming me for whatever he found necessary. But because of his lack of enthusiasm for my new style, his hate even, I felt exhilarated for a while. For a moment, my hair and I were together instead of having different agendas, ideas or wants. For a moment, my hair was mine, acting on my behalf instead of working against me, ticking down the final minutes, tightening its hold.

Had the thought ever occurred to me before, I would have acted upon it: My hair had the power to set me free. We had a formal to attend. I decided to visit the local hair salon to get my hair artistically arranged. I wanted something unique and different from the normal coifed presentation usually chosen by the Italian woman. I wanted to be just "off" enough but still be acceptable. I wanted to rebel just as much as I was able to in order to piss him off but not have him be able to say a word because I wasn't quite over the edge.

While I was waiting for my turn in the chair, flipping through a magazine, I rebelled. I knew then it would forever change. It was my epiphany. A heroine was born. The prisoner broke her chains.

I cut it off. All of it. That spot right underneath the earlobe was the last point that had hair covering it, leaving the rest of my neck bare and able to breathe. But it went shorter than that. My hairline at the back of my neck was shaved about an inch up into my hairline, cutting the rest of the hair to graze the top of the barely-there hair. I cut off the noose, leaving it on the floor at the *parrucchiere* in the Posilippo neighborhood off the bay of Naples, Italy.

— ReBecca Gardea —

30

Uke Can Do It

Music brings us pleasure and releases our suffering. It can calm us down and pump us up. It helps us manage pain, run faster, sleep better and be more productive.
~Alex Doman

Wow, exquisite pain comes after lung surgery. I spoke in whispers. My air intake was low on that thingamabob that measures breathing. Everything hurt. No one was allowed to make me laugh because that was too painful. If I could shapeshift, I'd be a howler monkey, but not during that long recovery.

Every day, I built up my breathing with light exercise. I'd go into the yard and walk across to the fence and back a few times. Did I say walking? More like stepping lively if I were a 150-year-old tortoise.

So, two weeks post-surgery, a box arrived. Inside, I found a ukulele. *Huh? Surely, it's a delivery mistake.* Then I thought, *Great. Some other house got my new UGG boots.*

But, no, the label was addressed to me.

Later, the phone rang. It was Molly from Paris. "I got a text that my gift was delivered. What do you think?"

"Molly, it's a super generous gift!"

But what I didn't say was, "I don't remember ever wanting one…."

Best friends can read minds, and she said, "You need something fun to do, and I've been playing it for over a year. I can help you learn. We can jam together on Zoom."

"Okay…"

Molly and I grew up in San Francisco and acted like twins for years. Then she relocated to Paris in 1996, and I moved to the East Coast that same year. Our communication grew spotty. We'd visit each other, but time passes, and lapses take over.

Now we're in our sixties, but once she heard about my surgery, she called me every morning. She organized a prayer time with six friends to beam me toward a successful surgery and recovery. Every day at 2:00 P.M. EST, no matter where anyone was, she ordered them to start their prayer engines.

I protested, "Oh, Molly, don't make everyone say the rosary. They can say their own prayers."

"No!" she said. "The rosary is powerful, and we have to do it together for group energy."

Her insistence surprised me as she is not religious, but I, her best friend, was having a cancerous tumor removed, and gosh darn it, money's on the table.

I must say, it eased my fear, and a feeling of protection came over me every day at 2:00 P.M. just knowing my friends were praying for me. My surgery was successful, but Molly wasn't finished yet.

So, back to the ukulele.

In one hand, I held my cell phone. In the other hand, I held this ukulele by the neck, a bit nonplussed.

Then Molly told me the backstory of why she so firmly believed in its healing power.

Like I said, we've had lapses in contact, and I had no idea she had been playing the ukulele for over a year. But here's why.

Her longtime relationship had broken up, causing her deep, emotional pain. She was living in Paris, far from her family and us, her childhood friends. She felt so alone with a broken heart. She took up the ukulele, playing as a diversion. Every day, playing songs on its melodic, sweet strings cheered her up. It was such an easy instrument to learn. She'd take it to the park or the beach and play for hours. For over a year each day, she made a musical gain, and every day her feelings of loss ebbed away.

"It saved my life," Molly said, "and I want it to save yours."

I fell silent. I was moved, inspired.

Here I am, a year and a half after my lung surgery, and most mornings I pick up my ukulele and strum. Then Molly calls me from Paris, and we yak about life. I've been taking online lessons and memorized a song or two. I'm not good enough to "jam" with others, but I do send video clips to Molly for her amusement. What should be a sixty-second rendition of "It's a Wonderful World" takes me two-and-a-half minutes because reaching for the right notes is still a stretch for my short, stubby fingers.

But I do agree with the late George Harrison who was crazy for the ukulele and owned a huge vintage collection. It's said he would show up at parties, giving out ukuleles and jamming on them with his musician friends. He once wrote, "Everyone I know who is into the ukulele is 'crackers.' You can't play it and not laugh."

And my own full, loud, throaty laugh has returned once again.

I'd like to learn a new song: "I Get By with a Little Help from My Friends."

— Suzette Martinez Standring —

It Takes a Village

31

Do You Want a Blanket?

*I thought faith would say, I'll take away the pain
and discomfort, but what it ended up saying was,
I'll sit with you in it.*
~Brené Brown

I pulled up to the entrance of the emergency room. My husband and I had tested positive for COVID-19 just one week earlier. For the most part, I remained symptom-free. Bob, on the other hand, had been experiencing almost every symptom and seemed to be getting a little worse each day. We had spoken to the doctor that morning. He suggested we have Bob checked out for possible dehydration. He told us that they might want to give him an antibiotic or a steroid.

I checked him in and went to park our car. We were told that the wait time was about three-and-a-half hours. When I returned, I found my husband outside on the sidewalk in a roped-off area, in a wheelchair waiting with other patients who had COVID symptoms. He was shivering and asked me if I had a blanket in the car. He explained that they were not allowed to give him one.

Frantically, I rummaged through my trunk looking for a blanket or a beach towel, anything that might help keep him warm. I had nothing! I went back to Bob and tried to figure out what to do. He looked at me and said, "I'm in trouble, Lori."

"No, I'll be right back," I told him as I rushed to the nearest drugstore.

I grabbed the five blankets that I found on the shelf and took them straight to the cashier. As she rang me up, the manager asked me what I needed all the blankets for. I explained that my husband was very sick, and all the COVID patients in the emergency area had to wait outside the hospital. I said, "My husband is not the only one sick and cold out there. I'm getting blankets for everyone." He turned to the girl who was ringing me up and said, "Give her 75 percent off. If her husband is sick and she's helping everyone else, I want in on that!" I started to cry as I paid and thanked him.

Back at the hospital, I wrapped up my husband and handed out the other blankets. As they wheeled him into the emergency room, I stood helplessly in the parking lot waiting for an update. Less than two hours later, a nurse ran out to get me. Bob's oxygen levels had dropped dangerously, and they were putting him on life support. I was able to quickly kiss him and tell him I loved him. The nurse rushed me back out as they ventilated him.

For the next seven days and nights, I practically lived in that parking lot, praying for my husband with family and friends. It just felt better to stay as close to him as I could. One of the nurses put a cut-out heart in the window so we could see where Bob's room was.

I asked my friends to bring blankets for me to give away. I knew that I couldn't do anything at that time to help Bob, but I could help the people waiting outside who were sick and cold. Conversation and encouragement seemed easy as we were all going through similar troubles. We also began giving away blankets at night to the other families waiting in their cars by the emergency room.

People started bringing bags of blankets for us to give away. One friend's nine-year-old son asked his mom if he could have people bring blankets for Bob instead of presents to his birthday party. He collected over 100 blankets and made encouragement cards for the patients.

On the eighth morning, Bob lost his fight with COVID. I got the call in the parking lot. I ran into the hospital, past the security guards and admissions nurse. They were yelling at me to stop, shouting that

I wasn't supposed to be in the building. As I stood in the emergency-room lobby, I realized that I didn't even know where to go. I had never been allowed in to see Bob or go up to his room. Finally, the doctor called and gave me clearance to go up. I stood and watched as they worked on my husband, trying to save his life for almost forty-five minutes. I knew that he was already gone.

That afternoon, blankets and money started pouring in. Small teams of friends and family were helping each night as we gave away blankets to COVID patients and the families in the emergency-room parking lot. Such an abundance poured out that we began sending meals to the doctors and nurses who worked in the ICU and ER.

It has been months now since Bob's passing, but the blankets continue each night, as do the friendships and connections that we have built in the parking lot — stories of hope and kindness in the midst of illness, separation and pain.

People are coming together, helping each other to make it through some of life's most difficult times. I can feel Bob smiling down on us, cheering us on to hope for the future, reminding us to keep our faith, choose kindness and help each other every chance we get.

— Lori Bryant —

32

Fire and Nice

All will concede that in order to have good neighbors,
we must also be good neighbors. That applies
in every field of human endeavor.
~Harry S. Truman

Why was our neighbor from across the street frantically pounding on our front door at night? She was screaming for us to open it. We ran to the door, and she said only one word as she took off running: "FIRE!" Then she let us know that she had already called 911.

We ran out just as the fire engines raced onto our street with their sirens screaming. The fire was huge! Flames were shooting wildly out the windows and through the roof of the hundred-year-old, three-story house next door. The flames were so tall they were visible a few miles away. Fire engines filled our entire street, from one end to the other, and even blocked the two cross streets.

My husband raced next door to be sure our neighbors had gotten out. All family members were outside and safe... including the dog. He ran to the houses on the other street that backed up to the house on fire and banged on those doors to be sure the neighbors were safe, too. They were. The air was thick with smoke, and it was hard to see and breathe as he came back down our street and arrived home.

We were almost grateful for COVID-19. Because of it, we were wearing our masks as we always did when we were outside, and that blocked some of the smoke we couldn't help but inhale. We sat outside watching the firefighters do the amazing job that they do.

Our street was crowded with fire trucks, eleven in all. One engine had a monster light on it that made the street bright enough that it looked like it was high noon on a sunny day. The paramedics and ambulances also came in case they were needed. Thank goodness, they were not. Our house became kind of a "safe house" with our next-door neighbors coming and going, as needed. It was a safe place for their dog, too. We made sure she had plenty of water, and she stayed in the house with our dog.

After around two hours, the fire was completely contained. Amazingly, the house was not a total loss. Most of it, while smoky and damp, was salvageable. And only a few important items were lost. The rest, like furniture and clothes, could be replaced. Only two rooms and a hallway would need to be reconstructed. The rest of the house could be cleaned and aired out. The fire investigators determined that the fire had been caused by a faulty appliance in one of the bedrooms.

The next day, our house smelled of smoke. The whole neighborhood smelled of smoke. Even we smelled of smoke! But, despite the tragedy — or maybe because of it — we have found many reasons to count our blessings and feel grateful. And, as we have found many times, when tragedy strikes people come together to help. Most people are good and want to do good for others. Coming to the aid of our neighbors during the fire and afterward became a blessing for us.

Our neighbors are also counting their blessings. First and foremost, no one was hurt despite the enormity of the fire and the challenges it will bring for some time to come. Everyone is okay. Their gratitude for the firefighters is overwhelming. They couldn't stop saying "Thank you." They have expressed their gratitude to us many times for opening our house to them that night and over the days that followed. It was a small thing for us, but tremendous for them.

They had no electricity. How can you keep your phone charged so you can keep in touch with family members to assure them you're okay? They charged their phones here. Where can your dog stay for a while and be safe? Right here at our house with our dog. What do you do with medications that need to be refrigerated? Put them in our refrigerator. Where can you meet with insurance investigators or others to sort things out? Right here. Or where can you lie down during the day when you need a break from sorting through the debris? Here. And on and on. They were small things but important.

In the days and weeks that followed, the goodness of others came through, too. A neighbor from a few streets over brought a basket full of home-picked fruit from the trees in their yard — oranges, lemons, peaches, and avocados. This neighbor didn't know the homeowners, didn't even know their names. But she brought the basket to share with them. Others in the area brought all kinds of things to share — some needed, some not (but it's the thought that counts). And our neighbors were and are so very grateful.

Things have settled down now. Our neighbors have insurance, so they will be provided a place to live while their house is being rebuilt. We will be without our neighbors for quite a while, but they will return. And then we will celebrate! They have such a positive attitude that all will be fine — and it will be. Good things can come out of bad things.

— Barbara LoMonaco —

33

Sweet Talking

*We must have a pie. Stress cannot exist
in the presence of a pie.*
~David Mamet, *Boston Marriage*

wo strawberry rhubarb sweet dough pies sat cooling on
the butcher block in the center of my kitchen. The pies
smelled heavenly and reminded me of the sweet aroma of
Grandmother's house on pie-baking Wednesdays.

I'd made hundreds of pies throughout the years, but I'd never
heard of sweet dough pies until I got the coveted recipe from a distant
cousin who was from New Orleans. She claimed sweet dough pies
were a specialty of the region.

With the COVID shutdown keeping me at home, I wanted to try
something new and different nearly every day. Cooking and baking
had always been a source of great satisfaction for me.

Now my mouth was watering as I smelled the cooling strawberry
rhubarb pies. It wasn't long before my husband, Ed, came sniffing his
way toward the butcher block. "Wow, these pies look as beautiful as
they are fragrant! When can we eat them?" he asked.

"They have to cool completely so all the juice doesn't run out of
the crust," I said.

"So, what are we going to do with two pies when there's only two
of us? Isn't our freezer full?" he asked with a broad smile.

"It's a new recipe for me, and I wrongly assumed it only made
one pie until I was knee-deep in rolling out the crust," I responded.

Ed was right. I was a whirlwind in the kitchen during these many confined months, and consequently our freezer was stuffed. Cooking and baking seemed to be the only things keeping me sane.

"Maybe we can share a pie with Sue and Scott," Ed suggested.

Since we'd moved in next door to them five years ago, we'd only said an occasional "hi" to each other across our respective driveways and exchanged cell-phone numbers in case of an emergency.

I decided Ed might have a point. Sharing my home-cooked creations with our neighbors could be a ray of sunshine for both families. Finding a sweet or savory surprise on the doorstep would perk up anyone's day.

My text to Sue: "I made strawberry rhubarb pies. Can I leave one on your front doorstep later today? If you're not comfortable with sharing homemade food during this time, I'll completely understand."

Her immediate reply: "Sounds yummy to me! I can't recall the last time we enjoyed homemade pie! Certainly a bright spot in long days."

It looked like I'd be sharing my kitchen endeavors after all, while nurturing my desire to cook and bake whatever struck my fancy.

That afternoon, I wrapped one of the pies in a fresh kitchen towel and placed it in the bottom of a large brown paper bag for easy handling. I set the pie on Sue's doorstep, rang the doorbell and returned home.

A few days later, Sue texted me. "Thank you for the pie. It was lovely! I've left a sweet treat on your front doorstep." She'd baked a type of refrigerator cookie I'd never seen. Currants were baked into a sweet, tender cookie that was expertly baked to be crisp on the outside and soft inside — a delightful treat with a cup of afternoon tea.

The following week, I left Twelve-Bean Sausage Soup on her front porch, and she reciprocated with freshly made, piping-hot biscuits to go with our soup that night. I sent a loaf of pumpernickel bread over to her family; she surprised us with banana-nut bread on my doorstep a few days later, which was made using a treasured family recipe. We finished out 2020 swapping family favorites, an exchange that went well into the Christmas season and into what we hoped would be a better 2021.

We learned our backgrounds were similar through exchanging our favorite family foods. Sue harkened from farm country in southeastern Minnesota and I'm from a farm community southeast of Seattle. It's an interesting twist for a budding friendship to blossom through the exchange of tasty foods during unusually tough times.

In essence, I have the virus to thank for a friendship that might not have otherwise happened. For me, the virus reminded me of the importance of sharing our bounty with others. Food is, indeed, a subtle yet powerful connection that I took for granted until the virus kept us from the joy of sharing a meal with those we care about and love the most. Who would have thought?

—Cynthia Briggs—

34

Chicken Soup for the Soul

A New Life

*Hope begins in the dark, the stubborn hope that if you
just show up and try to do the right thing,
the dawn will come.*
~Anne Lamott

My husband's sister-in-law succumbed to cancer at thirty-three years of age, leaving a confused son in the care of his father. This man was not capable of handling his own life without the crutches of alcohol and drugs, let alone the care of a small boy. He was a full-blown addict.

What to do with Todd became the topic of family meetings and discussions. Several of my husband's relatives stepped up to invite Todd into their homes and families, but they were not prepared for this over-indulged child. He was a headstrong boy, intensely competitive, and very troubled.

Knowing she was dying, his mother had smothered him with attention and love, but she did not look beyond the time when she would no longer be there. Todd loved toy cars and had every one imaginable — all he had to do was ask. He expected the world to revolve around him, and it did. He was often disruptive and demanding. These traits led to rejection by relative after relative who tried to foster him.

Ultimately, he went back to his father. Within ten months of losing his mother, he had been shifted back and forth no less than eight times to different homes of aunts and uncles and caregivers. Every time he was placed with someone, within weeks or months his father would be asked to collect him.

There was never any doubt that his father loved him. His promises of getting his act together were always sincere. Yet, each time Todd returned to his father, the situation soon became impossible. His father was a handsome man, popular and charismatic. He was a car salesman who left school at seventeen and started moving in the fast lane. Kevin met and married Iris when he was twenty-two, and Todd was born two years later. By the time he was twenty-five, Kevin was alcohol dependent. Iris became ill with colon cancer, and Kevin's way of dealing with the issue was to disappear in a fog of chemical bliss. Iris had few reserves to cope, and her pleas went unheeded.

After Iris passed, Kevin went on a drunken rampage and destroyed every memento of her. In his intoxicated state, he had unrealistic visions of the ideal life, filling Todd's head with unlikely tales. Todd heard the fantastic stories of how they were going to live the dream in an oceanside house — how they would wander the beachfront, collect shells and swim in the surf — an idealistic life. In truth, Todd lived in a house of cards that came tumbling down.

It was not unusual for this little boy to clean up vomit and excrement when his father went on a bender and passed out on the living-room floor, clad only in underwear. It was not unusual for this small child to be left unattended overnight. Several interventions did not solve the problem. Kevin refused to believe he was an addict. Todd was not only dealing with his personal world torn apart, but he was constantly taunted and bullied by his peers, being reminded that his father was the town drunk.

Our family of five — my husband, our three young children, and I — lived miles away from the rest of the family. Perhaps the best solution would be to remove Todd from his current location. After many serious discussions, we decided to take on the challenge. I insisted on safeguards for Todd, demanding that my brother-in-law sign over legal guardianship and give us the right to raise Todd as our own. We would give him a fresh start — a new life. His father would have visiting rights, but he would not be allowed to take Todd away.

We also determined that the choice to live with us must be Todd's.

When he was asked, he reached out as if he had found a life-saving raft in an ocean of despair. That does not mean he was not afraid — he was terrified. I was, too. What if I could not be the mother he needed? How would my other children accept him? There were no do-it-yourself books to read for advice. It was a time before family therapists were readily available — when commonsense ruled. We had to deal with it the best way we knew how; step by step, we would cope and learn.

The day he was to arrive, I prepared my daughter, age eight, and son, age seven (the baby was too little) to help them understand that their cousin was coming to live with us and would be like an older brother. Their little minds thought it was wonderful! Little did they know.

When Todd arrived, he stood in the doorway, his face white with fear. He knew, and I knew, that the next step he took would change our lives forever. At ten years old, he had already experienced more emotional trauma than most people do in a lifetime.

"Todd, come in," I said. "We are so excited to have you here. Come into the kitchen. I baked a cake." I hoped my words were welcoming and cheerful. Todd still stood rigidly on the doorstep, not moving. My daughter sized up the moment, walked past me, took Todd's hand and led him over the doorstep. As far as she was concerned, he was hers now.

The transition was rocky. In the first week, Todd and my two older children were playing in the basement, where we had set up a play area. I heard loud crashing noises. My two children rushed into the kitchen, crying. Todd was smashing all their toys. I sat with a child clinging to each knee, trying to calm them as I heard the chaos from below. I explained that Todd had lost all his toys and his mommy — and he was angry and sad. We could buy new toys, I told them. He just needed to break those toys to let out some of his sadness.

When he came into the kitchen, his face was streaked with tears. He apologized. I nodded and said, "I know," and gave him a hug. Over the years, I heard apology after apology. But the need for emotional outbreaks and angry releases became fewer. This troubled child learned to overcome his anger, his fear, his loss. In time, this resolve became his strength.

Todd was everything high-energy. To be around him was to sense his restlessness. If he was expected to sit and listen to a story, he would jump on the bed or run around it before leaping between or on the other children. The best tool we had was his bike. I would send him off to do ten trips around the subdivision to burn off his intense energy. This gave us all a few minutes of calm and helped ease my tension.

Our circumstances changed when we decided to move to the country and try a little homestead farming. It was as if Todd had found his calling. We bought him a calf, and the barn became his go-to place, the calf his beloved chore. He had inherited his father's good looks and charisma, and he made friends easily. He smiled often now. Rewards for showing his calf at our local agricultural fair, selling pumpkins to earn money, and playing hockey and other sports brought positive reinforcement into his life. For the most part, he became a healthy, well-adjusted young man.

When Todd was fourteen, his father died. Kevin had become less and less a part of Todd's life, yet that love between father and son was always present.

Our house was filled with Todd's teenage friends. I often counted the shoes at the door to estimate how many had slept over. At his graduation from college, I was as proud as any mother could be. At his wedding, I played mother of the groom, even though I was really aunt of the groom. When his children were born, the birth announcements listed me as their grandmother — the ultimate reward.

Sometimes, now forty-some years later, I watch this handsome man, his hair greying, and realize how blessed I am to have him in my life, grateful that the strength of our family brought him through. He is a devoted husband, and father of a son and daughter. He is confident and capable. He is still high-energy and uses it to operate a small business where he employs several people. He stands tall in the community and plays as hard as he works. His smile is still winning, and his blue eyes are happy.

Nevertheless, that vision of a small, lost soul on my doorstep will be with me always.

— Molly O'Connor —

35

Young Minds

*We have a powerful potential in our youth, and
we must have the courage to change old ideas
and practices so that we may direct
their power toward good ends.*
~Mary McLeod Bethune

I'd just entered a huge space with round tables, each seating ten, set up to feed the homeless of Philadelphia. Tired from a long day at work and an hour-long drive, I glanced around in search of my two sons. They'd be sitting with friends and strangers while my husband, my boys' father, served dinner to the masses.

I spotted them and approached that table only to be delayed by a young, heavy-set Black female. She pulled me aside.

"I wanted to tell you something…" she began, "…since you're the same complexion as me."

"What is it?" I asked.

"Well, I went to the table where your children are sitting and the three-year-old told me he doesn't like brown people."

My jaw couldn't have dropped any lower.

"This took me by surprise…" she continued, "…because you're Black. I just thought I should tell you."

Nothing I said could change something I didn't even comprehend. Neither of my boys went to daycare at the time, so where did he hear such a thing?

I apologized to her and found my two smiling boys seated with a rainbow of homeless folks doing their best to use decent language in the presence of a five-year-old and his little three-year-old brother.

After greeting my boys with kisses, I smiled and sat with the other guests for the next hour, thinking about how to approach this issue.

Later that evening, following story time, I broached the topic with my sons.

I turned to my younger child. "Did you tell a woman today that you don't like brown people?"

"Yes, Mommy," he said, with no remorse or nervousness in his tone.

"Why?" I asked.

Then, my older one piped in and told me the neighbor's older son had said it.

I was shocked. I'd been night-sitting brothers for my next-door neighbor, a single white mother struggling to keep food on the table. I didn't want to believe she'd say such a thing considering she'd asked me, a Black woman, to watch over her babies.

That night, after she dropped off her boys, I brought up this most difficult subject.

A string of "Oh my gosh. I never told them that. I'd never tell them that. Please believe me. I will get to the bottom of this. Are you going to stop having them over?" gushed out of her. She was rather distressed.

I assured her I'd still take the boys, and she promised she'd talk some sense into her older son. The next day, she told me that someone in her son's class baited him to say it. Then, her son dared mine to do the same. She apologized again and took them back to her house.

Now, I set to undo the damage. Adults often say parents cannot and should not reason with a toddler, but what else could I do?

I sat my three-year-old on my lap and said, "Do you love me?"

"Yes, me love you, Mommy."

"Is my skin brown?"

"Yes."

"So, it's not true that you don't like brown people, because you love at least one brown person, right?"

He nodded but didn't look so sure. "Well, I love Mommy but not other brown people."

"And what about you," I said to him. "Do you love yourself?"

"Yes," he said again.

"That's good," I said. "You are a lighter brown than me, but you're still brown. Since you love yourself, what you're saying about not liking brown people isn't true."

He stared at me, taking it in.

"And you love your brown brother and brown cousins, right?"

He nodded.

"Then, what that boy told you to say isn't true. So don't repeat what he said anymore, okay?"

He leaned into me and wrapped his arms around me as far as they would go. "Okay, Mommy, I won't say it."

"And don't believe it either."

He hugged me tighter and said, "You still love me, Mommy?"

"Yes, baby, I love you tons."

He never said those words again.

— Cassandra Ulrich —

The Pain of Serenity

I will not have my life narrowed down.
I will not bow down to somebody else's
whim or to someone else's ignorance.
~bell hooks

After the death of her mom, a fellow caregiver posted, "I miss my mom, but I don't miss being her caregiver." Her profound and transparent statement provided the raw, naked truth of the uncontrollable and chaotic reality of a caregiver.

It is certainly my reality as the caregiver to my ninety-six-year-old Queen Granny. I live an unpredictable, tumultuous lifestyle that hinges on the unrelenting disease of dementia. The disease's control over Granny's world creates a personal world of ever-changing emotions, unimaginable experiences, and agonizing decisions for me.

Each morning, I have no idea what the day will bring. Will it greet me with the required cleaning of uncontrollable body waste, or a mountain of food crumbs from late-night sneaky snacking? Perhaps I'll take a visit to a whimsical land where I chase after "walking socks," tuck in deceased loved ones for a good night's rest, or shovel snow in the living room. It may consist of reliving the stories of old, retold over and over and over again.

Other days, it's simply holding Queen Granny like an infant or listening to old gospel spirituals on the AM radio. Either way, each day brings about a different physical, mental and emotional challenge that's completely overwhelming.

With the plethora of emotions I experience, there are moments I would like to stay in bed, cover my head, and scream for it all to STOP! Praying she'll slip away peacefully into God's arms for eternal rest would mean the loss of my dearly loved Queen Granny, but it'd also mean an end to my unpredictable daily struggles of caregiving. Would her death provide a sense of relief, pain, or guilt for my silent prayers? The ranges of my emotions are extreme and contradicting. My caregiving responsibilities keep me on a roller coaster of ups and downs, and I don't know how to halt the madness of our deteriorating lives.

Watching Queen Granny deteriorate has been one of the most painful challenges I've experienced. Each day, I lose a piece of her to dementia; it is heartbreaking and gut-wrenching. She's no longer the vibrant Queen Diva I grew up with. Now, her eyes are glazed over as she fights between two unstable realities, tossed back and forth between her past and her present. Her inability to remember simple things like changing the channel or moving her limbs to walk is tormenting. This stage of loss has been the most difficult to witness.

I am losing my Queen to a dark, unknown place. Her feistiness and sassiness have been replaced with sleepiness and slurred, unrec-ognizable speech. The ritual of crowning her head with various wigs and hats is long gone. All that remains are the short, fragile strands of white-gray hair barely covering her scalp. Her Queen-like beauty routines of full-face make-up, polished nails and toes, with sparkling jewels adorning her ears and neck, are a fading memory. Now, she's slumped over, sleeping in her favorite chair for most of the day. At times, she's unable to remain alert to complete a casual conversation or a short game of Bingo. These odd behaviors are totally unlike the smack-talking, gossiping Queen Granny I know and love. She's quieter, weaker, and slower. Her requests have been replaced with subdued acceptance of whatever the day brings.

I don't know what's worse: observing her slow demise or dealing with the harsh demands and manipulative ways of this horrific disease.

Each progression has been challenging, and the stress and sadness eat at my peace. The monster of dementia has drained me in every capacity as I carry its burden. And not only has this monster created a frenzied life for me, but it has also brought strife and division within my family.

Some of my non-caregiving family members aggravate my predicament. I feel judged for every action and decision I make on Queen Granny's behalf. Their initial belief in the secretly whispered untruths from a tortured woman is infuriating. In my opinion, they show little concern for my wellbeing, and my need to vent occasionally is perceived as immature and negative. Yes, I should disregard the disapproving words and looks because they are clueless while living their own lives, far from my chaotic reality. At times, their lack of understanding and my anger toward them create a wall of pain between us.

There are times, I am viewed as selfish for wanting my life back. Is it wrong to place her in a nursing facility, to get back control over my life? Any choice I make affects Queen Granny. It feels like I'm disposing of the Granny who took me and my two siblings into her home when our mom passed. She kissed my boo-boos, and provided food, shelter and my basic needs. How can I break her heart and no longer care for her when she cared for me? These questions swirl around in my mind and keep me on edge. I want my life back, but what does that mean for Queen Granny?

I contemplate my choices. Keeping her means she's home and secure, but I'm overwhelmed and unable to provide the best care. Placing her in a nursing facility means she has twenty-four-hour care, but she's alone and without family. How can I find a facility that will treat her with the Queen status she deserves? Looking at the amenities and accommodations isn't a way to decide where she should live out her final days. I want to look inside the hearts of the staff and know they will care for her the way I do.

My heart is torn, and my torment is real. I attempt to remove emotions and think logically, but it's futile. I have only found one resolve: prayer. My prayers are for courage, wisdom, and freedom from guilt. In an attempt to find serenity in my pain, my solace comes from these familiar words: "God grant me the serenity to accept the things I cannot change, the courage to change the things I can, and the wisdom to know the difference."

It is my only path to peace and freedom from this chaotic, uncontrollable journey of dementia and caregiving.

— Nicko Rochell —

37

The ReedPop Note Fairies

Selfless giving is the art of living.
~Frederic Lenz

eing in the events industry was a high like no other. I was either in full work-until-midnight mode or participating in office hi-jinks when we weren't running a conference or convention. Our company, ReedPop, was dedicated to delivering the ultimate, inclusive fan experience. We ran over thirty global shows and had the largest pop-culture event in the U.S.: New York Comic Con.

There were some scheduling difficulties in 2020, and our Chicago, Seattle, and PAX (penny arcade) gaming shows were all happening within a two-week span early in the year. As the events inched closer, I noticed even our more chipper staff members looking exhausted. Being weeks out from a show can be very draining, especially when the A-list guests begin to cancel.

I decided the team needed a little cheering up. I devised a plan to type out anonymous notes to each team member and leave them on their desks. It was just a reminder about how much the fans appreciated their hard work and to highlight all their accomplishments.

As I came to work the following morning, the notes were all over their social pages. While a few had suspicions, I refused to acknowledge that I was the culprit.

Then, during two of our shows, the first death in the U.S. from COVID-19 occurred. Within a short time, our team decided to cancel our 90,000-fan Seattle show and move all other shows scheduled for the spring and summer to 2021.

With instructions to work remotely, all team members were quickly forced to shift focus. The thirty-day remote quarantine turned in to another thirty days. Morale was really low.

After receiving more heartbreaking news about a potential layoff, I kept brainstorming ways to cheer up the team. If only I could recreate the magic I saw the day after I wrote the notes.

At first, I thought, *I'll send postcards.* But this was early COVID times, and I wasn't sure if it was safe. Remember how we were all reading our mail with gloves on?

Later that day, my chat group had a Teams call. When only a few people remained on the call, I shared my idea about continuing the positive notes. My friend Sean suggested I send e-mails from an anonymous account. My roommate Britt remembered there was an e-mail database that would find our team of seventy-five people. Sean, Britt, and our other friend Camilla all wanted in.

"What should we call ourselves?" I asked.

"The ReedPop Note Fairies," Camilla answered. We decided to abbreviate is as RPNF.

We divided up the list among ourselves based partly on who we knew best. Once everyone had been assigned, we typed up individual personalized messages that capitalized on their accomplishments yet didn't give away our identities.

In only two days, the trial run was ready.

Immediately, there was buzz on Teams.

"Are you the RPNF?"

"What did your note say?"

"I didn't even know anyone noticed I had accomplished that!"

The chats were blowing up. Many people replied to the e-mails, talking about how bad they were feeling and how suddenly they felt seen, missed, and loved. It was incredibly rewarding.

As summer approached, no one had been given the all clear

to go back to the office. Unexpectedly, the company laid off about twenty people in our department. ReedPop West was disbanded, and co-workers who had worked there for over a decade were laid off.

There had been practically no heads-up. After months of hearing "We'll be okay," we realized things were falling apart more than was let on.

The ReedPop Note Fairies called an emergency meeting. "It's time for another round." These notes were more difficult to write. Again, there was an outcry of support. People felt appreciated. We were getting very honest responses about how they were hurting, but this helped.

As we ramped up for yet another round, we received a few messages from our team members asking us to send notes to certain people on the team who were struggling. Just seeing those requests helped us feel our work was appreciated.

After the conclusion of virtual NYCC (New York Comic Con), we agreed we needed to type out one last round before the year closed. The estimated release would be right before the holidays and would be one last acknowledgment going into a difficult time for many.

But as we approached Thanksgiving, our workload got to be too much, and we set it aside.

A week out from Thanksgiving break, I received a chat saying, "Are you safe?"

Confused, I went to respond, but then I heard tears in the living room. I walked out, but Britt was in her room with the door shut, which was quite uncommon. I texted her to see if something was wrong.

She came out crying. "I've been laid off," she said. I hugged her and checked my computer. I had received a message from my manager about a last-minute meeting, and my heart sank. "I'm next."

More than twenty people were laid off from ReedPop that day. As I lay crying in bed, I realized how many others were affected by this. Just like Britt and me, they had relocated across the country for this opportunity.

Then I got a text. And another text. And a few phone calls. They were from teammates expressing their sadness and acknowledging my contributions to the company. That's when I realized they were a very,

very small team now and also needed something to give them hope.

The following day, I wrote every person left at the company anonymously as the RPNF. I told them how they had touched me or our fans or clients. It was like my own goodbye to my time there and our time together.

Immediately after sending them out, I received responses acknowledging how they loved the notes. I reassured them that the RPNF would live on and encouraged them to reach out to someone in need. They might be surprised how much helping others can help them.

— Amber Curtis —

38

The Twinkle Heist

*Sometimes it takes only one act of kindness
and caring to change a person's life.*
~Jackie Chan

 o, ho hum. I didn't feel like decking the halls as I read the e-mail alert from my bank's fraud department. Twenty-seven hundred dollars overdrawn! This had to be a mistake. I called the fraud line like I was dialing 911.

I had been scammed! For years as a businessman, I'd protected the organizations I worked for from becoming targets of financial con artists. Thirty years ago, I left the corporate world to embrace my true calling. I became the year-round Santa who lived in my heart.

No sleigh swishes, no jingle bells. All I heard was the thump that landed in my throat and the plunk of my heart. Faster than Santa's sleigh would clock in, I was almost $3,000 in debt.

The COVID-19 pandemic had left a lot of folks, not just me, Santa Dan, out in the cold. When businesses and opportunities shut down, many of us were left scrambling to make ends meet. Our incomes were wiped away like chalk on a blackboard.

The entire country faced blizzard conditions of record proportion. An unexpected pandemic health threat took people, cities and air traffic by storm. My special appearances and Santa events were canceled. The smell of fresh baked cookies left the marketplace. Children's laughter faded from the playgrounds. This was a different kind of storm. This blizzard didn't drop snow. It dropped spirits.

I couldn't see a straight route through this mess. On my knee, when children's requests were beyond toys, we always made them known to God. But I didn't see how even God could help with my stupidity.

Finding myself almost $3,000 in the hole was like the Grinch stealing my Santa bag. The only thing I could imagine that would be worse was disappointing the thousands of well-behaved children who depended on me. I considered sending the guys behind this heist straight to the naughty list.

Looking to pick up some extra cash until the storm blew over was what got me into this mess. I received an e-mail inviting me to apply for a secret shopper position. Two weeks later, FedEx landed on my driveway delivering my instructions. The package wasn't wrapped with ribbons and bows, but it was as easy as pumpkin pie.

I was instructed to deposit the $3,350 check in the package made payable to me into my bank account. Once it cleared, the instructions said to take $3,000 and purchase three $1,000 money orders from a well-known national retail chain. Everything looked official. The store's logo was on the instruction sheet. My name, the bank's name and routing numbers were in place. They hadn't asked for any personal information. Everything appeared legitimate. I felt like I'd done my due diligence.

My job was a little naughty-and-nice surveillance to evaluate the friendliness and efficiency of one of the chain's local service departments. The store wanted to know if I'd received the quality service that they guaranteed their customers.

Once I completed my assignment, I paid the $75 fee to overnight the three $1,000 money orders to their Seattle office. The remaining $285 was mine to keep.

All had gone well. When I checked my e-mail again, I was excited to see one from my employer. "Good job! Your report was excellent. Your next assignment will arrive by FedEx on Friday."

Game for another assignment, I waited, patting myself on the back for the great job I'd done. I received an alert from my bank's fraud department instead.

My struggle increased when I discovered how little the bank was on my side. I'd been their loyal customer for many years. They gave me a few weeks to meet their deadline to have all the money back in my account or they'd label me a deadbeat with banks nationwide. They spoke as if I was the criminal.

I had rent to pay, and my bills were coming due.

I reached out to my daughter and son — not for money but kind words. They were heartbroken over the scam and the predicament that it left me in. Of course, they were willing to help. But I detected an undertone in their voices that was as heartbreaking as being conned.

I'd made a poor choice. The question that jingled through my mind was, "Is Dad capable of making his own decisions, or does he need our help?" I was disgusted with the situation, and now my kids were acting like my parents.

One mistake, and my independence was in question. I wondered if they'd start visiting more often to check up on me. More visits would be nice. But I know what day it is. I know where my keys are. I drive fine at night. There's nothing wrong with my memory or my decision-making skills. I'd been deceived by professional con men. It could have happened to anyone. And, according to the bank, it happened all the time.

"We see this four to six times a month at this branch," the fraud manager said.

I felt my face turn red, and my heart raced.

Unlike the banker, the police officer who filed my report was considerate. He said the same scam happened to his father. "Don't beat yourself up over this," he said. His kind words were a little late. I'd already been pulverizing myself over such a poor decision.

As the bank's deadline loomed, I reached out to my friends and the people I knew. I hoped to find enough odd jobs to dig myself out of the hole I was in. I needed work to help pay back the money I'd been scammed out of and keep current on my obligations. As word got out, a dear friend initiated a GoFundMe campaign.

I realized later that I was responding to my troubles as a frightened person who'd been hurt and was in need. But my friends responded to me the way they saw me. My friends knew me as the Santa who brought smiles and joy to many children over the years, including their own.

Within twenty-four hours, more than the $2,700 rolled in. My benefactor extended the time period, and within forty-eight hours it shot up to $4,300. In no time at all, I had more than enough to repay the bank and meet all my obligations.

Still, I felt stupid and ignorant. Of course, I thought I should have seen this coming. But when I couldn't see a way through the storm, it was the children who came to my rescue. The children I'd served for many years, the young and those now grown. Their kindness lifted my spirits and brought me joy like Christmastime filled my heart.

Sensing that familiar twinkle return, I choked up. I didn't struggle for words when I said a quiet thank you to God.

— Dan Short —

39

Teddy Bear Tears

Bears need people. People need bears.
~Pam Brown

I took a deep breath as I joined the line of mourners waiting to enter a funeral home in the heart of Detroit. I wasn't sure how I would react when I finally entered. It's not that I hadn't been to a funeral before; I've been to many. But I'd never been to one like this.

Death is never easy, but this was so senseless, so cruel, so wrong.

I looked up, and I could see bright red Lightning McQueen and blue *Paw Patrol* balloons floating in the front with big bouquets of flowers. My legs suddenly felt weak. As I steadied myself for what I was about to see, my hands tightly grasped a chocolate-brown teddy bear.

The coffin was white and small. Inside lay a handsome three-year-old boy in a white suit. He was the same age as my son. However, his energy, laughter, and dreams had been stolen during a reckless drive-by shooting.

I walked past to see his little hands folded, his little eyes closed. With tears in my eyes, I clung to the bear and kept moving past the coffin; the bear wasn't for him but for his older brother who was one of my freshman students. As I approached him, he looked at me with a mixture of confusion and sorrow that pierced my heart. When I gave him a hug, I quietly handed him the bear and went to find my seat.

This was the unofficial beginning of what has become known in my school as the Teddy Bear Project.

As a teacher, one of the hardest parts of my job is watching my students grieve and suffer loss. Some want to be held while their tears fall freely; others don't know what they want or how to process what they're feeling. I want to show them they're not alone and they're loved, but sometimes it's not easy or welcome in that moment. But it's needed.

When the school year began in the fall of 2019, one of my freshman girls lost her grandmother, and it affected her deeply. One day in class, she approached me with tears streaming down her face. She didn't say anything, just pointed to her tears. I excused her to go to our assistant principal's office for some privacy and a chance to grieve. When class was over, I went to check on her, but I didn't want to go empty-handed. I've always had the need to give people something, especially when they are sad. I looked around my classroom, and my eyes landed on a small stuffed unicorn I had at my desk. I grabbed it and walked to the office where I hugged her and quietly handed her the unicorn. Later, my principal told me it had made her smile.

That's when the idea for the Teddy Bear Project struck me with such force that I knew it had to be from God. After asking permission from my principal, I recruited my mother-in-law and best friend to help me collect new and gently used stuffed animals, mainly teddy bears, to have on hand for students and staff when they were grieving or just needed extra encouragement. Cards were made and attached to each bear and placed in a storage room at our school, ready when needed.

And they were.

Not long after, two of my senior boys were grieving the loss of a childhood friend who had committed suicide. With the help of our assistant principal, we opened their lockers before school one morning and placed a bear in each. I then went back to my classroom to finish prepping for the day. Minutes before the first bell rang, one of these seniors came into my room gripping the Winnie the Pooh bear he had found in his locker. He was one of our star basketball players and he towered over me. (I'd often solicited his help when hanging up things around the school.) He looked from me to the bear. He paused as he tried to find the words.

"Mrs. Harsany… thank you." And he leaned down and gripped

me tightly in a hug that spoke more than words. I hadn't known then, but later I found out that his mom had called him "Pooh Bear" when he was a little boy.

"We love you, sweetheart. Let us know if you need anything," I whispered as the bell rang.

And that's what the Teddy Bear Project is all about: letting people know that they are not grieving alone and that they are always loved and remembered.

Why teddy bears? Why not flowers instead? Well, flowers are beautiful, but they quickly die and are thrown away. When the funeral is over and the flowers fade, that is sometimes the hardest part of grieving because it feels like everyone else has moved on. However, the teddy bear is still there. A teddy bear can be held when someone needs to cry or scream alone. A teddy bear absorbs their tears.

Throughout the year, our administration and my fellow teachers would text me when someone was hurting, and I simply replied, "Teddy Bear Project is on it."

We would slip teddy bears on teachers' desks and in lockers for students who had lost pets, grandparents, cousins, aunts, uncles, and parents. We also gave them to students who were struggling in other ways as a reminder that they weren't alone.

And then COVID happened, our school closed abruptly, and we were in a new and uncharted situation: quarantine.

As we were scrambling to teach and reach our students in this new virtual setting, loss was hitting our students in many ways. Not only did many of them lose members of their family but, because of the quarantine, many of them were unable to receive the closure that memorial services often provide. I received the first text from our assistant principal just days after quarantine began: One of our girls who had recently lost her aunt had now lost her grandmother as well. I knew I couldn't get into the building to access my teddy bear stash. Even if I could, I was supposed to social distance and couldn't take it to the student. But I felt strongly that the Teddy Bear Project should continue despite COVID.

And that's when Amazon became my quarantine partner for the

project. Bears were ordered and delivered to the doors of our students. They were reminded that even in a pandemic, they were not grieving alone.

As restrictions loosened and we were able to venture out more freely, the Teddy Bear Project continued with personal deliveries. I'll never forget delivering a stuffed fox to the door of a freshman who had lost his little niece. He wasn't home, but his father answered the door. He looked at me strangely as I stood there wearing my mask and holding a gift bag. When I explained who I was and why I was there, he was grateful.

He reached out to shake my hand and then stopped as he said, "Oh, yeah, COVID."

I reached back and gently took his hand. "It's okay." We were in this together.

Throughout the pandemic, I've heard the slogan, "We're in this together" over and over. That's what the Teddy Bear Project is all about. Even though a simple bear can never replace what was lost, it reminds us that we're not alone, that our tears are not ignored, and that we are truly in this thing called life together.

— Elizabeth Harsany —

40

How Bigfoot Helped Me Through Quarantine

When life gives you lemons don't make lemonade,
make pink lemonade. Be unique.
~Wanda Sykes

It was insomnia that caused me to befriend Sasquatch. My seven-month-old infant never slept through the night, but now I couldn't either, kept awake by the anxiety that goes along with a global pandemic upending your life. Right around when our town of Sturbridge, Massachusetts started shutting its doors and my wife applied for unemployment benefits, our baby started refusing naps in her crib.

She craved constant movement, so I started driving her around in her car seat to get her to fall asleep. It was early in the pandemic, so I was terrified to be out of the house, irrationally worrying that coronavirus-infected air would attack us through the vents. We hadn't left our home in a week and navigating the eerily empty streets of the neighboring towns reminded me of an apocalyptic horror movie.

Then, instead of a zombie, I spotted Bigfoot.

A neighbor about three miles from my house keeps a six-foot-tall, bronze-colored statue of a yeti at the end of his driveway. The Brimfield Bigfoot has been there for years, but I didn't see him much since I usually take a left to go toward Boston on Route 20, and he was out in the less populated area to the west. Bigfoot is covered in painted shaggy hair carved into a heavy plastic. He is frozen in position like he's lumbering through the forest, and his simian face looks angry that you spotted him. In March of 2020, he started wearing a mask and posing with a new sign every day. The signs were usually some kind of punny encouragement to socially distance:

"Sasqwash your hands for at least 20 seconds."

"Safe distance = six (big) feet."

"Be the missing link. Stay home."

Around 8:00 every morning, I'd bundle the fussy baby into her car seat and wonder how Bigfoot would greet me that day. The signs were all handwritten, a human touch on my isolated drive.

"I may be a hoax, but COVID-19 is not."

"Squatch your desire for a haircut."

"If I can avoid people, so can you."

And then, on the morning of April twenty-third, he was gone. I joined the Facebook group for the Bigfoot's town of Brimfield and saw that that our beloved mascot had been stolen the night before. I was surprised by how much I missed Bigfoot.

After two days, I saw our yeti back in his rightful place, recovered by police from thieves thirty miles away. I learned that Bigfoot's owner was a guy named Todd who came up to Bigfoot's shoulder when posing with him.

More than one hundred comments on Facebook celebrated Bigfoot's return and revealed that I wasn't the only one who looked forward to seeing our mutual friend every day. Susan said it was a "day brightener" to hear Bigfoot was home. Melinda said she had felt sad when he was gone and was looking forward to seeing him on her way home. Others joked about his big night out in the city and wondered if he had been sprayed down with Lysol after his return.

Eric summed up what we were all feeling: "With everything going on in the world today, seeing Bigfoot and his messages brought something to look forward to as you drove East or West on Rt 20." I felt closer to these neighbors I had never met, knowing we were sharing an experience even though we were alone in our cars.

Bigfoot kept up pandemic-related messages through May, now with new heavy chains protecting him. This summer, he's moved on from social-distancing messages on signs to flags signaling his caregiver's beliefs and interests. Bigfoot held a rainbow flag in his hairy hand for a couple of weeks during Pride Month. In July, he switched between different pop-culture flags: one with the rebel symbol from *Star Wars*, another with the crest of House Stark from *Game of Thrones*, and a Wakandan flag from *Black Panther*.

I may have substituted human contact for glimpses of a mythological creature, but through knowing I'm not his only fan, Bigfoot has helped me feel human connection again.

— Sarah Prager —

Coping with COVID

The Vegetable Connection

It's difficult to think anything but pleasant thoughts
while eating a homegrown tomato.
~Lewis Grizzard

Corn, kale, beets, and basil were key to keeping my son and me connected during the pandemic. Adam and I split a produce share from a local farm, and the diversion, delight, and deliciousness brought to us during this tough time have been boundless.

I realized early in the crisis that things were going to be difficult for a while, so I bought a produce-share membership at a farm near my home, something I'd never done before. Worried that Adam wouldn't be able to easily source safe, fresh food in the city where he lives, I proposed a shared share: I'd do weekly pickups, package his portion, and arrange physically distanced deliveries. Adam was in, and excited. The farm I'd been driving by for years thus became "our" farm. During a time of isolation and uncertainty, it provided far more than nourishing food.

Pickup day is Wednesday, but engagement starts Tuesday when the farm sends out its newsletter announcing what's in the week's shares. When there are options — pickling cukes or zucchini? parsley or cilantro? — I scan the pantry and pick what pairs best. Choices made, I text Adam and tell him what he'll be getting. Sometimes, he texts first and asks, "What's in the bag this week? Doing meal planning."

Wednesday's my new favorite day. I have something to do, somewhere to go — and I get a goody bag. I tell the farm workers that every week, and they enjoy hearing it. And, being an efficiency nut, I build my daily workout into my "farm time," powerwalking there and back, mask on, neon-yellow string bag across my back.

Once, on the way to the farm, I came upon fifty-five used golf balls in a messy pile on the side of the road. I scooped them into the string bag to bring home to my husband. Usually there would be room left over after I picked up the veggies, but that was the day we also got watermelons. The veggies went in the bag, and I power-walked home clutching a soccer ball-sized piece of fruit to my chest. People here have been watching me run or power-walk every day for decades, and seeing me speed-perambulate across town with a bright yellow bulge on my back and toting a watermelon drew more smiles than raised eyebrows.

Share divvied up, I text Adam to see if he'll pick up from my house porch or I'll deliver to the front seat of his pickup parked at work a few miles away. The veggie connection continues all week through shared photos of culinary treats coaxed from our farm treasures. Egg pie with roasted tomatoes and radish greens; burgers with caramelized onions and sweet-potato fries; grilled squash skewers; spinach and arugula salad with sliced almonds and blue cheese; sauteed snap peas and jasmine rice; shrimp stir-fry with sweet and shishito peppers. We send our dinner photos to my eighty-five-year-old mom, who shares what she's conjured from her latest curbside grocery pickup: turkey tacos; tilapia with spinach and mushrooms; macaroni and cheese. We're not eating together, but our three households connect through food at mealtime and feel a family touch that might otherwise not happen.

Each week, when I pick up my vegetables I give them a loving pat, knowing they'll be woven into the happier threads of our family's coronavirus story, and I thank them. When the farm's workers planted this year's seeds, they could never have known the immeasurable value of the bounty that they and their seeds would yield.

— Lori Hein —

42

Be a Firefly

It's the teacher that makes the difference,
not the classroom.
~Michael Morpurgo

The Kennesaw City Cemetery is within walking distance of my home. I had a tree planted there in memory of my grandparents, Rose and Ben. One of the winding paths between the headstones is known as Rose Circle. It is the oldest part of the cemetery. Some of the grave markers date back to the 1800s.

I began walking there more often during the pandemic because the parks nearby were pretty crowded. I would check on my grandparents' tree as the seasons changed. One evening I saw fireflies twinkling above a single gravesite with that unmistakable glow.

Weeks later, as I returned to that section of the picturesque cemetery, I passed by that same gravesite and remembered the fireflies. The words "be a firefly" suddenly came to mind. I am a teacher, and I had been praying for some guidance from an angel statue at the cemetery. I was about to teach a hybrid class, with some students in person and some still at home attending virtually. I had many concerns and questions, especially about how to keep up with my increasing workload and keep my classroom safe. It felt terribly overwhelming.

I forgot about those words — "be a firefly" — until later in the day. But then, when I researched fireflies on the Internet, my search revealed that fireflies are often viewed as beacons of hope.

So, what did any of this have to do with me? Be a firefly? What do those words mean? I looked around my community. It was early fall. Downtown Kennesaw was having a contest inviting people to submit a scarecrow for a community vote. I took pictures of my favorites along Main Street. Then I thought, *These photos would be good to put in a slideshow so my students can enjoy these fun ambassadors of fall.* They could choose their favorites. And they could create a resume for their top choice using the usual format, but they could get creative with the writing part.

I downloaded the photos, created the PowerPoint, and previewed it. And as I looked over my first week of teacher plans, something occurred to me that hadn't until then. Fun is contagious. And it lightens the heart. And we needed that.

J.K. Rowling's character Albus Dumbledore said, "Happiness can be found, even in the darkest of times, if one only remembers to turn on the light." To be a firefly, you have only to be a light. This was a dark period that was affecting all of us. No one could have imagined how this would change our public education system, our families, our kids, our homes, and ourselves.

As I was wrestling with returning to the classroom or not, wondering if I could handle the demands of teaching two groups of students at the same time, I realized the first step is the hardest; it would get easier once I opened the door to my classroom and turned on the light. I was there to give the students both at home and in school something to look forward to each day, and at times it would be tough. But it would be worth it. Franklin D. Roosevelt said it best, "Courage is not the absence of fear, but rather the assessment that something else is more important than fear."

Later, I went back to that gravesite and read the epitaph. Rachiel J. Hayes died at age eighty-four in December 1899. I noticed no other graves near hers, not a husband, children, or other family. It saddened me to observe that. And I understood, especially now with COVID, how lonely life can be without interaction with others. Of course, I don't know Rachiel's story, and her life could have been very full. But as I looked at the graves that were clustered in family groups, I felt sympathy for her and wondered why she was alone. I made a mental note to bring a pretty wreath to place on her gravesite near the holidays.

Next, I walked farther back around the historic section respectfully looking at some of the epitaphs from the founders of our town who are buried there. I saw a gated area where the headstones were especially old. Directly behind those was a grave marker that read: *Thy memory shall ever be a guiding star to Heaven.* It was in contrast to Rachiel's epitaph. And I realized that life should be about who you touch. That's not something I should give up, not when I had the chance to be a firefly — a beacon of hope — for my students, and indirectly for their parents as well.

— Tamra Anne Bolles —

43

Travelling All Over Again

*The very least you can do in your life is figure out what
you hope for. And the most you can do is live inside
that place. Not admire it from a distance
but live right in it, under its roof.*
~Barbara Kingsolver, Animal Dreams

There are many things I miss about life before the pandemic, and one of them is travelling. Right off the bat in spring 2020, I had to cancel a trip to Atlanta, and after a while it became clear I wouldn't be traveling anytime soon.

Needing an escape from the safety of my own home, I opened the bottom drawer of my dresser where I stored my old travel albums. I hadn't looked at them in years, but I thought this was the perfect time. It was refreshing to get a break from my screens and flip through the pages of these albums by hand. I was taken back to my European adventures to Italy, Ireland and Spain, relaxing beach vacations to Cuba and the Dominican Republic, and North American city trips to Quebec City and Boston.

And within each of these photo albums were small mementos from each trip. In my album from Italy, there was the stationery from the hotel I stayed at in Rome and the flap of a matchbook from a restaurant I dined at in Florence. My album from Boston had my baseball ticket stub from the game I went to at Fenway Park and my train ticket to Salem.

My album for Ireland included a few postcards I picked up there, including one poking fun at the Dublin transit system that featured a skeleton waiting at a bus stop and one of an old Guinness ad. And my album from beach trips included the fluorescent-coloured wristbands from the all-inclusive resorts — the golden passes that gained me entry to everything on the grounds.

My trip down memory lane ended prematurely, however, because my albums only went up to 2010. I had done many trips after that year, but I didn't have any physical albums to show for it. Why? Well, if video killed radio, then digital has definitely taken a heavy toll on print, including photo albums.

I'm not on social media, so for my first few trips after 2010, I uploaded pictures to an online album and shared the link with friends. That practice soon fell by the wayside because I was too busy after returning from these trips, so there are hundreds of pictures on the memory cards from my digital camera and on my cell phones. These include trips from everywhere from the Czech Republic and Curaçao to New Orleans and Newfoundland. Colour me embarrassed. I've done nothing with this treasure trove of memories.

With time on my hands during the second wave of the pandemic, and travel always in my heart, I have started to go through my travel pictures from the last decade. And like I used to do in the past, I am picking out the best ones to have them printed so I can start putting together physical travel albums once again. I also have a whole box of keepsakes from my trips (currently bundled together with elastic bands) to include in these albums, such as my Viking Museum pass from Stockholm and my ticket stub for a Broadway musical in New York.

As we have seen firsthand, technology changes rapidly, so who knows if we'll still be able to access pictures from our online albums, social media accounts and electronic devices decades from now. With printed photo albums, though, we'll always be able to hold them and flip through them, regardless of the digital advances that may come.

It took a pandemic, but I'm glad that I've gotten back into this old pastime of putting together travel albums again. It has not only helped me to reconnect with cherished memories and mementos from my old trips, but it has given me a tradition to continue when I'm finally able to travel again.

— Debra Rughoo —

44

That's Ms. Mommy to You

You can learn many things from children.
How much patience you have, for instance.
~Franklin P. Adams

I sat in bed with my tearful fourth grader, massaging her shoulders as she nestled between my legs, hunched over her math worksheet. "You've got this," I assured her.

"Can you do that thing where you tap your fingers at the bottom of my back?" she requested. It occurred to me that I had a new currency, a bargaining chip to entice her to complete the second half of the rounding exercise.

"How about this?" I countered. "Do the rest of these problems, and then we'll listen to that relaxing music your teacher posted in the Google classroom, and I'll finish your backrub."

It was the second week of remote school, and we subsequently began to incorporate massage into our daily routines — before school, during movement breaks, and after completing the least desirable assignments. I felt like a boxing coach hopping into the ring between rounds. I included her favorite back-tickling techniques but also deftly integrated brain-balancing exercises to activate acupressure points for concentration and frontal-lobe functioning, and joint compressions to help ground her proprioceptive nervous system. It was similar to that early 2000s cookbook where parents snuck pureed vegetables into their kids' ketchup.

As an early-childhood music therapist, I was no longer able to teach my in-person music classes. During the spring, when remote learning was more of a laissez-faire event, I'd fit in weekly Zoom music classes. But as the structure of learning intensified in the fall, I found myself incapable of doing anything aside from parenting my two daughters.

For the first time in my life, I was a stay-at-home parent. I relished the stereotypical perks — sweatpants couture, copious espresso consumption, and no more morning rushes — and settled into my new role with optimism.

I diffused uplifting essential oils. We organized my fourth grader's work environment to be tidy, inviting, and distraction-free. We played Disney music during independent work breaks to "pump ourselves up." I became so attuned to Google classroom notifications on my iPhone and laptop that I nearly developed a sixth sense, leaping up to print literacy PDFs mere seconds after they were posted.

"Mommy!" my fourth grader hollered as I writhed on the living-room floor, stretching to alleviate the low back pain that had cropped up as a result of my newfound sedentary lifestyle. "I need you to print this weird paper that has a picture of an elf on it!"

"Already did it!" I called back. "It's on the right side of your Chromebook on top of your clipboard!"

I sprinted up and down the stairs, locating pencils, pouring water, and retrieving printed documents while reminding my daughter to "listen with attention!" as she wound three feet of strung beads around her wrist. Occasionally, I would help my ninth grader identify universal themes from her Honors English assignment or assure her that her hair looked awesome and that the girl named Rhiannon was probably just bored and not actually throwing shade. I could simultaneously shush the barking dog and identify which child's voice droned from my daughter's Chromebook by her downward inflection of "Mrs. Myyyyers?"

It wasn't long before my delight in my new status began to wear on me. I was exhausted, frustrated, and unfocused. "You'll never get this time back with the kids," I repeated like a crazed un-Zen mantra when the chaos became too much.

Intellectually, I knew I would never regret our midday walks and morning snuggles, but the extra fifteen pounds, aches, pains, and ebbing creativity left me feeling resentful. I had always worked; this was brand-new territory, and I wasn't sure I liked it.

Whether I "got to" be a stay-at-home mom or "had to" was irrelevant semantics. Either way, I was one now. Shaming myself into gratitude or trying to find a silver lining had meaning, of course, but were ultimately useless details.

"I don't have a life purpose," I choked in the direction of my laptop screen as our couples' therapist sympathetically regarded me from his side of the Zoom meeting. "I'm used to having a life purpose. I know this is important work, but I never wanted to be a stay-at-home parent. I'm failing at my new job."

"You need to remember that what you're doing isn't parenting," he said gently. "This isn't normal. Very few people are good at what you're doing right now. Being a good parent may mean that you're not actually a very good teacher for your child."

His words comforted me and also made me think. It hadn't dawned on me that the absurd hodgepodge of daily activities I performed in the presence of my children wasn't actually parenting. But as a music educator and participant in parent discussions about schooling, I realized that these tasks were certainly not teaching, either. When it came down to it, my new role was neither SAHM nor homeschool teacher. I was more of an administrative assistant cum barely qualified life coach.

After our therapy session, I gave myself permission to be mediocre. "Good enough" became my new motto. I used fewer words in lieu of rambling diatribes and injected tough(er) love into my pep talks about attitude and participation.

My husband and I encouraged our fourth grader to have compassion for her remote teacher — whom I pictured to perpetually have her head in her hands — as she urged (begged?) the kids to pay attention, share their work, and turn their screens back on. Eventually, our daughter became more comfortable with the daily schedule, gained confidence, and started taking pride in her contributions to class discussions.

"It feels better when I try!" she crowed. As for me, I tried a little less.

At first, I wondered if her lack of cooperation was due to laziness or incompetence. Ultimately, I decided there was likely another culprit: a fried nervous system permeated by an undercurrent of constant low-grade anxiety and grief over the loss of normalcy.

I've tried to find some middle ground between hovering and abandoning my overwhelmed child to the Chromebook wolves. I avoid being a pencil-fetching, snack-cart operator but know that if I leave her to print and retrieve her own materials, she'll lose the thread and wind up frustrated and emotional.

"I need you to print this honeybee sheet," my daughter whispered to me.

"It's printed and already on your desk," I whispered back from my yoga mat.

It may be wishful thinking, but I'm pretty sure she gazed at me as though I were a remote school wizard. "Thank you so much," she replied with genuine gratitude.

Whatever my job was — parent, teacher, administrative assistant, or slightly woo-woo remote-learning facilitator — maybe I wasn't a complete failure at it after all.

— Stephanie Sprenger —

45

Wedding Cake & COVID

*Creativity involves breaking out of expected patterns
in order to look at things in a different way.*
~Edward de Bono

"**W**e need to talk about COVID." My fiancé stood on the other side of the counter as I stirred the low-fat enchilada sauce. Our wedding was in less than six weeks, and everything we ate had "low" in front of it: low cal, low fat, low sugar. I was excited for the wedding and secretly excited for the carb-heavy meals to come. No more sweat-inducing nightmares of stuck zippers and last-minute alterations.

"What about it?" I asked.

I never stopped stirring, and I certainly didn't look up. I knew my facade of composure would slip if I did.

"It's getting serious. We need to start talking about an alternative plan."

I sighed and twisted the knob to simmer. The conversation was unavoidable. Our wedding was scheduled for late April, and until March my thoughts had been consumed by centerpieces, seating arrangements and the room temperature necessary for cakes with whipped topping. Two weeks earlier, my co-workers had thrown me a bridal shower with chocolate fountains and advice from the people I spent forty hours a week with. At that time, COVID was just a conversation next to the water cooler. It was not yet a way of life.

Wedding stuff had all seemed so serious and important until mid-March. Prior to COVID, I could spend hours going down the rabbit hole of wedding jitters and overthinking. Were my shoes too tall? Should we practice our first dance? Would the flights land on time? It was unreal to now be having a conversation about whether there would be a wedding at all.

There was about a week of limbo, and then the news abruptly shifted. What was once a scary possibility became an alarming reality.

When my fiancé came home a week early from a business trip, I knew that the jig was up. The truth I had been running from had finally caught me.

"We need to talk about COVID," he said.

Our conversation that night grew heated as I insisted that we should "cross that bridge when we get there." Everything felt so out of my control. The last thing I wanted to add was predicting the peaks and valleys of a pandemic and whether we'd be able to squeeze in a wedding. It felt silly and self-indulgent, but then again so many elements of weddings are.

When his mother arrived from Chile, we were waiting at the airport armed to the teeth with hand sanitizer. It felt like a science-fiction movie as we walked through an eerily calm LAX. A year ago, I had imagined his mother and I flitting around Los Angeles in my final unmarried days, running in and out of shops, fussing over details and having garbled heart-to-hearts through our language barrier.

None of that happened. We got take-out, returned to our apartment, and kept an eye on the news. We quietly sipped coffee like fiends as shops closed and the public panic intensified. People were scared. I was scared! How could I daydream about tulle and toasts when people were afraid for their jobs and health?

More than anything, I wanted to assuage my guilt. I still wanted to get married. I still wanted to see my family and friends celebrate our love story that was almost ten years in the making. The world felt like it was falling apart, and while I was scrabbling to come to grips with our new normal, a tiny part of me still felt sadness for the day of love that seemed like it would no longer come. I wouldn't even articulate these feelings aloud for fear I would seem as silly and superficial as I felt. I desperately wanted someone to tell me that I wasn't terrible for having these thoughts in the midst of a crisis, but nobody did because we were all too damn busy being scared.

I sent a long message to my wedding party that we might have to make a few changes, but the wedding was still on at that moment. I even did a walk-through with my wedding planner. We all wore masks and stood six feet apart. We played it safe while simultaneously pretending that it was planning as usual.

A week later, we received a refund from the venue and discussed backyard alternatives. Finally, with all options exhausted, we pulled the plug. We sat around our living room table and crafted what we hoped was a thoughtful message to our friends and family that we had reached the difficult decision to postpone our wedding. We collected our refund from the bakery and took the complimentary pieces of would-be wedding cake in plastic to-go containers.

When the fear reached a fever pitch, we put his mother on the next plane home. We were afraid that if we waited any longer, she would get stuck in our apartment eating leftover wedding cake and reading about COVID thousands of miles from home.

We spent the next few days scouring the Internet for a place where we could get married. No longer concerned about fanfare, we just wanted our union. We had been waiting what felt like forever to become husband and wife, and one more month seemed a month too long. When even Vegas chapels closed their doors, we felt completely out of luck.

On our planned wedding date, I awoke with a heavy heart. I had already imagined I would spend each hour looking at the clock and thinking of what I should've been doing instead. Ten o'clock brunch with bridesmaids. Eleven o'clock make-up, and so on.

Instead, my fiancé woke me up with breakfast in bed and flowers. I was determined to mope, and he was determined to make it a day of love. We didn't get married then but, on that day, I had never felt surer that he was supposed to be my husband.

A few days later, a co-worker informed him that a neighboring county was doing drive-up weddings. We just had to register online and give them a call first thing Monday morning. If we were lucky, we'd get a spot. My emotions had been on a roller coaster for a little over a month, and I felt far too fragile to get hopeful.

Monday morning came, and like kids on Christmas, we were up earlier than usual, doing our best to seem nonchalant. At 8:00 A.M. sharp, we began calling. I was on hold for so long that I thought they forgot about us. When I finally heard the intake of human breath, my heart skipped a beat.

In what seemed too easy after the past few weeks, they gave us a date. It was our anniversary.

We drove to the site and, in a parking lot surrounded by other couples who had decided that love couldn't wait, we were married. Our witness held an iPad to capture the ceremony, and the tiny speakers blared with cheers around the world from family and friends in celebration of our love.

— Lauren Morton —

46

As Screens Come Up, Walls Come Down

Communication is merely an exchange of information,
but connection is an exchange of our humanity.
~Sean Stephenson, Get Off Your "But"

Afflicted with cabin fever about a month into the pandemic, I tapped out a note to my journalism friends from Ohio University, where decades ago we had chased stories and dreams. "If your Zoom dance card isn't full, a few of us thought it might be fun to reconnect over drinks and the miles at 5:00 P.M. on Saturday," I wrote.

Seconds later, Scott quipped, "Sounds great! I'll pick up the check."

"Can't wait to see all your tiny, smiling faces," responded Dee Dee, signaling the beginning of regular Zoom dates, the rectangles multiplying as old friends joined the periodic video calls.

I never thought it possible to be cloistered and connected. But, to my surprise, my relationships today are more intentional and emotionally intimate than ever.

Every night, shortly after 5:00 P.M., my social-worker son calls from New York City to chat about his work counseling HIV-positive adults, the latest adventures with Link — his roommate's deaf rescue dog — and that night's vegan recipe. My phone, markedly quieter before the pandemic, now dings daily with text messages from my college roommates, my older son, or friends from across town, on the other side of our rural road or on the opposite coast.

"Can't sleep! So excited for a new beginning." A neighbor interrupted my sleep with a 5:30 A.M. text on Inauguration Day.

"Hot Pockets recalled. That's IT. That's my bad-news tipping point. I'm out," texted a close friend from L.A. in one of her hilarious messages.

And every few weeks, my journalism-school friends gather to check in on each other, analyze the day's headlines, and renew friendships that began over all-nighters pulled together producing a daily student newspaper in a small Appalachian college town. Scattered now from Manhattan to Seattle, these are some of the most fascinating people I know — curious, inquisitive, compassionate and unfailing in truthtelling. They are the storytellers who will chronicle the unfamiliar road we're traversing for the pages of history.

Stories and news bring us together like hummingbirds to nectar. But it's friendship cultivated over forty years that keeps us moored.

"We know each other the way children who grow up together know each other," said Anne, a health reporter.

Still held largely captive in our homes, we talk about our lives in isolation and playfully tease each other. "None of those classes helped you, Larry, because you didn't go to them," Peggy, a contact tracer, told an AP reporter, to laughter from the group.

"We've come full circle," I told Theresa, a space reporter at *Breaking Defense* who was carded when she showed up early for "senior shopping" at her neighborhood grocery store.

During our college days writing and editing for *The Post*, we stood on the cusp of careers that would bring us into the lives of readers. These days, we find ourselves peering into each other's lives. After her son suddenly lost his job, a friend fought back tears and shared her worry about his future. As writers who respect facts, we're dismayed by those in our own families who embrace unfounded conspiracy theories. Choking back disappointment, we canceled Christmas plans with relatives after a new surge in the virus.

During these socially distant times, we show up for each other — and show vulnerability. We've learned to be gentle with ourselves. Every video call now ends with two words: "Love you!"

Turning wistful as the conversation wound down one week, Larry quietly urged us to live life without hesitation. "The road behind us is longer than the road ahead. Embrace every moment. Find that moment of joy."

As I clicked "leave meeting" on the laptop screen, I realized the pandemic will end eventually, but friendship may be the one immunity that lasts a lifetime.

— Teri Rizvi —

47

Make-Believe & Magic

Creativity doesn't wait for that perfect moment.
It fashions its own perfect moments
out of ordinary ones.
~Bruce Garrabrandt

We were gutted when we received the cancellation e-mail. Yet it seemed selfish to mourn the loss of a mere holiday during a pandemic. Then again, it was our thirtieth wedding anniversary, and we'd planned a once-in-a-lifetime cruise with destinations close to our heart. It was a "meant-to-be cruise just for us," which included Croatia where we'd gone for our first holiday abroad together and Lake Bled in Slovenia where we'd honeymooned.

We'd booked it in August 2019, anticipated it, planned it. On the day of our anniversary, we were scheduled to be in Venice, where we'd gone for a day trip on our first holiday in Croatia. We intended to splash out in the café with the orchestra and have coffee and cake in St Mark's Square.

But the world had turned on its head. I had asthma and was terrified of catching COVID. For months, I stayed in the house, my routine ripped asunder.

When I went grocery shopping for the first time in months, I felt terrified — not only of the virus but of people. It gave me a new fear that I was becoming agoraphobic.

The loss of a cruise was insignificant compared to all these scary feelings and what others were experiencing. But my husband Robert and I felt low, depressed, and then guilty about feeling that way.

We pulled ourselves together and formulated a new plan. We'd go back to doing what we'd done as children and play "make-believe."

For the full week, we pretended we were really on the cruise and shared our "experiences" with our friends on Facebook. It was so heart-warming when they got into the spirit of it, leaving comments such as "Enjoy" and "Weather looks gorgeous. It's raining here."

When we posted old photos of us in Venice in our twenties and said, "This holiday's taken years off of us, 34 to be exact," a friend quipped, "And added a few inches as well."

Another friend said Robert looked like a model from Grattan in his 1980s photo and asked us to let them know if we found a good restaurant as it was their silver anniversary the next week.

At the start of our make-believe adventure, we poured a drink and clinked glasses when we were at the "airport" at the beginning of our journey.

We researched the destination we had been scheduled to visit on each day and watched videos of the place. Then we dressed up in holiday clothes, sunhats and sunglasses and took selfies of famous landmarks from each place, usually behind us on our TV, and posted them in Facebook.

On the actual day of our anniversary, friends and family dropped off presents. Others had traybakes and champagne delivered. They were really inventive.

For me, that's one of the few positives of the pandemic: the creativity of people in finding solutions. It shows the resilience of the human spirit.

One friend gave us T-shirts emblazoned with a photo of us on our wedding day and the words "Pearl Anniversary: The One Where We Were Quarantined" on it.

We also had Zoom get-togethers with family and friends on the actual day, but we didn't forget to post our "cruise update."

Some nights during the week, we got dressed up for dinner as if it were a formal night on the cruise, with me in my posh dresses and Robert in his tuxedo and bowtie. As it had been ages since we'd had a chance to put on "going-out clothes," we really enjoyed it.

During the whole experience, we had great fun, finding suitable photos of each destination, whether new ones from the Internet or actual old ones of us.

We loved deciding what activity we would be getting up to on that day. Would it be sightseeing or a sail-away party? Would we be eating pizza or ice cream?

Doing this gave us a project and a purpose, and it pulled us out of our self-pitying moping.

We realised it's only one holiday and, hopefully, we still have it to look forward to one day in the future. We are very much counting our blessings of each other, family, friends, our imaginations, sense of humour, and a determination to have some fun, no matter what.

We discovered that we are never too old for make-believe, and it's still possible to create our own magic in an uncertain world.

— Sharon Haston —

48

Pandemic Delivery

The appetite is sharpened by the first bites.
~Jose Rizal

We were careful. We wore masks and spread hand sanitizer around like it was Christmas cheer. We had one of the last cans of Lysol seen in captivity. Anyone who so much as touched the doorknob got the soap-and-water treatment.

And we got sick. All four of us, in separate rooms, but joined together by the same mysterious disease.

The pandemic had invaded our home.

Lying in bed, counting on the CPAP machine I used for sleep apnea to breathe for me, I realized that if anyone in my family took a turn for the worse there was nothing I could do. I was too weak to know, too tired to help. I mechanically took the medicine my sons had given me because they wouldn't go away until I swallowed. The fluids they pressed on me were like lava in my mouth. My throat felt scorched.

I was freezing cold, and then the fever engulfed me like the fire.

One day, somewhere in a faraway world, I heard, "Our food is here!" Then I heard the rattle of bags and the laughter of a new discovery. "Mom, do you want something to eat?"

No. God, no. It had been three days.

Sleeping and not sleeping, the sounds came again through the haze. "Our food is here!"

Everyone had been sick, but slowly I realized that the sound of the shower running in the morning and the evening, spreading healing steam in withered lungs, had stopped.

"Our food is here!"

They were better. Healing. They could eat. But what did they find? It seemed like years since we had seen the outside world or gone to a grocery store.

"Our food is here!" Gleeful sounds replaced the shower running, the coughing, the shuffle of feet too tired to take real steps.

"Drink this. Do you want something to eat?"

No. God, no. It had been... four days? More?

My sons were grown. And resourceful. And in a world where we were the lepers of old — the unclean, the quarantined, not allowed to mingle with society — they provided.

Bags rustled. Footsteps headed to the kitchen. "What did you get?" The question sounded like a Christmas morning question from long ago.

Every day, we plodded through the house, my husband and me, trekking through the house like pilgrims, sitting in armchairs until we could go to bed again. *Keep moving, keep moving,* the Internet told us. *Keep moving so that it doesn't settle in your lungs.*

So there we sat, staring at the clock, willing the hands to move even one tick, not wishing time to pass in case that was the time when one of us got sicker, but willing the days to go by and relieve our suffering.

The picture that penetrated my isolation was my older son, man-sized and strong, pressed against the front door with his eye to the peephole. Our younger son ran in, waving his phone like an Olympic torch.

"They're almost here! They're almost here!"

And, in a minute, "Our food is here!"

Quarantine meant waiting until the delivery car drove away and then rushing out the door like the Brinks truck was dropping off gold bars.

"Our food is here! Mom, you need to eat."

Even after all the fasting days, I couldn't imagine eating food, not even the canned alphabet soup Mom had given me years ago when I stayed out of school with the flu and spelled my name with the letters. Now, I couldn't stand the thought of it in my mouth.

But my family was hungry, and even with their hands full of takeout bags of chicken and burgers, they reached out to me. Remembering the years of making special tea, toast and scrambled eggs when they were sick, I held out a hand for a bite.

Tears came when I thought there was no moisture left inside me. The face of COVID for me isn't the parched tongue, cracked lips, or seventeen pounds of fluid my body boiled for fuel.

It's the picture of two young men peeking out the front door, well enough to eat and strong enough to provide.

— Amy Mullis —

The Bread Bandits

Food is love. Food has a power. I knew it in my mind,
but now I know it in my heart.
~Jael McHenry

I t started with a single bubble. Then another. Then a third. By the fourth bubble, I began to celebrate. The sourdough starter was... starting!

Early in the pandemic, bread was hard to come by. I was ordering it online and it wasn't being delivered. We had gone a few weeks without fresh bread and had used up our stores of sliced bread, French bread, even some English muffins in the freezer. I had made a beer-bread mix that was in the cabinet, and it gave me an idea. What if I ordered flour instead?

Of course, flour was also out everywhere. A nationwide shortage. So, I looked to see if I could buy it online in bulk. I could, but it came in fifty-pound bags. Fifty pounds gave me pause. That's a lot of flour! But I decided to go for it. We didn't know how long we would be in quarantine, and we were going to need some bread.

It arrived two days later, the size of a pillowcase filled with flour. I didn't have a lot of yeast (also a nationwide shortage), so I looked up how to make a sourdough starter. It starts with some sugar, flour, and pineapple juice. I ran downstairs to the canned goods. Luckily, I had a can of chopped pineapple! I drained the pineapple and then mixed the three ingredients together. Then we had to wait.

And wait.

And wait.

Every day, adding a little more flour, taking a little bit away, we waited for bubbles. Sourdough starter is a way to activate the dormant yeast that is already in flour, but you have to wait until it ferments a little. When the bubbles arrived, I knew we could begin. As was custom (according to the baking websites I visited), we named our sourdough starter. By family vote, it was given the name "Gluttony."

I had never ventured into the world of bread baking. I had made cookies and cakes but never anything that required yeast. I decided that Friday would be my baking day, after I finished teaching my online lessons. I tried a number of different recipes and settled on one that used sourdough starter and a little yeast, too. The first couple of batches of bread weren't great. A few adjustments were needed. Maybe try it with a slightly hotter oven. Maybe let the bread rise a little longer. Maybe put a tray of water underneath or mist it with a water bottle before baking.

After a few weeks, I had a reliable pair of loaves that we enjoyed eating as a family. It felt good to be able to provide for my loved ones. We would eat the two loaves throughout the week, as toast or sandwiches, or to mop up some homemade soup. I loved making the bread from start to finish, from mixing the ingredients to kneading to waiting for it to rise, separating it, and waiting again. Baking the loaves made the house smell wonderful.

Then we had a freak storm, and the neighborhood lost a lot of trees. A tree landed on a neighbor's car. It was Friday, so I made an extra batch of bread. We left it on their doorstep and rang the bell. I figured that they could use a little cheer given the circumstances. Then I thought about all the other people in our community who could use a pick-me-up of fresh bread. A neighbor who had lost her job. A family that just had twins. A friend who was working really hard as a counselor.

Just like that, The Bread Bandits were born.

Every Thursday night before I would begin baking, we as a family would sit down and think about who was really struggling that week. We would choose two people to deliver bread to the next day. I would bake four loaves of bread (keeping two for the week), and we would pile into the car. We would drive to the house, ring the doorbell, drop the bread on the front step and run. The bread would come with a little note that said, "We hope you enjoy the fresh baked bread. Love, The Bread Bandits."

We did it every week for months, keeping a list of people whom we had visited. We weren't really that stealthy — a lot of people knew our car — but they were all very appreciative. Sometimes, it is just nice knowing that someone is thinking about you.

Before I knew it, we had to buy another fifty-pound bag of flour.

— Darcy Daniels —

50

Let the Music Play

Music is the moonlight in the gloomy night of life.
~Johann Paul Friedrich Richter

I hated doing dishes. I grew up with stern grandparents who felt that every member of the family must "work," no matter their age. For me, starting at age seven, it meant washing dishes.

Three times a day, seven days a week, I did the dishes. For a few years, I stood on a stool with an apron tied around my neck. Gran hovered over me, giving non-stop instruction. A forgotten spoon or a dirty glass would earn me a sharp smack or a pinch on the arm.

I hated doing dishes.

When I first lived on my own, I refused to do the dishes for several weeks. The dirty dishes become a science project. I think that was somehow in defiance of my grandmother's rules, despite the fact that she had no way of knowing what I had done. As years passed, I finally viewed doing the dishes as a necessary yet unhappy chore and tolerated my time at the sink.

When COVID-19 entered our world, many of us were required to tighten our belts, shelter in place, and pause the busy lives we led. We began to relearn some of the things lost to us from our own childhood. We began to cook again, sit around the dining room table together, and redefine relationships.

We made dirty dishes.

One morning, having procrastinated until there was not a clean spoon to be found, I resigned myself to the inevitable. The neighbors on either side were mowing, it was noisy, and I was cranky. My head was hurting.

I had received a pair of Bluetooth headphones for my birthday, and it occurred to me that maybe they would help pass the time and cut out the noise while I did the dishes. At that moment, I was willing to try anything to get out of my own head.

I popped them on and hit Play on my phone's music program. I selected Shuffle and began filling the sink with hot, soapy water.

At first, I was busy getting things organized and not paying attention to the music. I mindlessly hummed along, doing the glasses first, and then the plates and silverware. I felt the tension growing in my shoulders.

The next song cued up, and suddenly I was seventeen again. The old rock anthem brought a photo album of people and shenanigans to my mind's eye. I could smell the municipal swimming pool where we spent endless summer afternoons. I tasted the root-beer floats we made under the blue twilight of the end of a summer's day. I could feel the wind on my face as we cruised the main street with our friends, windows down, without a care in the world.

The next song talked of a dark, deserted highway, and there I was slow dancing with my crush at a dance in middle school. I could see myself dressed in red with a big white camellia in my hair, giggling in the bathroom with my girlfriends.

For the next hour, every song was a time capsule, every melody a window into bits and pieces of my past. I sang at the top of my lungs, danced in place as I washed, and used the pancake turner as a mic as I belted out one beloved tune after another. Sometimes, I laughed aloud at the memories; other times, I got lost in what-ifs. I thought of people I had not heard from in many years and those who had fallen along the way.

A few songs opened doors I thought had been long sealed shut. I wept at the image of my first love in his naval uniform, how he looked when he swept me into a kiss and the music seemed written just for us. I smiled through tears when I heard the song that was playing when my late husband proposed to me.

Finally, the dishes done, the kitchen clean, I was just about to hit the Power button when I heard the first notes from the orchestra. The first time I'd heard it, sitting in a darkened movie theater almost forty years ago, I was brought to tears by its beauty and soulful notes. The world-renowned opera singer ended the song with a note that seemed to hang in midair. It held me captive, powerless to breathe until the note ended.

As the note faded away, the floodgates opened, and I let go of all the bad memories of my childhood. I cried for that kid I used to be, for the people long gone and lost to me. I cried because I was thankful that, for whatever reason, my lesson came wrapped in the one thing that has been a constant friend in my life.

Since that day last fall, I have come to see those headphones as a time machine, a therapy session, and good medicine all at the same time. When the silence of living alone during a time of isolation gets to be too loud, I just... hit Play.

— Cj Cole —

Chapter
6

Attitude &
Perspective

51

"Bike Ride, Kids?"

I don't ride a bike to add days to my life.
I ride a bike to add life to my days.
~Author Unknown

hen our three kids were young, we'd ask, "Bike ride, kids?" They'd enthusiastically don helmets and jump on their bikes. Our family would set off into the sunset, winding through nearby developments. (The kids were not joyful because of superb parenting but because we lived a mile from LeBron James. When we rode past his gate, the boys hoped that LeBron would appear like Cal Ripken did on a commercial, asking if they could play ball.)

Bike riding cured all ills then. An upsetting test? A mean kid? Your basketball team did not score as many points as LeBron did? "Bike ride, kids?" was the fix. We'd slather on sunscreen and pedal, breathing in the smells of fresh air, spring flowers, summer grilling and campfire s'mores. It was our sailboat through small storms, the way our crew stayed afloat.

But as the kids grew older and busier with school, teams and activities, "Bike ride, kids?" was no longer a rallying cry. Life was changing. Even LeBron bolted from us, announcing he was taking his talents to South Beach. My crying boys tore down their posters and sold his jerseys for a dollar in our garage sale. We moved, too, for a job transfer.

In our new home of northern Virginia, with our lives full of work, horrendous commutes, and adjustments to new schools, family bike rides fell off the radar. Saying "Bike ride, kids?" to middle-schoolers triggered a "No way." A breezy bike ride was not the ticket during those turbulent teenage years. Besides, bigger wheels mattered: driver's ed. And so it went. They headed off to new lives at college... without their bikes.

Then we braked, like everyone, as the world crashed to a screeching halt in 2020. In January, I was shocked when a longtime friend, a fifty-five-year-old healthy pastor, suddenly died of a "flu." I was devastated. How in the world...?

Then the world learned of COVID, and we clung to safety nets: mask, distance, wash hands, wipe groceries. No movies, shows, or restaurants. Our kids returned. My older son's senior year in college blew up. My younger son's dream internship on Capitol Hill and a study-abroad program were canceled. My high-school junior daughter's school shut, too, and her spring musical was canceled. In my best Carol Brady voice, I said that while we had been robbed of milestones they'd looked forward to, they weren't alone. Other kids were feeling this loss, too. At least we were alive, getting through this together. But with our family sequestered, how to cope?

"Bike ride, kids?" I found myself saying.

They looked up from their phones as if I'd announced a presidential run. "No, Mom," they said. Zoom classes. Homework. Busy night ahead on social media.

"Fine. With or without you," I said, quoting from the prophets U2. (I'm prone to speaking in song titles.)

So, my husband and I set out without them, biking through the spring, talking about trauma, disaster, fear, grief, and anger. The bike rides felt stressful, dodging people walking, running, biking, and skateboarding. But the road was more dangerous. Cars zoomed through crosswalks or came too close. And, emotionally, it was impossible to relax, I couldn't get the scenes out of my head of sick people lined up in parking garages, healthcare workers crying, and kids without parents. I felt their grief.

By late spring, we had a daily time and route for our rides. We rode past the overgrown grass and dandelions by the closed-school sign, past a sign announcing a drive-by fifth-grade graduation, past the yellow tape — like a crime scene — cordoning off a playground, right to a new home development under construction. We rode to foundations poured, workers hammering, Mike Bradys in hard hats hunkering around maps, and past the model-home sign, "By appointment only."

Soon, instead of curing ills, "Bike ride, kids?" — they always said no — became about shutting out the world. A full hour respite. We hadn't made sense of the news anyway; what could we say? Life was surreal. The Brady Bunch was now in a horror flick that Stephen King couldn't pen. At least we'd made it to summer.

"Still they ride," I said, quoting a Journey song as we pedaled on through the early fall to watch the builders putting up insulation. The first new homes had closed, and we spotted smiling families putting up Halloween decorations, pumpkins and hay on porches, with hearty maroon mums planted in their landscapes. Life was being added.

Weeks after a Zoom Thanksgiving with family in Ohio, we learned my mom's husband had a tumor and would need brain surgery at Christmas. Without their kids, grandkids, friends, church, prayer groups and book club, they didn't have much help. Even our Christmas presents to them, mailed two-day priority, arrived three weeks later. Not even the mail could be counted on. We could only send prayers.

As the U.S. death toll climbed toward 400,000, and the Capitol was stormed, with police officers attacked, we were horrified again. Why was nothing making sense? There were no answers, only praying when stress-pedaling, wearing our winter coats on our trusty old bikes as blustery air chilled us.

Before long, though, we saw dozens of families moving into the new development. Then, early spring came and we rode past homes sprouting daffodils, green yards, a family's trampoline, kids shouting, dogs frolicking, and runners whooshing by. Parents swung toddlers on a new playground, chatting with their neighbors and talking about schools from six feet away. Cars bore license plates of Texas, Maryland, and California; new people were moving to the D.C. area. Children scurried, making fast friends. Perhaps it was a year's isolation, but everyone now waved, even little ones yelling "Hi!" from upstairs windows.

"We've watched an entire neighborhood built from the ground up," my husband called to me on one ride, enamored with the construction.

"Why am I excited for these people? I don't even know them," I called back, admiring a wreath, waving to a mom sitting on a driveway with her daughter, playing dolls the way I used to with my girl. The cycle keeps going.

At the pandemic's one-year mark, when the ride was routine, I suggested we try a mindfulness game.

"What?" my husband said.

"Let's see if we can find something we haven't noticed before on this ride!" (I'm not only prone to speaking in 1980s songs but also spouting ideas from Oprah's shows. Or Oprah's books. Or Oprah's podcast.)

He sighed his okay. Clearly he did not aspire to ascend to Oprah's level of mindfulness.

But since I'd already noted all the new houses' stone, brick or siding, decorations, and flowers, I only noticed this: All the portable toilets in the development were blue, except for one green one. My husband saw this: the building of a new road behind an old one. I yawned. (This is a man who once read a whole book on the building of roads. Of course, I once read a book on Oprah.) This is what had become of us on our bike ride. Portable potties and roads. Oprah would be disappointed.

The next day, after I said, "Bike ride, kids?" and they said, "No," we pedaled anyway, rolling right to the new development. I suggested the mindfulness exercise again. But as I was mindfully looking for life, I failed to be mindful of the MASSIVE TRUCK SUDDENLY BACKING UP INTO ME. About to be smashed, I overcorrected and swung my front tire at a seventy-five-degree angle over a curb. As it had been decades since I popped a wheelie, I crashed, shooting out of the seat and landing on my left leg, hip and arm. (Good news. As I lay in a heap, the truck driver finally stopped.)

"Wipeout," I said, like the old song.

"Are you okay? Geez! Be freaking mindful of trucks!" My husband shook his head, helping me up. But weirdly, as I hobbled up, shaking off the dirt, gratitude rushed me. I was not currently dead! Nor in an ambulance. The bike was intact. All limbs working. I'd dodged catastrophe with merely muddy jeans, scrapes and bruises, and was ecstatic.

At that unplanned moment, I noticed spring's light peeking through the clouds. Hope. Vaccinations had started! My mom's husband who recovered from brain surgery and was now in grueling chemo and radiation, was awe-inspiring, speaking of his faith, and the grace and strength God gave him daily. Our girl's entire senior year in high school, which had been virtual, was becoming hybrid for the last quarter. She'd picked her college for the next year, and our middle son was back at his dorm, hoping for a graduation, too. Our oldest son had graduated via Zoom (confirmed when the college diploma arrived in the mail). I felt so grateful for everyone. Slowly, the world was rebuilding, resilient, fighting for life anew.

Easing back onto my bike, I thought of big and small things that we take for granted. Like seeing our precious families and friends. Like having a graduation, a prom, a bed or toilet paper or bikes, or a hug. Like meeting a new neighbor with the promise of a new home — or watching an old neighbor return to fulfill his promise to his old home, leading Cleveland to our first-ever championship in 2016. (It is still replayed in our house. My sons want me to add here: LeBron is the GOAT — Greatest Of All Time.)

As I coasted down a low hill feeling the wind hitting my face, it finally felt mindful. In a year where "I can't breathe" referred to George Floyd and people on ventilators, I inhaled, feeling grateful for that breath at that exact moment. "Thank you, God," I said into the wind gust. A bumpy bike ride doesn't cure all, but it sure soothes the weary.

Back in our driveway, neighbors called over: "Did you hear about the prices of bikes? Since the pandemic, it's a supply-and-demand issue. Some people are paying $1,000 for 'em!"

Our eyes darted to the kids' abandoned bicycles in the garage.

"Kids!" I called. "Can we sell your bikes?"

— Kristine Meldrum Denholm —

Another Glorious Year

Sisters make the best friends in the world.
~Marilyn Monroe

L ooking at the card, I understood the significance after all these years. Aunt Anna had laminated it as a gift to my mother, a tribute to surviving tough times.

It was Mom's fiftieth birthday party, and the house was filled with relatives and friends who had come to wish her well and acknowledge that survival. Everyone knew that many of those fifty years would have tested the endurance of a superhero.

But Mom had survived them all — years of a bad marriage followed by the struggle of being a single mother raising five sons; the death of one of my brothers at age twenty-one; and the subsequent loss of his young son, her grandchild, who was taken away and withheld from the family. Those were hard years, before anyone had ever heard of grandparents' rights.

For nearly two decades, the pain and struggle were addressed in the simple dime-store card I was now holding almost like a talisman, something mysterious.

And, in truth, it *was* something mysterious, a legend spoken of for ages in our family. However, until that moment, I'd never actually seen proof of the legend. But there it was, a worn card of fairly heavy cardboard, with a faded cartoon on the front of a bedraggled bag lady wearing an equally downtrodden look on her face. Opening the card, I saw the magic words that I had been told about so often: "Here's to another glorious year."

Underneath those words, years were marked in pen, counting down the 1960s and 1970s. This card had traveled between Aunt Anna and Mom during those years of hardship, black humor shared between them, a tradition continued annually until the year that Mom remarried—this time a good marriage to a good man. Anna, who happened to have the card in her possession then, decided that this tradition could safely end.

Mom had always been close to her sisters, especially Anna, whose quirky sense of humor was infectious. Aunt Anna was a big part of my childhood and lived with us during the first years after my father abandoned us. Anna cheerfully took on the role of being an additional parent to my brothers and me.

These two sisters relied on each other. It was the 1960s, and we were fairly poor, but I never knew that or of the sacrifices that my mom and Anna made for the rest of us. Only later did I hear about the meals they skipped so that we kids could eat. "I'm on a diet," Mom would say. Being so young, it never occurred to me that my bone-thin mother really didn't need one.

Occasionally, my father would breeze in just to taunt my mother about having to struggle so hard financially. I have crystal-clear memories of the hundred-dollar bills he would flaunt and the twisted look of triumph in his eyes—the cruelty of a person with a very small heart who felt pleasure in hurting others.

Mom would send him on his way with a defiant faith that God would take care of us without help from this man. God couldn't have picked a better person to be mother to her brood in such trying circumstances. She made sure that we were well-provided for before God even got a chance to help out.

Aunt Anna had her own dark times. She had married Uncle Aaron, a man who was good as gold and everything that my father was not. But he had been called up to serve in Vietnam, and those years in the jungle and return to civilian life were their own journey through the dark — one which he and Anna walked with the same faith that sustained Mom.

And, of course, there was the card.

It started with Anna — then living on her own and waiting for Aaron's return — seeing the card and deciding to send it for the soon-to-dawn year of 1966. And so it was that, two days after Christmas 1965, Mom received the card with the bag lady and gallows-humor greeting of "another glorious year." And, with that, they began a tradition that became a sustaining lifeline — two sisters standing with each other through the hardship, sending a card back and- forth year after year, a card of few words that spoke volumes.

Every year, Mom would either get the card just after Christmas, or, if she had received it the previous year, send it to Aunt Anna. And each time, whatever sister happened to be sending the card would mark the year — a little nod that another rough one was over. And although she spoke of the tradition, my mother didn't share the card with her children. It was a private moment shared with her sister.

And so the card, much spoken of, was never actually seen by me until the fiftieth birthday party many years later.

"What are you looking at?" Mom asked. I hadn't noticed her walk up, engrossed as I was in the card. "Oh, the card," she said with a nod. "Isn't it nice of Anna to have it laminated? That card means a lot to me." Before the card was laminated, Anna had marked the year one final time and wrote that she thought it was fitting that Mom keep it as a family heirloom.

We both studied the card, lost in thought. And then, looking up at each other, the emotion caught us both, and we could not speak. Across the room, Anna and Aaron were smiling and laughing — happy and as much in love as when they first met. There was my stepfather, Edward, the good man who was throwing the party for my mother and loved her with all his heart.

On the wall was the picture of my brother Jay in his military uniform — the best friend to us all, lost just as his life was beginning. The flag that had been presented to Mom at his funeral stood in its display case. Beside it was a picture of Jay with his son — the son who we knew would find us and reconnect one day. He actually did, finally, in 2020.

The little card was an unlikely bearer of a message of hope, family, and God. But, most of all, it was an annual reminder of love. The bag lady and simple message showed that genius springs as much from the heart as from the mind. Another glorious year?

Yes, another glorious year.

—Jack Byron—

Check Engine

God never said that the journey will be easy,
but he did say that the arrival will be worthwhile.
~Max Lucado

Ten years ago, I reached an emotional place where life was becoming very difficult to navigate. Even though I was a self-proclaimed eternal optimist, the odds were stacked against me.

I was happy to accept a new job on the other side of the country in a city where many of my friends already lived, I loaded up my car and headed toward what I hoped would be a new and rewarding adventure. My old car barely made the trek, but I arrived safely, anxious to start my new life. Two days after my arrival, the promised job fell through. Having spent every dime to make the journey, I wondered how I was going to survive. To make matters worse, a polite police officer pulled me over to let me know that if I was planning to stay put in my new home state, a new license plate would need to be issued soon.

After securing a place to sleep on a friend's couch, I mustered up what little gumption I had left and started to put the pieces back together. I needed a job. I needed a second chance. I needed a new license plate. And I needed some faith.

After botching a job interview, I went to the parking lot outside the building, sat in my car, and cried for an hour. Finally, I turned the key in the ignition, only to be greeted by the illuminated Check Engine light. I stared at the message and quickly made an important decision:

The light and what it represented were either going to make or break me. Realizing there wasn't much more I could take, I vowed right then and there that I would make it through this rough patch somehow.

Knowing how sad my spirit was, I agreed to attend a local church service, accepting the invitation from a friend after her third request. I was stubborn in my initial responses, insisting that nothing would be solved by going to church. Still, she persisted.

My obstinance diminished quickly when I was greeted with open arms by smiling strangers who all seemed to be exuding the same love of life I once did. I was drawn in, recognizing how extraordinary the closeness of their community was. It was apparent how much they genuinely cared for and about one another. I was invited to join them for an after-service meal where I ate the best food I had tasted in two weeks. When prompted by questions about how I ended up sitting at their table that day, I broke down and revealed all I had endured and all that stood before me. I got especially choked up when I explained how the Check Engine light felt like the final straw.

On my way out, a woman stopped me. She handed me a piece of paper on which she'd written a verse from the Bible. I recognized it at once, as I had memorized every word of it as a child when my Sunday school teacher had challenged us to pick our favorite verse. It's from 1 Corinthians 2:9 and it says, "However, as it is written: What no eye has seen, what no ear has heard, and what no human mind has conceived — the things God has prepared for those who love him."

I looked at the words and let them seep in. I also accepted one last hug and promised to return the following Sunday.

I faced the dreaded emissions test in order to get a new license plate from the DMV, so the next morning I climbed into my old car with determination to turn the odds around. I was broke, but I refused to be broken. I took a breath, said a silent prayer, and turned the key.

To my surprise, the Check Engine light remained dark. It was gone. I turned off the car and turned it back on again, just to be sure. Within seconds, tears of joy filled my eyes as I saw the small miracle for what it was: the reappearance of faith. I felt a deep flood of relief as I drove to the DMV with a sense of confidence I had feared was gone. An hour later — after passing that emissions test and getting my new license plate — I was on my way to becoming an official resident of the new state I was living in. It was a beautiful place where I knew that, no matter what, I was going to be okay.

— David-Matthew Barnes —

54

Pretty in Pink

Children see magic because they look for it.
~Christopher Moore

I t was around noon on a Friday, exactly one week since I sat in the infusion chair getting my second round of chemotherapy. I came downstairs from taking a shower and was right on time for my "I have breast cancer at thirty-three during a pandemic" pity party. It hit me like a ton of bricks. The all-too-familiar wave of sadness and anger washed over me, instantly changing my mood. I was aware of it today, though. I was prepared for it. During the first round of chemo, I let it get the best of me and snapped at everyone I love. On this day, I chose to sit in it in silence, in the comfort of my back patio, letting the sun warm up my soul.

I thought about how unfair it is. I've always worked hard to live a healthy life, and yet cancer found me. It isn't fair that my joyful four-year-old daughter has to deal with grown-up emotions. I stood in the shower earlier and put my hands where my breasts used to be. I've only done it a couple of times because it feels so foreign and makes it all too real. Then I caught a glimpse of my bald head in the mirror as I was drying off and thought, *Wow. I look sick.*

I walked down This Isn't Fair Lane and ventured into Loneliness Plaza. I tried to remember the last time I gave my sister a hug. It was when I had breasts and hair, that's for sure. I thought about my in-laws living in agony in another state, unable to visit, to hug their own son, to see with their own eyes what we're going through and offer help.

I took a detour through Gratitude Circle for a moment and watched my parents kick a soccer ball around the yard with my daughter. I thought of my hard-working husband upstairs in his office putting in long hours, paying the medical bills, and being the best support person a girl could ask for. As much as I wanted to stay in Gratitude Circle, though, I found myself pulled into Anger Alley. "How can this be happening? How is this real life? And why is it happening during a pandemic?" the voices in my head shouted.

Not only did I have to worry about the cancer attacking my body, the loss of body parts, and the poison being pumped through my veins, but I had to experience some of the most frightening moments of my life completely alone. My husband wasn't allowed in the hospital when I had my double mastectomy. No one was able to sit next to me the first time they hooked me up to the IV and released the chemo drugs. It had been over two months since my diagnosis, and I hadn't been able to see anyone in person except my "pod."

Don't get me wrong: I was beyond grateful for my pod. My husband, daughter, and parents were the most amazing support system and beacons of light, but I missed my friends. I missed my sister and her family. I just wanted to hug my nieces. I missed my grandparents and cousins and aunts and uncles. I believed with every fiber of my being that our isolation was the right thing to keep me healthy during chemo, but that doesn't mean it didn't suck. It really sucked.

I was brought back to reality by the sound of, "Mama, it's your turn!" and saw my daughter kicking the soccer ball toward me. Physically, I was starting to feel better from the last round of chemo, so I shook off the gloom and played for about ten minutes, and then I was exhausted. But I played nonetheless.

Later that night, as I was changing into my pajamas, my daughter looked at my chest and said, "Mommy, I can still see your lines." (That's what she calls my mastectomy scars.) "Will they go away?"

I responded, "No, honey, but they'll fade over time, so they won't always be such a dark pink."

I expected her to respond with something like, "Oh, that's good," or to ask me again, "Will your boobies grow back?" Instead, she said sadly, "Oh, but I like pink. Pink's my favorite color. I hope they stay pink."

Then I realized how much of what we feel is about perspective. I looked at my scars and saw pain and loss. My daughter looked at my scars and saw the same Mommy she's always had, but with really cool pink lines.

I smiled at her and said, "You know what? I like pink, too."

— Randi Grant —

55

Theatre of the Mind

*Mental illness is so much more complicated
than any pill that any mortal could invent.*
~Elizabeth Wurtzel

I stood anxiously at the emergency-room reception desk speaking softly to the receptionist. I did not want anyone else to hear my reason for being there. I also kept a watchful eye on my thirty-four-year-old son, who was having a psychological episode.

Six months prior, my son had been diagnosed with paranoid schizophrenia. My son refused the doctor-ordered sedative and said he just needed to get back on his meds. After the nurse left the room, my son asked me to get him a soda. A few minutes later, his nurse approached me at the vending machine. She said my son wanted me. I was shocked to see my son being restrained by four security guards, screaming for me to get him a lawyer. He said his civil rights were being violated. The doctor was holding a syringe and informed me that my son had just tried to hang himself with the TV cord.

My son was sedated and connected to an EKG monitor. His hands and feet were bound to the bed railing with restraints. It was heartbreaking to see my son in that state. I was shaken and started to cry, so I stepped outside his room in the hallway to collect myself. When I came back into his room, I saw his face was red and appeared to be swollen. He was sweating profusely and had urinated on himself. Thinking he was having an allergic reaction to the sedative, I called the nurse. When I looked closer, I saw he had somehow managed to get a cord attached to the EKG monitor, wrap it around his neck and the railing, and try to choke himself to death. This was the first of a series of suicide attempts.

Two months later, the state highway patrol found him semi-conscious in his car on the shoulder of the highway in 100-degree weather, close to death from heat exhaustion. He had also drunk antifreeze. He was unconscious in the intensive care unit for three days.

In one of his counseling sessions, I learned he had been hearing voices since the age of eighteen. I felt like a terrible parent because I had missed it. He said he never told anyone about the voices because he did not want people to think he was crazy. I also learned he had used methamphetamines and other hallucinogenic drugs "to drown out the voices."

One night, I felt as though my husband and I were in a horror movie. We had returned home from an evening out and had been home about twenty minutes when my husband heard noises outside our house. He called me downstairs. I heard them, too, and got my gun. I called out, "Who is it?" I got no response, but the noise persisted. Suddenly, our cable and side porch light went out. When I tried to dial 911 on the home phone, it was out, too. I called out, "I have a gun, and I'm calling the police."

Then I heard a knock on the side door and a voice said, "Mom, it's me. Call an ambulance. I need to go to the hospital. I'm having a bad episode."

My first instinct was to open the door, but my husband stopped me. He said, "You don't know what that boy is on. Don't open that door. Call 911." I used my cell phone to call 911 and told the dispatcher, "My son has mental illness and needs to be transported to the hospital. He is not a threat and has no weapons." My fear was the police would shoot and kill my Black son.

After the ambulance left, the officer on the scene told us my son had admitted that he had tried to hang himself on the side porch with cords from our porch light and cable. When we checked the porch, we saw a cinder block from the back yard and cords dangling from the ceiling light. The emotions I felt are indescribable. I could not understand why he would come to my home to commit suicide. I thought about how I could have come home and found my son hanging from the porch ceiling. Or how I could have shot him, not knowing it was him, if he had tried to break into the house.

I have come to realize how difficult it is for a paranoid mind to see logic and reason and how the torment drives them to want out of their life. For instance, when he was in the car with me, he constantly looked at the side and rearview mirrors, suspecting cars were following us. Once, we were driving down the highway, and a cop car was parked on the shoulder. He said, "See, Mom. I told you they were following me." I said, "But they were already there when we passed by." He would not hear it. In his mind, it was all a part of the conspiracy to make him think they were not following him. He has made freedom-of-information requests with all branches of law enforcement demanding to know if there is an active case against him and accused law enforcement of systematically harassing him. He claimed they were surveilling him and had recruited private citizens to do the same in an effort to drive him crazy.

One day, the police came to my home looking for my son because he had sent an e-mail to the Chief of Police saying he could not take it anymore and was going to kill himself. I had no clue where he was. All I knew was his paranoia about his roommates plotting against him kept him away from his residence. He went days without sleeping and slept many nights in his car. I called my son to see if he was alright and tried to find out where he was, but he would not tell me. The next day, I received a call from the hospital. He had cut his wrist and taken an overdose of pills. Fortunately, he was at a friend's house, and they called 911.

After one of his suicide attempts, I asked him why it happened when he seemed to be doing so well. He said, "I was fine—until I wasn't." When I wrote this story for Chicken Soup for the Soul in 2020, my son had gone eight months without a suicide attempt. He was taking his medication and talking to a therapist twice a week. He had lived in the same residence for seven months, which was a first, as his paranoia had caused him to leave every room that he has rented in the past three years.

I was so grateful he had finally accepted he had mental illness and was willingly treating it. He had arrived at a place where he thought life was worth living and he was working hard at it.

Unfortunately, I found him dead of an overdose of his prescription psychiatric medicine in February 2021. I take comfort in the fact that he gave it his all. He fought his illness, just as someone would fight cancer or some other chronic and possibly fatal disease. For me, his mother, that will have to be enough.

— Angela Ayres —

56

Fight Like a Girl

*A strong woman knows she has strength enough
for the journey, but a woman of strength knows it
is in the journey where she will become strong.*
~Author Unknown

"Y ou fight like a girl!" The boy laughed as he ran away after delivering that statement like a rock to a pane of glass. And, like glass, I was shattered. It laid waste to my belief that I could do anything that my young male classmates could do, and my innocence faded into the blackness of nonexistence.

Through the years, I pushed that memory into the crevices of my mind as life replaced it with tasks, goals and accomplishments. Days melted away, and my life became a welcome movie that replayed daily. Then my movie reel snapped, and the film flipped out of control as I was met with the news: "You have cancer."

A grueling year and a half of surgeries and complications kept my happy ending at bay. Then came periods of calm intertwined with interruptions of relapses. Three times in my life, I have heard those horrendous words spanning nearly a half-century of battles. And their power never waned. But through my faith in God, I never allowed them to leave me in darkness.

Every instance becomes an opportunity to explore new avenues in life. To meet new people. To remind myself how strong and determined I am. To show myself and the world that nothing is impossible. Nothing is final. Nothing is predetermined.

After one of my battles, someone asked me, "How do you keep going and not give up? How do you do it?"

Instantly, I was taken back to that playground of my youth. Suddenly, those stinging words held new meaning in my heart. A sly smile formed upon my lips as I turned to face my friend.

"I survive because I FIGHT LIKE A GIRL."

— Pastor Wanda Christy-Shaner —

57

Container of Hope

*Hope itself is like a star — not to be seen
in the sunshine of prosperity, and only
to be discovered in the night of adversity.*
~C.H. Spurgeon

ome years ago, I was extremely sick and hospitalized for weeks. A stubborn infection in my stomach seemed resistant to all antibiotics, and the next step was to remove a huge portion of it and install an ostomy bag.

Day after day, I dreaded when the doctors would come into my room because they always brought bad news. It seemed like they did not know what to do to help me.

As a cyclist, I was used to robust health, and the idea of having my body altered both scared and demoralized me. I had already been in the hospital so long that I became deeply discouraged. One of my doctors had told me I would probably be unable to continue cycling unless I could learn to do it with the ostomy bag. It seemed like life as I had known it was over.

That afternoon, I had an emotional breakdown in the shower as the water washed over a body that I no longer recognized. It was a moment of profound despair, and I wondered if I would ever get well.

Later that day, while I was lying in my bed, a man with smooth, beautiful skin who was wearing a cool Indiana Jones–type hat came into my room with a Tupperware container filled with goodies of all kinds. By then, I was used to a number of people showing up in my room for a variety of reasons, so I assumed he was a volunteer stopping by to drop off some snacks.

The man told me he had gotten approval from my nurse, and I could have any of the snacks in the container, either for myself or to share with visitors and family. I was surprised when he set the container on my bedside table and told me the whole thing was mine.

Then the man stood by my bedside and looked directly at me with that smooth, kind face and said something I will never forget. "God told me to come to this room today, to tell the person here that they are not to lose hope."

My first thought was, *Wow, this Demerol is awesome!* I told him that sounded great, and that it was easy to lose hope after being in the hospital for so long.

He said, "Yes, it is very easy to lose hope, but I am telling you that God told me to come to this room today to tell you that you are not to give up hope."

We made small talk, and after a few minutes, the man turned and left. Soon, I drifted into a narcotic-induced sleep. When I awoke, I thought I had had a great dream.

Then I saw the container on the bedside table. It was all real. A total stranger had appeared on my darkest day to tell me that God had sent him specifically to my room to tell me I was not to give up hope.

I did not get well suddenly. In fact, I still had a long way to go. But after my visitor, something changed in me. The same doctors came in with the same discouraging news each day, but it no longer affected me the same way. I suddenly felt like I had insider information, and that what I knew was the most important thing to know, more so even than anything the doctors knew.

What I knew was that somehow, in some way I did not yet understand, I was going to get well. I had not been given some new medicine; I had been given hope, and it was the most powerful medicine of all. After that, everything else was just details to be worked out over time.

I eventually recovered completely and without the need for surgery. I resumed cycling with no restrictions and quietly dedicated my next finishing medal to the doctor who had told me I would probably never ride again.

It has been many years now, but I still have that snack container. It is an enduring reminder through all the challenges of life to never give up, even when I do not yet see how or when help will arrive.

The snacks and puzzles are long gone, but the container is not empty.

It is filled with hope.

—Dorian Leigh Quillen—

I Woke Up!

Like the wind that carries one ship east and another west,
the law of autosuggestion will lift you up or pull you down
according to the way that you set your sails of thought.
~Napoleon Hill

M y eighteen-year-old grandson, Andrew, fidgeted as he sat on an uncomfortable exam table. A straightforward surgeon announced that the lump and testicle he'd removed a week earlier was cancerous. I watched my daughter's face crumple, tears streaming down her face.

The doctor was still talking. "It occurs most frequently in young men between the ages of eighteen to thirty — usually painless."

I had to keep myself together for my daughter and Andrew. I swallowed my own shock and fear. As a retired pediatric nurse, I listened intently because my daughter, Margie, had stopped comprehending. Although I slowly digested every word, I was terrified about what lay ahead. Andrew was my first grandchild, son of my first child. When he was born, I was in the delivery room, one of the first to hold him and kiss his little forehead.

The surgeon said his office would set up the initial oncology appointment. "We're going to do a CT scan and draw some blood before you leave to determine the staging of this cancer." The doctor stood and opened the exam-room door. "I'll see you again tomorrow to go over the tests. Hang in there, Andrew."

While walking down the hall, Andrew turned to his mother. I

heard him say, "Thank God, I had pain. It got me to the doctor faster." These were the first words he uttered after hearing the diagnosis. At the time, we didn't realize that his attitude would set an example for the entire family.

Andrew's testicular cancer had metastasized. We prayed. Everyone we knew prayed. One day over dinner, Andrew bowed his head and gave thanks for the outpouring of support. His attitude was infectious.

When he had a port put into his upper chest, Andrew pointed out, "Grandma, this port means fewer vein sticks, and you know how I hate those!" He managed to find the positive.

Chemo began. His body hurt, and his hair started to come out in clumps; he had the remainder shaved. As Andrew joked and laughed with his nurses, he became a favorite on the unit. Each day, after six to eight hours of chemo, he personally thanked each caregiver.

When cancer proved to be more tenacious and aggressive, Andrew was outwardly unfazed. He reassured all of us. "Don't worry, we'll get 'em in the next round."

Andrew was drained of stamina and perpetually fatigued. He began to have severe reactions to the chemo, causing the nurses to spring into action with other drugs to combat each reaction. After each incident, he rewarded the team with a weak smile and a thumbs-up. He spoke slowly, "I sure am glad you guys know what you're doing!"

After nine weeks, Andrew completed his last infusion. With the battery of blood tests and scans in a folder, his oncologist took my grandson's case before the tumor board.

In a few days, we had an appointment with another oncological surgeon who explained a relatively new radical surgery to give Andrew a better chance of long-term survival. With the daunting risks in mind, the difficult decision was made to proceed, and the surgery was scheduled. Andrew was quiet on the car ride home.

A week later, after a six-hour surgery, the young doctor came to update us. Several family members huddled with the surgeon outside the crowded waiting room. While we listened intently to the doctor, a team from the operating room dressed in green scrubs wheeled Andrew past us, taking him to the intensive care unit.

Andrew was awake and flashed a smile. He held up both thumbs. "I woke up! I'm still here!" he said triumphantly.

—Nancy Emmick Panko—

59

Healing

*I found that with depression, one of the most important
things you could realize is that you're not alone.*
~Dwayne Johnson

Depression knocked on my door one ordinary Tuesday.
I recognized him by his hooded gray sweatshirt and worn-out jeans.

He sat on my couch and kept me company while the rest of the world
went about its business.
I thought he would leave the next morning, but he overstayed his
welcome, like unwanted houseguests often do.

Each day, Depression bombarded me with the same insensitive questions.
"When are you going to get off this couch?"
"Don't you know that people are counting on you?"
"What are you crying about now?"

I had no answers for him, so he wrapped me in a blue blanket and
sat even closer.
Eventually, Depression became bored with tormenting me.

That's when he went after my children.
He stole my son's sense of humor.
He swiped my daughter's sparkle.

He kidnapped my son's passion for life.
He stripped my daughter of her creative spirit.
I was desperate to help them, but Depression tied my hands behind
  my back.

That's when I finally found my voice and called out for Healing.
She was not far away and waited for us just down the road, her eyes
  filled with hope.

When Depression's back was turned, we escaped his hold on us.
Healing led us to her refuge. Comfy chairs. Soft color on the walls. A
  "Welcome" sign.

She wore a kind expression and had a warm touch, but, most of all,
  she held the answers we needed.
Some solutions were buried deep; some were right before our eyes
  that we had not noticed before; and some were scribbled on little
  blue slips of paper that saved our lives.

She gave back my son's smile.
She gave back my daughter's art.
She gave me back my children and my life.

Healing is here for all of us.
We just need to find our voices and cry out for her.

— Erin Solej —

60

The Cooky Book

*Our most treasured family heirloom are our sweet
family memories. The past is never dead,
it is not even past.*
~William Faulkner

"Which ones shall we make first?" Mom asked me while browsing through cookie recipes. It was the Christmas season — time to bake.

When I was a kid, my mom had an extensive collection of cookbooks in her kitchen, which she used to prepare both daily family meals and decadent holiday treats. She gave me a copy of her favorite basic recipe collection, *Joy of Cooking*, when I was in my early twenties, since she viewed it as an essential item for every household. Her own copy had a broken binding from decades of use, causing loose pages to fall out whenever she took it off the shelf.

For me, the most beloved of Mom's cookbooks was *Betty Crocker's Cooky Book,* which she always brought out around the holidays. I loved to help her bake, and perhaps as a result of my enthusiastic participation, the pages of Mom's *Cooky Book* were caked in flour, butter, and sugar. Some of the photos were almost comically discolored from frequent and longtime use. For instance, the photo of Chocolate Crinkles had morphed into a sickly shade of green. Mom and I always laughed when we saw this, although it never stopped us from wanting to bake these delicious, chocolatey delights.

At some point after Mom died more than eighteen years ago,

I asked Dad for her copy of the *Cooky Book*. He never baked — or cooked, for that matter. During their years together, Mom — even when she was sick — did all the food preparation, and Dad — well, he has always loved to eat.

Dad said no. He wasn't ready to part with any of Mom's cookbooks. Initially, I was upset that he wouldn't give just this one to me. In time, I understood — perhaps more than anyone else — the memories associated with Mom's cooking and baking. After all, I wanted to hold on to them, too.

In recent years, Dad's health has declined. At first, doctors thought it was Parkinson's disease that caused his gait to change and his thinking to muddle. Then, they decided it was something called normal pressure hydrocephalus. Next, they suggested, perhaps something more vascular in nature? Or maybe a combination of several things. He is an unusual case, his doctors comment — which doesn't surprise me at all.

A couple of years ago, when Dad inquired about what I wanted for Christmas, I asked him again for Mom's *Cooky Book*. By then, he seemed to have misplaced his sentimentality for it — and possibly the book itself, mentioning that it was probably in a box in his garage somewhere and pretty worn-out.

My own health has declined in recent years, too, and I am feeling worn-out myself. Just like Mom, I was diagnosed with cancer in my thirties. First, a rare, slow-growing cancer was found in my lung; then, at age forty-four, my lower back pain turned out to be sarcoma cancer — which is also rare but much more aggressive. Finally, before my hair had even fully grown back from sarcoma treatment, my doctors found invasive breast cancer.

While I try to live my life as fully as possible, my cancer treatments have been complicated in ways that even I, a writer, have a hard time describing. Suffice it to say that cancer has been life-altering — and not in a positive way.

When a yellow Jiffy envelope, clearly containing a book the size of the *Cooky Book*, arrived from Dad, I put it under the Christmas tree with a smile. I had recently completed nine miserable months of chemo and radiation, and there wasn't much I wanted or needed that hadn't already been showered upon me by caring friends and family during that time. But when I opened that much-anticipated gift on Christmas morning, it wasn't Mom's discolored, flour-, butter-, and sugar-caked copy of the *Cooky Book* that I pulled out. It was a brand-new one, still sealed in plastic.

Although Dad's heart was in the right place, this new *Cooky Book* wasn't at all what I had in mind. I could have bought one like it for myself years ago. But there have been so many things in my life that haven't turned out like I meant for them to. So, I flipped through the pages to the Chocolate Crinkles recipe. When I squinted a little at the photo, I could almost see a greenish tint. If I concentrated hard enough, I could almost hear Mom laughing about it.

As Dad's physical health has declined, so has his cognitive state. In the past, he was well known for recognizing everyone's birthday — family members, friends, ex-colleagues, even people he hadn't seen for decades. He developed a tracking system, and each month he sat down in front of his computer, logged into a Jacquie Lawson e-card subscription, and scheduled a series of animated, electronic birthday wishes to auto-send on the correct dates. These e-cards, and Dad's unwavering commitment to them, are the subject of many jokes between my two brothers and me. But if there has been one thing we can count on for our birthdays since Mom died, it has been this.

Soon after that Christmas, during a period when Dad often couldn't find words, drove his car through his own garage door, and got lost in his own neighborhood, Dad forgot my birthday entirely.

Since then, many medical events have occurred. His brain surgery, believed at one point to be a potential miracle cure, was scheduled right after my breast cancer surgery. Soon after that, he took a disastrous fall that we're not sure he'll ever fully recover from, although he has fought valiantly to do so. He continues to be physically impaired and somewhat cognitively disoriented, but memory is a funny thing. I suspect Dad's mouth would still water at the mention of his favorite *Cooky Book* selection — the molasses cookies — that Mom always baked for him at Christmastime.

When we finally moved Dad into an assisted living facility, I came across Mom's *Cooky Book* while packing. It was shoved behind a bunch of Dad's old magazines on a rather chaotic shelf in his office. I quietly took it home with me where it joined my own unused copy.

I am currently between treatments and considered "stable," although I feel anything but. Similar to Dad, I am generally a little off-balance these days. I don't know what to make of everything that's happened or how to prepare for what comes next. Even Mom's *Cooky Book*, nestled on my orderly shelf of cookbooks, can't seem to offer what I truly desire.

Instead, I pull out my pristine copy of the *Cooky Book*, which, in many ways, has begun to grow on me. It is immaculate, brightly colored, and free of any unintended ingredients. Come what may, I know that it is time to move forward. Perhaps I can entice my kids to bake with me, as I once baked with Mom. I envision a kitchen filled with warmth, laughter, and Chocolate Crinkles. We can even make some of the molasses cookies for Dad.

— Lisa Pawlak —

Moving Forward

A Mother's Love and Courage

Darkness cannot drive out darkness; only light can do that.
Hate cannot drive out hate; only love can do that.
~Dr. Martin Luther King, Jr.

It was a beautiful sunny day in spring when my mother, June Lorraine Overton Wright, revealed to me an incredible story. We were sitting on the small front porch of my grandmother's home, a place where we often sat and talked.

I had recently become a teenager, and I guess this was a milestone for my mother. She said, "Kelvin, I am about to tell you some things that I need you to know. No one else, not even your grandmother knows about this. I have never shared it with anyone except for your great-grandmother who you never knew."

There were children nearby laughing and playing. Cars were whizzing by on the busy one-way thoroughfare of Jonathan Street, which served as the main road from downtown to pass through the Black neighborhood of Hagerstown, Maryland. It was always an area full of activity. But as my mother began to tell me her story, all the sounds faded as Mom's soothing, yet commanding, voice continued.

I knew that my mother was about to tell me something very special and important. She had my undivided attention. As she leaned closer toward me, she said; "You're thirteen now and I need you to know how you got here. I need you to know the circumstances of your birth."

She explained that at age sixteen she was enthusiastic about her future. I had already known that my mother was a brilliant student and gifted vocalist who sang at churches and social events. But as she continued her story, I learned that she had aspired to become a psychiatrist, even though her mother wanted her to study music in college and become a professional opera or gospel singer.

The revelation was not a complete surprise to me since music had always been part of the fabric of our family. My grandmother played organ and directed the choir at our family church. Before that, my great-grandmother played piano and sang at the same church. And it was easy to understand my mother's desire to become a psychiatrist. She was always eager to provide wise counsel to me, my friends, and people who needed advice on important life decisions.

As she continued her talk, she explained that she had become friendly with a pastor's wife at another church in our small community. She and the wife would often walk downtown on Saturday mornings to go shopping. One Saturday morning she was a little late arriving at the pastor's house to meet his wife. The pastor opened the door and said his wife had already left. He asked her to come inside and wait for his wife to return. June, in her innocence thought nothing of his invitation to go inside the home.

As my mother's voice became more intense, she told me the pastor, a man she respected, sexually assaulted her. Her first instinct was to fight but she was fearful he would hurt her for resisting his advances. So, she reluctantly and silently lay there, enduring the pain and degradation. Afterwards, she ran home.

So many emotions and thoughts were racing through her head. Fear, heartbreak, humiliation, and confusion flooded her mind. She repeatedly questioned herself: "Did I cause this? Did I do something to provoke this? Did I wear the wrong clothing?"

She thought about telling her mother but she was afraid of how her mother would react. She considered telling the police but she believed that would only make matters worse. She concluded that it would boil down to her word against the pastor's, and he was considered a pillar of the community.

June kept the secret locked inside her. She never visited the pastor's wife again. She kept busy with school and music. She tried to focus on her future. She was not going to let the terror of rape keep her from achieving her goals. She still had big dreams. But her dreams turned into a nightmare when she discovered she was pregnant.

It was the summer of 1954. June was a sweet sixteen-year-old girl who now faced the scorn of so-called friends and disappointment from her mother. Her mom demanded to know who the father was but June never uttered a word. She persevered through the alienation from her mother and school friends. The only one who stood by her side was her grandmother, who constantly prayed with her and for her.

My heart broke for her as she told me that one day she arrived home from school and saw her suitcase in the middle of the living room. Her mother, a domestic worker, explained that she and one of her wealthy bosses gathered enough money to fly her to Nebraska to have an abortion. They wanted her to go to college and study music. A baby would derail those plans and ruin her chances of becoming successful.

What my mother told me then was a display of her courage and her faith in God. She calmly but firmly told my grandmother; "No I'm not going to Nebraska and I'm not going to have an abortion. God is telling me this is the only child that I'm going to have." And with that, the matter was closed.

I was born five days after my mother celebrated her seventeenth birthday. She said she immediately felt an overwhelming love for me. She was faced with a seemingly insurmountable task: "How do I help my son become somebody when I have not done anything to be somebody?"

My mother worked very hard every day of her life to never become bitter but to always become better. She worked her fingers to the bone to instill in me an abiding love for her, for God, and my family. And while she never achieved her goal of becoming a psychiatrist, she became my greatest counselor.

And true to what God told her, she never had another child biologically. During a brief marriage, she was unable to have a child. Years later, she learned about a baby girl who was being abused and neglected by her birth mother. Mom stepped in and adopted the baby girl. That baby girl became my sister.

My mother poured life into me. She poured faith into me. Against all odds, this courageous and loving Black woman managed to help me become who I am today. Not a day goes by without me thinking about her.

I miss our talks. I miss her smile. Before Mom passed in 2005 from cancer, we spent the last two months of her life rejoicing over her triumphant life. Our family held a party for her in a conference room at the hospital that was caring for her. Some of her closest relatives and friends gathered around to thank her for being their advisor, counselor, and trusted friend. To them, she was the unlicensed psychiatrist who gave each of them the best therapy they needed during troubled times — her love and encouragement.

And I must stress to everyone, do not get it twisted; I am not a product of rape! I am a product of a mother's love and courage!

— Kelly Wright —

Small-Town Heartbreak, Big Apple Dreams

I wake up every morning and say to myself,
"Well, I'm still in New York. Thank you, God."
~Ed Koch

How many times have you bounced back from something you swore was the end of the world? I know I have. For me, it was when my heart was broken at age twenty-one.

Ethan and I had been dating for more than three years. Our relationship was filled with laughter, fun and adventure. We did everything together from skydiving to buying kayaks, biking, parasailing, you name it. He truly was my best friend.

About two years into our relationship, Ethan enlisted in the United States Air Force. He moved to Texas and then Seattle while I was in college in Wisconsin. At first, our big life changes brought us closer together, but about a year into his enlistment, the distance between us felt farther than those 1,700 miles.

I felt that something was off when I talked to him one Thursday night. We both said "I love you" before hanging up but I could almost hear the emptiness in his words.

I didn't hear from him for three days even though I called him and sent texts. On Sunday, I went on a bike ride to clear my head. On a back road in central Wisconsin, my phone rang, and I came to a stop.

It was Ethan. As my heart raced and my hands shook, I said, "This isn't going to be good, is it?" I heard a sigh in his voice followed by a quiet "No." I explained that I would call him back and sped home in the sunshine with tears streaming down my face. The two-mile trek felt like an eternity.

Bursting through the kitchen door, I explained to my concerned-looking parents that Ethan was about to break up with me. I quickly went back outside and paced back and forth on the backyard patio. Then I called him.

We both knew everything was about to change. Time froze. As I stared down at my bare feet on the warm patio brick, he said it. "I can't do this anymore. The distance."

That day, we were on the phone for more than two hours. The irony of such a perfect, breezy summer day was like a slap in the face. There was no arguing between us, just pure heartbreak.

So young and naive, I thought, *Where will I go from here? When will I find this kind of happiness again?*

We hung up the phone, and I went to be alone in my room. The day turned to night, and my parents' hearts broke with mine. With periodic check-ins, they let me cry on their shoulders with absolutely no judgment.

I went to work the next morning at the golf course where I tended bar and tried to act as if nothing had happened. But my puffy, red eyes told a different story.

Luckily, I was scheduled several hours that week, which helped keep my mind from wandering. I'd be lying if I said that week flew by, but with the help of Taylor Swift songs (clichéd, right?) and good people by my side, I got through it.

One week after my heart was torn out of my chest, I received yet another phone call that would change my life forever.

The call came when I was working a closing shift at the bar, and all my managers were having their after-work drinks. We weren't supposed to have our phones on while working, but as someone in her early twenties, of course I did — and of course I checked it.

My phone read "Missed Call" from a number I did not recognize. I stealthily looked up the number out of sight from my bosses.

The call had come from Manhattan.

A few months prior, I had applied for an internship at the *Late Show with David Letterman*. As I applied, I sent the position posting to my mom and Ethan with a text that said, "Applying to this… ha ha yeah right."

Now was about the time they'd be making those interview calls. My heart started racing.

Trying not to get my hopes up, I stepped outside into the humid heat and called the number back, fully expecting it to be a telemarketer. Instead, I reached a voicemail with only a person's name: Matt S****.

Still trying to hide what I was doing, I went back inside to Google his name. A Twitter page appeared before my eyes with his job position: receptionist at *David Letterman*.

As the webpage fully loaded, a voicemail appeared on my phone. At that moment, I gave up all efforts at being sly.

I went up to my bosses and said, "I know I'm not supposed to have my phone, but I think I just got a call to interview at *David Letterman*. Can I go outside?" In unison, the three of them shouted, "Go!"

Out the kitchen doors I went. The smell of stale cigarettes from a co-worker's previous smoke break lingered as I listened to the voicemail.

"This message is for Shelby. This is Matt S**** at the *Late Show with David Letterman*. We got your application and would love to schedule a time to interview."

The rest of the message was a blur as I teared up. Small-town Shelby Krommenacker had an interview in New York City for a position on one of the world's most well-known late-night talk shows.

This doesn't happen to people like me, I thought. Immediately, I called everyone closest to me. Of course, when you have the biggest news of your life to share, nobody answers.

Life consistently works to test our resiliency. Roadblocks happen to each and every one of us. The great part about it is that we have the option to view the roadblock as an opportunity rather than a limitation.

Isn't that wonderful?

Little did I know that my heartbreak one week would turn out to be the top dog of unanswered prayers the next. Closing my chapter with Ethan, although tough, led me to begin my journey on the nothing-is-impossible train.

Rather than sitting back and sulking over my breakup, I prepared harder for that interview than I had prepared for anything in my life.

It was my time to shine.

— Shelby Krommenacker —

Validation

*Self-esteem comes from being able to define the world
in your own terms and refusing to abide
by the judgments of others.*
~Oprah Winfrey

It was gone. All of it. In a few short hours, my house had been totally consumed by fire. I went to work that morning, fresh from an argument with my husband about the best way to rework the remaining turkey from Thanksgiving for dinner. It was an argument worth having because everyone knows that reheated turkey with Stove Top stuffing is infinitely better than turkey salad.

By early evening, I'd said a million prayers of thanks that those weren't the last words I shared with my husband. As we stood in front of our burning home, our arms around our teenage son, I was certain that there was nothing else that I needed from the building that had been our home.

The fire wasn't a tragedy. No one was hurt, harmed or killed. Our home was insured, and we were quickly resettled into a nearby luxury apartment complex. We were abundantly grateful that we had emerged intact, with only our possessions gone. Over the following months, we would spend hours trying to create a list of belongings that we had accumulated and lost. I vowed never to let things overrun our lives again. I pledged to embrace a more minimalist life that would not be cluttered by "stuff."

The first week following the fire was one of the most difficult. It was nearly impossible for me to wrap my brain around the fact that nothing in my home remained. I asked my husband several times to retrieve the mail that I'd left on the side table in the dining room. In my mind's eye, I could see clearly where it was. I remember when he said, "Tracy, it's not there. Everything's gone." I don't know why it was easy to grasp that there'd been enough heat to melt a computer, but difficult to acknowledge that mere envelopes had not survived.

My personal hoarding revolved around paper. For as long as I can remember, I'd held onto pieces of paper long past their usefulness. I saved records for the "just in case" inquiry when I would have to prove something. Store receipts and tax records confirmed my honesty. Birthday cards and personal letters verified that I'd mattered to someone and that I was loved. Certificates and awards affirmed that I was special, gifted. Diplomas attested to my intelligence and accomplishment. Pictures celebrated moments of happiness, however fleeting. Documented workplace slights were preserved in preparation for termination or litigation.

It was on the third day after the fire that I awoke and suddenly realized I had no proof of anything. Although I had a driver's license and credit cards, I had no real proof of my life. No proof that I had done anything except breathe. No proof of the textures — hopes, loves, dreams and fears — that make a life. No proof of education. No proof of love, as all the sweet notes and greeting cards were gone. No documentation of success as every award bestowed was now a memory. No proof of my creativity, as my unfinished poems had perished. No proof that I had tried and failed — I had saved all my rejection letters!

Who was I without some "seal of approval?" I had no proof that my life had contributed more to the planet than it had taken. My breathing changed. I began to question all that I ever thought I was.

I felt a strangely familiar terror. Perhaps in the deepest recesses of my being, there was historical trauma associated with the loss of documentation — documentation of freedom, of ownership, of self.

I had a startling realization. Not only was my documentation gone, but so was my ability to languish in the familiar comfort of the past. When my self-esteem was lagging, I could re-read old birthday cards and love letters. I'd re-read journal entries that held my fear, brokenness, abandonment and sadness so I could recapture old pains and remind myself of my inadequacy. When I was overlooked or undervalued at work, I could review my graded "A" papers from high school and college. The thought of not being able to curl up in the papered corners of my past jarred my inner being in a way that I had not anticipated.

Yet, as quickly as this fierce sense of desolation came, another feeling slowly began to replace it. For the first time, I questioned the validity of my "papers." A certificate proclaiming I was great did not mean I was. A love note had not guaranteed that I was safe from betrayal. None of these papers was proof. At their most fundamental level, they were merely snapshots of a particular time in my life, someone else's opinion of the me who I had been. Why had those pieces of paper held so much value to me? When had I relinquished my self-identity to others and settled for their definitions of me as validation of my worth?

I'd been hoarding not just paper, but other people's opinions of me. Now I could reimagine myself. I liked how it felt to have no remnants of the thoughts of others, good or bad, hovering around me. I liked the sense of beginning again, with the only evidence of my character being my actions of the day. My mind felt lighter than it ever had, and I felt a sense of freedom that was new and exhilarating. I declared my intention to resist ever being held captive by documents again.

It is sometimes hard to let go of old habits. Although I work against collecting the clutter of other people's feelings about me, I occasionally open a drawer to find it stuffed with holiday and birthday cards. However, today I can let them go more easily, knowing that the only opinion worth cherishing, the only validation I need, is mine.

— Tracy Robinson Whitaker —

64

Recipes for Healing

Comfort food is the food that makes us feel good — satisfied,
calm, cared for and carefree... Finding comfort in food
is a basic human experience.
~Ellie Krieger

When my wife Jenn committed suicide in September 2018, it left a deep and profound hole in my life and that of my daughter. In the months following her death, I found myself in a dark place that felt devoid of hope or light.

Throughout more than twenty years together, Jenn and I had spent countless hours in the kitchen creating. I was sure that had ended until I came upon a simple black folder while cleaning my library. It contained over two dozen recipes for comfort foods written in my wife's handwriting. They spanned our years together and had everything from katsu chicken to chocolate-chip cookies. My wife had written comments in the margin about each dish. Some of the comments regarded the recipes; others were humorous observations made at the time about their creation.

When I began cooking, I discovered the light away from the darkness in which I had been living. While making my wife's "Finally Meatloaf" (thus named because, after years of tinkering, she had finally gotten it how she wanted), I found myself overwhelmed with feelings.

As I gathered and mixed ingredients per my wife's writing, a hundred memories of standing next to her in the kitchen flooded back. As the meal cooked and the aroma filled the house, I recalled dozens of warm memories from our past family meals.

Slowly but surely, with time and the help of that simple black folder, I have dug myself out of the dark, hopeless place I had fallen into. In the end, I learned that sometimes the longest lasting expressions of love and affection can be nothing more or less than a really good meatloaf recipe.

—Steve Coney—

65

My Treasure Map

*It must be borne in mind that the tragedy of
life doesn't lie in not reaching your goal.
The tragedy lies in having no goal to reach.*
~Benjamin E. Mays

ehind the open door to my bedroom, attached to the
wall with red pushpins, is a piece of white poster board.
Pictures and words are glued to it, and black checkmarks
are plentiful. This is my treasure map.

Several years ago, shortly after going through surgery and months
of radiation and chemotherapy for breast cancer, I crashed and burned.

I should have been happy. The treatments were over. The surgical
site had healed.

Instead, a door somewhere in my subconscious flew open from
the stress of coping with my cancer diagnosis. All the feelings, worries,
and fears that I had pushed and shoved into that overstuffed, emotional
closet came bursting out, burying me in their debris.

It took a huge effort to get through each day. The world was dark.
I didn't care about anything.

I visited a counselor at the nearby cancer center.

"You need to make a treasure map," she said, handing me a Kleenex
for my tears.

"How do I do that?"

"First, you make a list of the things you want to do or accomplish
in the future. Then bring it here next week."

That afternoon, I started small and wrote, "Walk for twenty minutes each day" and "Finish the book I started." Then I began thinking a week and then a month ahead, writing, "Visit SeaWorld," and "Start attending yoga classes." And, finally, I was looking a year ahead: "Finish writing my novel," and "Go to cheer for Diane." (My sister was training for a sixty-mile walk to raise money for breast cancer research.) I felt a little better.

When I showed my counselor the list, she told me to buy a piece of poster board and cut out pictures of the goals I had written. That would be my treasure map, my working plan to navigate my way into the future.

At home that day, I cleared off the kitchen table and hauled out a stack of old magazines. At first, I felt silly looking for pictures, like I was back in kindergarten.

But as I found what I was looking for, I became more interested. When I finished with the magazines, I looked through my computer's clip-art files and printed the ones I was missing. I added captions to the pictures and framed a few quotes in flowered borders. I got out stickers of shimmering butterflies and found Magic Markers to add color.

As I glued and arranged, I began to remember. Before the cancer diagnosis, I had wanted to travel to see the Grand Canyon. I had forgotten that. I had wanted to learn to use my fancy camera. And to visit New Orleans. I had forgotten those, too.

As I worked on creating the treasure map that evening, my world began to brighten. It was the strangest thing. Maybe it was because I realized that I had something to look forward to. Maybe it was, for the first time in many months, immersing myself in something that was simple and fun. I don't know.

It has been many years since I created that first treasure map, and I'm now well into my second one (this time on bright, fluorescent yellow poster board and adorned with jewels and diamonds and as much sparkling bling as it will hold). Of course, I still add pictures and check off the things I have done.

But I'm sure that following that early treasure map made things happen. My sister walked the sixty miles for breast cancer twice, and

I was there each time waving a huge yellow banner to cheer her on. I completed my first novel and was awarded a publishing contract. And early one spring, my husband and I drove to New Orleans where I sat in the sun on the banks of the Mississippi, savoring the almost mystical flavors of café au lait and warm beignets sprinkled with powdered sugar.

I plan to continue following my dreams, guided by the pictures on my treasure map. I continue down the pathway of my life from one "treasure" to another, happily checking them off with a black marker that I keep nearby.

—Michele Ivy Davis—

66

Relief Within My Heartache

What a lovely surprise to finally discover
how unlonely being alone can be.
~Ellen Burstyn

My mother, sisters, and best friend are here now, and I go sit in the bedroom, pretending I'm packing up. Instead, I sit on the bed, staring out the window, listening. I hear the bags and boxes being filled up by my best friend and then picked up and carried down the stairs and into the truck by my sisters and mother. Footsteps and grunts go down the stairs. I hear, "Turn, turn," and "Okay, I got it, I got it."

The bed of the truck makes loud sounds each time a bin is dropped into it. I can hear it all from outside the window, and what I hear is permanence.

In the heat of battle, I had packed up to leave three times before. One time I even stayed away for a month. I always returned though, and all my things went back into their accustomed places.

This time is different. I hear myself leaving with every noise from my helpers. With each trip they take to fill up the truck with my life, a piece of hope leaves, too. The relationship, the comfort, the memories, the future — are all now changed for good.

It's over.

I hide in the bedroom, crying, but I hear whispering in the kitchen.

There are a few things they are unsure of. I wipe my face when I hear, "Kiki, can you come out here for a second?" My mother, sisters, and best friend are by the cabinets where I had put some of my things. They look at me lovingly, and they're quiet. I try to look at their eyes in an effort to figure out what they want to know.

I can't tell if they're going to laugh or cry.

"So, um, what's the plan for the canned goods?" my oldest sister asks.

"Yeah, specifically, the black beans there." My other big sister points toward the cans.

"As well as the four opened containers of half-eaten almond butter," my best friend notes.

My mom looks at me, and her eyes say, "I didn't want to make you come out here to deal with this." She's ready to defend these cans if I need her to.

I look at their faces and then at the pile of pantry items that I, at some point, had apparently prioritized to make the big move with me to my sister's basement. I cry and say, "The almond butters can go to the trash, but the black beans are coming with me." They pause and exchange looks with each other.

I realized the absurdity at last, and I burst out laughing. We are all in hysterics now. "Black beans are a necessity; got it," someone jokes. We keep laughing, and they don't ask questions. Into the truck the special beans go.

It wasn't about the beans for me, though. It was about making choices that bring me joy and do not compromise my wants or needs. He hated beans, and we could never have them in the chili.

Relief comes in the most unexpected moments by the most unexpected things.

Today, relief within my heartache comes from a few cans of beans.

— Kellie Burley —

67

Omens of Happiness

The good and the bad things are part of life. Accept it.
The bad is a learning process, you will surpass it.
If you do you will be happy and it will be a good thing.
~Ann Marie Aguilar

I've never really been one to believe in omens or the like, but I do think our brains sometimes use whatever is out there in the world to deliver a message to us.

Sometimes, those "messages" come twice on the same day.

When I moved into the bachelor apartment where I would end up living for the longest amount of time I lived anywhere, I was not a happy fellow. I'll allow myself a touch of drama and point out that if you've ever been asked to move out and then were introduced to the more handsome and blonder fellow about to take your former role of boyfriend, then you might well have permission to enter a bit of a funk. Or, at least, I certainly did.

The apartment I could afford on my retail salary was a rather dingy bachelor pad on a busy street in a dodgy bit of the city. It had a good layout but very little else going for it. Plus I had very few belongings because I'd gotten rid of them when I lived with my ex. His stuff was nicer than mine.

The end result? I had a bachelor apartment and not even a bed.

I bought a few things right off: the bare basics with which to cook and eat a meal, a teakettle—an absolute necessity in my life—and, because beds are expensive, I bought a cot. I worked out my budget and tried to figure out how many months it would take before I could visit Ikea and start over.

The apartment looked horrible. I washed the walls; it didn't help much. It was empty, and for such a tiny place, it managed to echo. I had CDs and some VHS cassettes, but no way to play them; clothes, but no way to hang them; and books, but nowhere to shelve them. I could fix all these problems one at a time. Coat hangers were cheap enough, certainly, but it meant sandwich lunches and rice dinners pretty much nonstop for the next six months or so.

On my first day in the bachelor pad, after I had figured all this out, I was overwhelmed. I felt worthless—something quite common then but happily not so now.

So, I went for a walk in my new neighborhood.

The first of the two "omens" that greeted me did so right out my front door—or, rather, the apartment building's front door. A bird swooped by me, landed in the giant flower box outside—which was full of dried-out dirt and weeds—and tugged out some twigs. Then it shot past my head again to the corner of my ugly building where it was building a nest in a nook formed by the light fixtures and the brickwork.

I watched it for a bit, having nothing better to do and nowhere to go, and at some moment I realized that the bird, one tiny piece at a time, was making a home.

I sighed, rolled my eyes at the sky as if to say, "Message received," and then went for my walk. I was mulling finances, trying to figure out the order of importance of what I needed, and thinking that it was going to be a lean year. I'd recently gotten my yearly raise (which wasn't much) and knew, given what I was worth an hour, it was definitely going to take a while to gather my own twigs.

That's when I saw the dime. I picked it up, popped it in my pocket, and had a brief smirk over having begun my new home-improvement, savings-plan project.

That dime moved from pocket to pocket as I went to work the

next few days, and I pulled it out about a week later when I was doing laundry in the dank basement of my new building. I noticed something. It wasn't a dime. It turned out to be a pre-confederation nickel from Newfoundland, the last province to join Canada in 1949 until Nunavut entered in 1999.

On a whim, I checked one of the coin books at work and learned the nickel was valued around $25 in mint condition. I remember looking at it and thinking how it didn't look like much of anything but had more value than it seemed. In fact, it was worth more than it literally said it was worth, stamped right there into the face of the coin.

There were many times during that first year when trading in that nickel for even $20 would have been a godsend. But it's still sitting in my library in the home I share with my husband today. Every time I notice it, I smile.

It's a physical reminder that I — and everyone I know — am worth more than you'd think at a quick glance.

Well, maybe not that more handsome, blonder guy.

— Nathan Burgoine —

68

Desperate Times, Hidden Treasures

Your talent determines what you can do. Your motivation
determines how much you are willing to do.
Your attitude determines how well you do it.
~Lou Holtz

In late summer 1988, I went with a friend to look at a new development in our town. On a whim, I put down a deposit for one of the homes, and then I proceeded to work every bit of overtime I could to save up for the down payment. Six months later, I had my down payment and then some. The "then some" included a case of carpal tunnel syndrome (also known as a repetitive strain injury, or RSI), an occupational hazard for secretaries who spend their days at the keyboard.

I had to rely on disability insurance for my income, and the contribution from my roommate helped, but it was significantly less than my regular paycheck. The "then some" was quickly depleted, and my savings account was soon empty. In addition to worrying about my disability, I was fearful of losing the home I love that I had worked so hard to buy. It was a frightening time. I needed to do something fast.

But what? Even if I could physically do something else, I couldn't get a part-time or temporary job and still be on disability.

Like many people with an RSI, I felt the pain most acutely at night. Thankful that I didn't have to get up for work in the morning, I spent long hours of my nights reading. I didn't read engaging fiction or even sleep-inducing non-fiction. Instead, I read phone books.

As my friends and neighbors did, you might ask, "And *that* didn't put you to sleep?"

No, it didn't. It actually gave me a lifeline to save my house and stepping stone to a new career.

As I pored over those pages each night, I found organizations that would provide food, help paying utility bills, and even mortgage assistance. All night long, I made lists of the organizations and their phone numbers. During the days, I called each of those numbers, applied for whatever aid I could over the phone, and found rides to other sources of assistance, with the firm goal of saving the house I loved so much. Because I couldn't drive myself any longer, friends took me where I needed to go. Bit by bit, I was able to restore some stability to my life and, most importantly, keep my home.

During that time, voice-recognition software was coming into its own. One of my many phone calls led me to meet one of the developers of a voice-recognition program. He listened to my story, and I was fortunate to be selected as a beta tester for him. Soon, I was dictating my many lists of resources into a Word document. It felt like a miracle to have a way to create something in writing, and my lists grew.

One day, as I shared with a friend how I had scoured phone books to find resources to help me, he suggested there must be other unlucky people who had found themselves on disability or out of work and making less than they used to. He said I should collect my lists and share the information. It was a great idea, and soon my lists became a pamphlet. This was so well-received that I decided to go one step further. I'd write a book on how to "survive" disability.

It took some time to organize all my notes into appropriate chapters and teach the voice-recognition software how to recognize the words I wanted, but in-between surgeries to correct my carpel tunnel syndrome, I "wrote" my book and was surviving disability. In addition to chapters on finding sources for food, clothing, paying bills and rent or a mortgage, I also delved into laymen's experiences with workers' compensation and touched on Social Security Disability.

When I finished the book and it was published, I was pleased to have created a good resource for people with disabilities. However, since most of my readers were out of work or on limited incomes, the sales didn't increase my bank balance much. Surprisingly, however, the book did open other doors.

After the surgeries, it was clear that returning to my profession as a secretary was no longer an option. I needed a career that wouldn't involve me using my hands very much, and I wanted to work with people with disabilities. Although I had personal experience, I needed some formal education.

With my first book in hand, I was accepted into a counseling program. Because my advisor was impressed with my book, she suggested that in lieu of an oral practical final exam, I write another book — this one about the struggles students have coping on their own and keeping up with classwork. As I had with my first book, I set to work writing for high-school students with disabilities who were transitioning to college as well as college students with disabilities.

I graduated with high marks, and my second book was later offered as a resource to students with disabilities. After I finished graduate school with a master's degree in counseling and special education, I started my career as a counselor, focusing on people with disabilities. With a steady income from my new career, my beloved home was safe, and I survived disability.

About the time I was starting my counseling practice, I met an author who offered a writing challenge: Write a thousand words a day for seven days. For me, it would be a triple challenge. I'd never written fiction, I'd be "writing" using voice recognition, and a thousand words sure seemed like a lot. Since I loved reading fiction, I jumped in with both feet. It didn't take long for me to eagerly return to my story, writing day after day, page after page. In short order, I fell in love with my characters and didn't want to leave them at the end of the first book. The next thing I knew I was writing a series!

Here I am now, living in my beloved home, the author of nonfiction and fiction books. It's not a booming career bringing in millions of dollars, but it fulfills my love of creating, growing my own ideas, and offering entertainment to my readers. My days and nights recovering from carpal tunnel were painful and frightening, but my determination to keep the home I loved opened doors that I would never have dreamed of.

—Regina Schneider—

69

Do You Have a Pen?

*Magic exists. Who can doubt it, when there are
rainbows and wildflowers, the music of the wind
and the silence of the stars? Anyone who has loved
has been touched by magic.*
~Nora Roberts

This couldn't be happening, could it? Not our marriage!
Not us — two professional therapists with four wonderful
children and twenty years together. How could our marriage possibly be falling apart? How? And, more importantly, why?

When it comes to divorce, people rarely come up with satisfactory
answers to these questions. Certainly not answers that wash away all
the pain and grief. Yet we keep asking the how and why questions,
holding onto a glimmer of hope that there was an explanation around
the corner that would somehow turn our reality into something less
gritty, less painful, less real. But it's hard to move forward when you're
consumed with the past. So, eventually, you stop asking those questions because, if you don't, you fear you'll go crazy. For me, it was like
being confined to a jail cell of my own construction, while the key to
the door lay at my feet all along.

Once I made the choice to unlock the door to my cell, I faced
that looming darkness, hoping for daylight to come as I cautiously

took tiny steps to face a new day, a new way. I started returning calls from friends who had been reaching out to me. I found a new church. Eventually, I started attending singles' events and joined a divorce-recovery support group.

I learned that many divorcés declare they'll never marry again. I understand the desire to protect yourself from repeating your worst nightmare, but, for me, protecting myself wasn't recovery. I loved all relationships — those with my friends, my children, my family. And I loved marriage, too. Even after going through the deepest downward spiral of my life, I still held out hope of finding love again. I started dating for the first time in twenty-five years and discovered that, in my fifties, I got just as nervous asking a woman out on a date as I had decades earlier.

I also learned that "the right one" doesn't always come along easily. Or soon. Or how you might miss your big opportunity to discover the right one if you're still nervous and fearful of rejection when a likely candidate presents herself.

Luckily, I was able to harness my nerves and fears one morning in church when Jeanne sat down a few seats from me. We had been introduced to one another months earlier by a mutual friend at church. I had admired Jeanne from afar as she sang in the choir but hadn't gotten past my nervousness to approach her. But now here she was, sitting just a few seats away. As I waited for the service to begin, my heart began racing as I rapidly ran through different scenarios for how I might begin a conversation with her.

We glanced at each other (full disclosure: I had been glancing at her a lot) and said hello. Then she asked, "Do you have a pen?" Having just one pen, I offered to share my pen so that each of us could write notes on the church service handout.

For the next hour, my connection to this attractive woman was confined to a pen travelling back and forth between us. It was the first time I wished a church service would last longer. I needed the time to muster the courage to talk to Jeanne once the service ended. We attended a mega-church, and it was quite possible I wouldn't run into her again for months if I didn't take advantage of this opportunity.

So, when the service ended, I asked if she wouldn't mind sitting and talking for a while. She agreed, and it was great. But the next service was about to start, and we had to leave. Once again, I felt anxious about when I'd see her again, about asking her out on a date, about letting this opportunity slip away. So, as we were leaving, I asked her if she would like to continue our conversation sometime soon, and she agreed.

Jeanne and I began dating, and it felt right from the beginning. Jeanne was interesting and fun, compassionate and kind. We had common interests and similar life experiences; we were both divorced with four children. But there was one big difference between us: She kept losing pens, while I always had one ready to offer. It was a difference I was willing to accept.

When our first Christmas together arrived, we exchanged a few modest presents. When it appeared our gift-giving was over, she gave me one more present. I opened the present to find a bag full of pens, which I managed to spill all over the floor. It was easily my favorite present from her. Then I had one more present for her. When she opened it, she found a gold pen with the words "Do you have a pen?" inscribed on it. Three years later, we used that pen to sign our marriage license.

— Marvin Yanke —

Editor's note: Marvin reports that eight years later, he's made a hobby of collecting pens from restaurants, hotels and events so that he'll always have one to share with Jeanne. He hides them at home where Jeanne will likely find them. Their junk drawer is overflowing with pens.

70

Windblown Message

Never lose hope. Storms make people
stronger and never last forever.
~Roy T. Bennett, The Light in the Heart

My husband and I embraced and sobbed when we learned our home of twenty-eight years had been destroyed in the northern California Camp Fire. The souvenirs of our fifty-plus years of marriage along with generations of irreplaceable memorabilia and family heirlooms no longer existed.

Several weeks after the fire, we were allowed into the area where our home once stood. We had purchased shovels, boots, respirator masks, protective gloves and plastic storage containers to take to the site of our former home. We were given disposable hazmat suits at the check-in point where we had to provide proof of residence before being allowed to proceed. I felt like an outsider in the place I had called home for thirty years.

The drive to our homesite was heart-wrenching. The area of the once forested Sierra Nevada foothills was desolate, with the charred remains of old-growth Ponderosa pines and cedars. Chimneys stood on demolished homesites, and the charred, hollowed remains of vehicles stood next to piles of debris that had once been garages. Some vehicles had been abandoned on the side of the road.

I had researched online what items would not be destroyed by fire and was prepared to find as many as possible while digging through the remains of our home. Weeks of rain had turned the ashes to lye that encrusted the few things that survived the fire. Tears streamed down my face as I dug into the crusted debris. Every item I found was a treasure to be restored.

After hours of scavenging, we loaded the cast-iron and dense metal items we had rescued into plastic containers and loaded them into our two vehicles. I stood in the driveway and looked at the rubble that was once our home, wondering how long we would be living in hotels, where we would find another home, and how we could start over. It was a hollow feeling, and I questioned my strength to survive the oncoming challenges.

An afternoon breeze started and unearthed partially burned pages from books that had been buried under metal items. They drifted across the charred remains of homesites. I thought about the books I had lost and the comfort they had given me, along with copies of the *Chicken Soup for the Soul* books that contained stories I had written.

As I turned to leave, I noticed a piece of paper with charred edges stuck to the top of my boot. I pulled it off and read the printed message: "If life seems difficult, I pause and reflect on the blessing sometimes hidden within every circumstance. With renewed faith and courage, I begin again."

I framed that piece of paper and put it where I could see it often in every hotel and motel room we stayed in during the coming months. The framed message now sits on a shelf in the home we settled into four and a half months after the fire. It sustained me during that time and has helped me through the long emotional recovery process.

— L.A. Kennedy —

A Silver Lining

*Walk on, walk on with hope in your heart
and you'll never walk alone.*
~Rodgers and Hammerstein, Carousel

I've never believed that every cloud has a silver lining and I don't agree with that familiar adage, "That which does not kill us makes us stronger."

My husband's debilitating dementia had no silver lining, and it made neither of us stronger. John's decline was marked by suicide threats, crying jags, and psychotic episodes that landed him in the geriatric-psych unit for weeks. Once, he even managed to hurl himself out of a reclining wheelchair. He knew he was losing his mind, and he objected.

John, an NYU professor seventeen years my senior, had always been the composed one — a steady ship in calm waters with his confident stride and ever-present briefcase. When we had first started dating thirty-six years before, I'd had my share of relationship failures but he was steadfast and knew what was right for us. After we'd been dating for a few months, John went out west on a fly-fishing trip. I missed him terribly. He called late one night, from, I kid you not, Last Chance, Idaho. "I've been thinking about you," he said. "I'd like to spend more time with you. In fact" — there was a pause — "I'd like to spend the rest of my life with you."

I was speechless, terrified that this was too good to be true. I panicked that I would ruin our relationship by panicking, and he would get sick of my panic and leave me. This created more panic.

All the same, that August we got married and moved into a fifth-floor Chelsea walk-up. The panic moved in with me.

Eventually, it occurred to me that John wasn't going to get spooked by my panic attacks. He loved me whether I panicked or not.

"You're playing to an empty house," I told myself. "Why don't you just relax and enjoy the relationship?"

That was some of the best advice I ever got.

From the beginning, John expressed unshakable confidence in my dream of becoming a writer. Not only did he think I would be a writer, but he believed I already was one, even before I demonstrated the talent or tenacity. That someone believed I could actually accomplish anything was a novelty for a girl who had grown up with a conspicuous lack of abilities or even intelligence, at least that anyone took note of. My first husband, whom I married at nineteen, said I was an idiot to think I could ever be a writer.

John not only believed in my dream of becoming a writer, but he believed in me as a person, in my innate goodness. If faith is the evidence of things not seen, then he had more than confidence in me — he had faith. And because of his faith, I became the person he believed me to be (almost) and the writer he believed I would become.

Then John had a stroke. Now, I had something concrete to panic about.

My efforts to keep John alive and safe felt like trying to outrun a truck that was careening downhill. The stroke was followed by multiple falls, fractures, seizures, and surgeries. Eventually, he could no longer walk. The cost of hiring round-the-clock nurses was out of reach, so I placed John in a memory-care facility close by and visited him every day. I brushed his teeth, played Bach and Jessye Norman, and reminisced about the past. Our separation made me feel like I was leaving this man who had always stood by me, or that we were leaving — or losing — each other.

"I couldn't find you," he'd cry when I visited him. "I didn't know where you were. I didn't know who I was."

For John, I existed in a dream: an apparition of memory, love, and self, miraculously appearing out of nowhere and then vanishing just as mysteriously.

Sometimes, I'd hold his hand. "You're magnificent," I'd say. And then he'd have more than himself for just that moment; he'd have us.

As time passed, I witnessed fragments of his mind fall and shatter, like pieces of an antique lamp. He was a brilliant man, and some of the pieces glittered.

Ultimately, everything faded from his mind: his passion for teaching, his joy in his students' success, people and places from the past. But when all that had vanished, he still knew me and our daughter. The details of our lives — where we lived and what filled our days — eluded him, but he knew who we were and what we were to him.

Still, I was not prepared to call that a silver lining. It was a titanium lining, at best. Titanium, I knew, blended strength and practicality with a high melting point — just like me, since I've been known to blow a fuse now and then.

"Are we married?" I asked him one day after yet another stint in a geriatric-psych hospital. It had been two years since he'd moved to the memory facility, and he was fading fast.

John gazed at me fiercely in spite of the haze of dementia and truckloads of tranquilizers and anti-psychotics he was on. "Absolutely," he said.

Three days later, he was dead.

His death brought new questions and dilemmas. How could such a tremendous (though diminished) personality simply vanish? Could he still see me somehow? Would we meet again at a trout stream one summer evening — he casting a fly, me reading on a grassy bank nearby?

A friend told me her late husband returned as a thrush one spring morning and trilled a song to her from the treetops. Was the bird singing outside my window actually John?

At John's burial, our friend Gary, who knew John years before I had, said a few words. "When I met John, he was a kind and serious man but emotionally heavy," he began. Old friends who had gathered around the gravesite nodded knowingly.

"In the periodic table, there are transitional metals like silver, gold, rubidium — heavy metals," Gary went on. "When John met Pammy, his soul lightened. Nitrogen, hydrogen, helium — these are the elements he inherited when he fell in love."

There was laughter and camaraderie, but I didn't feel any stronger. I wondered when I would recover.

Yet, with time, John's confidence in me, his very essence, has become a part of me, of who I am, and how I make my way through the world. Gradually, I have grown more serious, more solid.

I still panic about nothing, but every once in a while I catch a glint of those transitional metals Gary spoke of at the gravesite that day: gold, rubidium, and, yes, silver.

— Pamela Jane —

Chapter 8

Meet the New You

72

The Fire Within

Redemption is not perfection. The redeemed
must realize their imperfections.
~John Piper

hite fluorescent lights flooded my squinting eyes as the *click, click, click* of cold, metal handcuffs shackled my wrists and ankles to a gurney in the trauma bay of the hospital.

Sharp pain in my knee. "You have the right to remain silent."

Dull pain in my shoulder. "Everything you say can and will be used against you in a court of law."

Stabbing pain in my tailbone. "You have the right to talk to a lawyer…"

I would learn later that I had blacked out, left my friends in my apartment near campus, got in my car, and drove over thirty miles before running a red light and colliding with an Uber driver and his three passengers at over eighty miles per hour. They were all injured.

Then I hit a median, flew over the top of two cars, and landed on my roof after flipping twice in midair. I would lose my driver's license, internship, and job, and serve time in prison while incurring tens of thousands of dollars of legal and medical expenses.

At that moment in the hospital, however, I knew none of that. All I knew was that everything hurt and I had double vision. For the first time in my twenty-two years of life, I was in handcuffs. I spent three nights in the hospital and one night in jail before my teary-eyed parents picked me up, thankful that their only son was alive. I had an eye patch, a limp, and enough guilt to make me wish I hadn't survived.

I quickly learned that no matter what happens in your life, the world keeps moving forward, with or without you. That weekend, four days after I was released from jail, I returned to campus and took my final exams for the fall semester. I passed them all but then put school out of my mind; I had a situation on my hands.

How did this happen? This was not me. I didn't drive drunk. I didn't even drink that often. I was a full-time accounting student, a part-time salesman at one of the major wireless carriers, and a competitive powerlifter. I had an internship and a fruitful career path at one of the Big Four accounting firms. My hobbies were going to the gym, reading books, starting to write (and abandoning) a novel, and working on my car. That's it.

By the time the next semester rolled around, my hobbies had become attending AA meetings, going to rehab, and trying not to break down every time thoughts of the people I had injured came to mind. No driving. No working out. No drinking with friends. In rehab, I was diagnosed with bipolar disorder and obsessive-compulsive disorder. Turns out, drinking while experiencing a manic episode is a recipe for catastrophe. While a part of me was relieved to have a diagnosis to help explain how I ended up in this situation, another part of me struggled to come to terms with the fact that I have a mental disorder, that I'm broken in some way.

At the time, it felt like the only part of my old life I still had was my mind, and therefore my ability to read. So, I read. A lot. This became my lifeline when the coronavirus pandemic sent my classes online.

Filling my mind with the wisdom of men and women greater than myself is what allowed me to keep my sanity through this living nightmare. I read fiction that taught me empathy, how to see the world from someone else's point of view. I read accounts of tragedy such as Viktor Frankl's *Man's Search for Meaning,* which taught me two things. First, people throughout history have gone through trials much more difficult than my own — trials they were forced into, not trials brought upon themselves by their own hand. Second, the only way I was going to make it through this was if I forged meaning amidst the calamity.

I knew what the meaning of my old life was. It was the epitome of the American status quo. Go to college. Pick a marketable major. Get a good job. Live a good life. That was the idea, at least. Not anymore. With two felony DUIs and prison time on my background check, I lost my internship and any chance at a future in accounting. I quit my sales job and took a semester off so I could go to prison, something that wasn't even in the realm of possibility for the old me.

What do you do when your plans are dashed, your future uncertain, and your faith in yourself is shaken? You stand up straight with your shoulders back. You do the next right thing. You lift your eyes to the mountain you must climb and you climb it, one rock at a time. What once seemed insurmountable will in time become manageable. On the other side of your mountain, you will find the path leading you where you need to go.

What remains when the external accomplishments that your identity is based upon disappear? The answer is *you*. The essence of your being. Sit down. Close your eyes. Breathe. Turn your gaze inward, look deep into your soul, and search for the crackle of flame burning within. That's you. The voice in your head and the tingling in your fingertips? That's life, coursing through your veins. Feel it. Cherish it. Do not take it for granted, for none of us knows the time nor the place when our flame will be extinguished.

What is the meaning of my debacle? Is there even meaning to be found in the aftermath of a drunken collision for me, the man responsible for it? Some would say no. I, however, believe that there is.

Coming so close to losing my life helped reveal to me what truly matters. Not money. Or status. Or material possessions. None of that matters when you look death in the eye. Don't look outside yourself for fulfillment, or you will never find it. Everything your soul needs can be found within. When disaster strikes, you'll learn who is really there for you. Treasure those people.

What is my meaning? To live my truth. The written word is my medium. I feel called to write, to share my story with the world. I finally fulfilled my dream of finishing a novel, with many more to come. This brings me more joy than any job or internship ever could.

I hope that, in reading my story, you may learn from my mistakes and apply my experience to the struggles in your own life. Whatever you have to do, whatever challenges you must face, do it with the faith that no matter how impossible it may seem today, you will grow through it, and you are not alone.

—John Apel—

73

Epic Anyway

I've learned that "making a living"
is not the same thing as "making a life."
~Maya Angelou

I sighed as I tried to focus on my yoga mat. Since the gyms were closed, my new normal was fitness by the pool at my apartment complex. On any other day, this would have been enjoyable. Ideal even. But in the midst of trying to find some sort of Zen, my mind kept wandering. There was just too much to think about. Disease. Chaos. Societal breakdown. Doom. Fear. The Unknown. Murder hornets. How could I survive when I could barely snag a roll of toilet paper?

I found my sweaty feet losing grip and was brought back to reality as I quickly moved to avoid falling on my mat. The whole mindfulness thing really wasn't working.

The year 2020 was supposed to be epic for me. I had finally gotten my content-creation business on track to where I wanted it. I had found some great brands to collaborate with and arranged some really incredible international trips I had been trying to put together for years. It seemed like everything had fallen into place. All my hard work had finally come together and paid off.

And then, almost in an instant, everything fell apart. Since the beginning of the lockdowns, it seemed as if all the projects I had worked so hard for were disappearing by the day. Trips and treks were canceled or postponed as international borders were shut, businesses were closing, and people were sheltering in place.

Our way of life, our normal, had almost ceased to exist. Cities looked like ghost towns, like something in an apocalypse movie. Human contact seemed to be a relic of the past as Zoom meetings from isolation became the new disease-free way to communicate. Friends and families wanted to stay in their bubbles. People were placed into groups: "essential," "non-essential," "masker," "conspiracy theorist." We became more divided than ever, all while more events came into play. We saw natural disasters, protests, riots, cancel culture, political divides and millions of jobs lost. Meanwhile, the death toll climbed, and there seemed to be no end in sight.

And, everywhere we turned, it was in our face. Was there anything else to talk about?

There comes a point in time when obstacles force us to change. We can either be consumed by them and let them destroy us, or we can respond by getting creative, adapting and changing our path. I was riding that fine line and realized I had to make a change, and fast.

I realized that I couldn't change the world around me. I had no control over that. But I could change myself. I could change the course of my life. I realized that wasting time by trying to salvage past projects was not in my best interest.

I took to my yoga mat again. This time, with an open mind.

It took me a while to get some clarity, but I finally had a breakthrough. I felt stronger, happier and more confident with each movement as I became more and more comfortable with my decision.

I was going to look into alternative career options. I had been a personal trainer before, and the thought of getting back into something health and wellness related intrigued me.

Of course I had questions. How was I going to do this? Was I too old? Was I smart enough and strong enough? How would this affect my content career when, and if, things got back to normal.

I had to put those fears aside. If there is anything that 2020 taught me, it's to accept and embrace the unknown. So, with great enthusiasm, excitement and a hint of anxiety, I signed up for an EMT course to begin my journey.

From the first day in class, my sense of wonder and passion for learning and helping others were evident. I once again felt that fire to not only succeed, but to fully immerse myself in the subject. I dedicated my time to learning everything I could about the subject. When I wasn't in class, I was watching videos, listening to podcasts and reading books at home about health and wellness. I felt like I was living out my purpose in life again. I felt that fire light up inside me.

And the passion and hard work paid off. At the end of the year, I had earned my EMT license and began to look for options in the industry. This was only the beginning, and there were so many options and directions I could take it. As the year wound down and the chaos settled my content career seemed to come back. But the experience at the EMT academy gave me a desire to help people and make a difference. After another session of soul searching on the mat, I decided I could do both. I could continue my content business while also making a positive impact working with the community. I decided that even though being a field EMT wasn't exactly for me, I could still make a difference by being an advocate for health and wellness through my content career.

I learned so much from this experience. Life can literally change overnight, so it's important to get creative and adapt to the new situations. Learning new skills will open your mind and doors to new opportunities, even if every one of them seemed to be closed.

So, I was wrong the whole time. The year 2020 was epic. Just in a different way than I had planned.

— Kirsten Alexis —

74

Bold Progress

When we show up, act boldly, and practice the best ways
to be wrong, we fail forward. No matter where we end up,
we've grown from where we began.
~Stacey Abrams

ivorce propelled me to the barber's chair. For several weeks I had toyed with the idea of taking off ten years' worth of locs, wondering what I would look like with a tapered fade and a new color. I stood in the mirror and pulled my waist length hair into a ponytail and pictured myself bald. I never thought I would be here, and by "here" I mean a thirty-one-year-old divorcée in the throes of a pandemic.

I threw out the idea in casual conversation with friends and family and was met with resistance.

"But you've been growing it for so long! Do you really want to waste all that time?"

"Aren't you afraid you'll look like a boy?"

"What if your head is a weird shape?"

"Look, I know you're going through a lot but isn't this a little extreme?"

They were right. I had no right to be so bold. Still, Pinterest became my secret obsession. I typed "short haircuts for Black women" into the search bar and marveled at the kaleidoscope of colors, designs, and styles. If only I had the confidence these women had.

Besides that, my locked hair was my best beauty feature. It was a testament to my patience and creativity. More importantly, it was an homage to my Blackness. My natural state was a way for me to buck a beauty standard that placed a perm in my hair at the age of ten. It was a physical manifestation of the ancestors I had never known and a continent I had yet to visit. If I cut it off, I wasn't sure who I would be.

That is, until one Saturday morning I sat at my kitchen table to sign a petition for an absolute divorce just as the COVID-19 death toll hit its summer high in August 2020. Not even my family knew of the official separation. I deleted pictures of my ex-husband and me from social media because I was too ashamed to say that my courthouse wedding barely lasted two years.

Here I was, signing for an unwanted, new beginning as the world around me crumbled. At that moment, everything got heavy, especially my hair. The urge to get a pair of scissors had my fingers itching.

Then it hit me. The world as I knew it was gone. A divorce and a pandemic completely reshaped everything. This "new normal" extended far beyond wearing masks and closing a joint bank account. I was holding onto a past that would never return.

I opened Instagram, searched the hashtag #DMVbarbers, and came to a page that I liked. In a matter of minutes, I set an appointment with a man named Wes and a week later I was sitting in his chair, showing him the cut and color I wanted.

There was no countdown or final confirmation. Wes took his shears, stretched a loc taunt at my right temple, and in one swift motion — snip! He handed me the hair as if it were a receipt and pulled another loc to do it again. I massaged the loc, feeling the experiences and trauma of the past decade between my thumb and index finger. When I first started my locs I told everyone that I would never cut my hair. Now the sound of Wes cutting them off one by one was strangely therapeutic.

I stood in front of the mirror after a wash, dye, and tapered cut. It was much shorter than I thought it would be and redder than the picture I'd downloaded. I turned my head to the side and took in the outline of my nearly bald head — I looked more like my younger brother than I realized. I ran my fingers across my scalp, making sure that it wasn't an illusion.

"I like it," Wes said.

I smiled, "I do, too."

As I walked out of the shop with my locs bundled in my hand, a cool breeze slapped the back of my neck. I was surprised by the lightness and the freedom of it all. I got in my car, took off my mask, and pulled down my sun visor to look at myself in the mirror. I laughed. It was funny how I'd feared a disconnect from my Blackness without my locs. It turned out that my wide nose and full lips were more pronounced without my mane.

I'd done something I never thought I had the confidence or courage to do — I transformed without permission. It was a small bit of joy in a spiraling world, but it was still mine. I took out my phone and snapped a picture. It took less than I realized to be bold.

— Morgan Cruise —

75

Rainbows Along the Way

Stay afraid, but do it anyway. What's important is the action. You don't have to wait to be confident. Just do it and eventually the confidence will follow.
~Carrie Fisher

I was a teenager in love — in love with Ralph Macchio, the star of *The Karate Kid*, and his crane kick. I loved martial arts. I even joined the karate club in college.

But life got in the way. My crane kick became a distant memory. I was too busy graduating from college, getting married, having kids, and paying the bills.

Imagine my sheer joy when, decades later, my six-year-old expressed interest in martial arts. A perfectly timed Girl Scout outing to the local taekwondo school proved to be the match that lit my daughter's flame. She followed her dreams, and her older sister followed her. I watched as my girls, dressed in their pure-white uniforms with a menacing dragon on the back, punched and shouted in unison with twenty other students. It was like a scene straight out of *The Karate Kid*.

I was itching to get onto the mat, too, but I was a forty-year-old mother and a school psychologist. With all my responsibilities and at my age, how could I even consider martial arts?

The kicker was that I also had a chronic medical condition that affected every aspect of my life and made even standing a challenge.

That condition, postural orthostatic tachycardia syndrome (POTS), can cause a host of symptoms, the worst of which are fainting, light-headedness, fatigue, and shortness of breath. I sat on the sidelines, a stark contrast to my life as a kid when I was usually on a skating rink, court, field, or ball diamond. But, at the time, I believed a POTS-sufferer belonged in a martial-arts uniform as much as an NFL wide receiver belonged in stilettos.

Fate stepped in. The instructors invited parents of students to one free class a month. I left my "mom hat" at the door, leaped onto the mat, and joined immediately after my first class. It didn't take long before I walked, talked, and breathed martial arts.

I loved taekwondo, but my body didn't. Martial arts involved being on my feet for a long time, elevating my heartrate, getting overheated, and doing a lot of head movement. Each of these had the potential to trigger POTS symptoms.

I was a yellow belt (the first belt earned after beginning as a white belt) when I faced my first significant battle — The Gladiator Games, a local martial-arts tournament. Besides being forty-one, a newbie martial artist, and a POTS patient, I also had performance anxiety.

The battle didn't begin well. I lost my registration ticket — the one my instructor had repeatedly warned the young students not to lose. After admitting my mistake, I realized it was a molehill, not a mountain. The event host quickly printed a new ticket for me.

My first event was board breaking. I hoped to break eight boards because I had broken five during practice. My nerves got shakier as the stack got higher. But I psyched myself up, focused, clenched my fist, raised my arm, and smashed down into the stack. I stared at the pile in amazement.

Only three boards broke.

My next event involved performing a form — a prescribed series of movements. I knew I was ready, but my stomach and legs didn't want to prove it. My ever-increasing heartrate was no help. But I stepped into the ring, faced the three glaring judges, and performed the form better than I ever had. I surely earned gold.

The judges disagreed.

My last and most anticipated event was sparring. I donned my protective gear only to realize I had forgotten one critical weapon — food. It was well past noon, and I hadn't eaten since breakfast. Low blood sugar and POTS do not mix, but there was no time to eat.

I fought hard the first round — too hard. I had the girl on her heels, but I also had my heart nearly pounding its way right out of my chest. I gasped for air and was lightheaded and fatigued. Thankfully, the bell rang. I got a much-needed break.

I sat in the corner of the ring while the referee and my master stared at me with wide eyes. I needed to catch my breath. I could survive one more round. I'd pushed through before.

The referee suggested I forfeit. My master agreed.

My heart sank. How could I quit? I had just won the first round — only one more round for gold. But my body would not cooperate. I would need more than a minute in a chair to recover from the two minutes in the ring. I took what may have looked like the easier route, but it was torturous.

I quit.

The referee grabbed my hand and my opponent's, triumphantly raised hers, and left mine hanging as low as I felt.

My first tournament didn't turn out how I dreamed, but it started me on a road of growth that was well worth the bumpy ride. Like losing the registration ticket, I made other mistakes. Some mistakes were easily corrected molehills; others were mountains. Mistakes are part of life, especially when you're stepping out of your comfort zone. I grew to accept my mistakes, learn from them, and keep kicking.

I may have broken only three boards at my first tournament, but I never stopped breaking through obstacles. I had plenty of them. The most significant was a dysfunctional body and a busy life balancing home and career. Not to mention, I was no spring chicken. But you never know what you can accomplish unless you keep trying despite any obstacles in your way.

My form didn't earn gold at that tournament, but not earning gold is okay as long as you did your best. Every day that I showed up to class, regardless of how I performed, was better than never stepping onto the mat.

I also learned the art of self-control. There were times when I could push myself to finish a class, test, or sparring match. Other times, I had to slam on the brakes before I even started.

One of the most beautiful aspects of being in a battle I could not win by myself was feeling love from others who supported me along the way. My family, masters, and fellow students helped me stay on my feet and picked me up when I fell.

Three years after I quit my first sparring match, I earned a black belt in taekwondo. If I had not battled POTS while training for my black belt, the road would have surely been easier but I might have missed out on the personal growth and beautiful relationships I developed. Furthermore, overcoming the obstacles made the accomplishments that much sweeter for me. I learned that the storms of life make the rainbows shine brighter.

— Diane DeCaprio —

76

Miles of Me

One run can change your day,
many runs can change your life.
~Author Unknown

Before becoming a dedicated runner, I had always bought my running shoes from the nearest store, more concerned with color, style, and price than about getting the right fit. But one of the first pieces of advice new runners receive is to get shoes that fit well no matter how they look. If that ugly neon-green pair will fit you better and won't give you blisters, they will serve you better than the cute blue pair. And a second piece of advice: You should never have to break in a pair of running shoes. They should fit you well from the first mile.

I remember walking into a real running store for my first fitting. It wasn't a store at the mall. It was a store dedicated to runners. As a new runner who was ready to invest in myself, I felt self-conscious as the young, fit specialist asked questions about my running routine.

"How many miles do you run?"

"Oh, about ten miles."

"A day? That's great!"

"Um, no. I run about ten miles a week."

I was still starting out, and it seemed incomprehensible that I would run more than ten miles a week.

But that first pair of "real" running shoes showed me the way to myself. I was so lonely as a stay-at-home mom after I left teaching.

My identity had been wrapped around who I was as a teacher. But, I discovered, I didn't have the same confidence now that I was a mother.

As a new mother, I never felt like I was doing anything right. I was tired from the late-night feedings and I was lonely. The stay-at-home mothers I met always seemed to have it all together, from the mothers at the local toddler gym to the perfectly coiffed mothers in my Mothers of Preschoolers group. I, on the other hand, was always running late, with my hair in a messy bun and my body squeezed into my jeans. Who has time to put herself together when rounding up three children to make it to a meeting to talk about motherhood?

But running showed me that being alone wasn't a bad thing. Those solitary hours spent running gave me time to regroup, find time for myself, and enjoy the time when someone wasn't demanding my attention.

Running taught me discipline because it meant saying yes to myself every time I laced up. Training runs strengthened my determination to accomplish goals. It gave me courage to step outside of myself and who I thought I was. I could be more than a teacher. I could be a mother, an athlete, a dream chaser.

That first pair of shoes carried me through all those training runs that brought me to the starting line of my first half-marathon. Since then, I've run numerous races, including more half-marathons. In the past ten years, I've changed my shoes more times than I can count and changed brands as I became a better runner. But that first pair of shoes will always be my favorite.

Those running shoes pushed me out of my depression when I suffered postpartum depression. They were my best friends when I felt so isolated as a stay-at-home mom watching all my friends return to work. They taught me to be comfortable in my skin. I wasn't and will never be the fastest, the best, or the strongest runner. But I was and still am determined.

Those first shoes were reliable and dependable. They carried me on many a treadmill run and were with me as I ventured off the treadmill onto my neighborhood roads for the first time. They carried me past soccer fields, on paths, and in and out of cul-de-sacs. They carried me through sunny days, snowy days, and rainy days. They didn't care which season I was in; they would be there ready to go. I could be in the infancy of motherhood, the season of chaos with four children at home, or a season of illness.

My shoes didn't care if I was having a good day or a bad one; they would take me wherever I needed to and for however long I needed to run. Running made me a better wife, mother, and person. With each run, my shoes reinforced that it was okay to take care of myself so that I could take care of the most important people in my life: my family.

They were with me when I began to up my mileage, showing me how much more I could do — not just in running, but in my life. If I was willing to show up for myself every day, I could reach my goals, whether they be in running, in my career, or in the type of mother and wife I wanted to be. We ran hundreds of miles together, and whenever I needed them, they were waiting for me. They carried me through my first half-marathon, showing that when I showed up every day for myself, I could accomplish great things.

Most recently, my latest pair of running shoes were waiting for me when I received my cancer diagnosis. They were there through the months of chemotherapy and radiation. They were there when I felt like I couldn't do more than walk around the neighborhood clutching my husband's arm. They were there as I finished treatment and became stronger. They are there as I find myself learning to run again.

Now I run for fun and sometimes for survival. When depression threatens to overtake me and tell me I'm not good enough or that my family would be better without me, there my shoes sit, waiting to tell me differently.

— Heather Martin Jauquet —

77

Soldiers Don't Smile

*A gentle word, a kind look, a good-natured smile
can work wonders and accomplish miracles.*
~William Hazlitt

I'm not the kind of person you'd look at and think, *That girl looks like a soldier.* It's not that I wasn't fit, but at 5'2", decked out with designer clothes, high heels, plenty of jewelry, and a thick Jersey accent, combat boots weren't something I aspired to wear. All that changed on September 11, 2001.

I lived only a few miles outside New York City. I was enrolled in college, but suddenly my world (as were the lives of many others) turned upside down. College seemed less important and donating blood was simply not enough. Somewhere among the images that flashed across the TV were soldiers, and I thought, *I want to be one of them.*

I had the insurmountable task of convincing my parents that this was a good choice. It's not that they weren't proud; they were concerned and scared. It was tough to put into words, but deep down inside, I knew joining was what I wanted and needed to do. I didn't even watch military movies growing up, and here I was ready to put on a battle dress uniform (BDUs) and train for war. Within weeks of 9/11, I enlisted in the Army with the support of my family behind me.

The lifestyle change of civilian to soldier wasn't a smooth transition. My biggest challenge was military bearing. I smiled too much.

Apparently, soldiers don't smile, but this Jersey girl couldn't help but smile — and boy, did I pay for it! My "pearly whites" earned me plenty of extra "smoke sessions" — that's when drill sergeants get creative and find any number of ways for you to work out. Muscle failure is their goal, and they achieve it as often as possible. You have no choice but to dig deep and push your strength and endurance to their limits.

I had a lot to prove — not just to the drill sergeants but to myself and my family and friends back home. No one really thought I'd be a good fit for the military. To be honest, I didn't know if I'd be a good fit either. But what I lacked in prior military knowledge, I made up for with fierce determination. Our battalion's motto was "Always Forward." It was not only a call to motivation and an appropriate response to cadre but also served as a personal reminder to never quit.

Not even nighttime granted a respite from our demanding drill sergeants. You'd be lucky to sleep more than four consecutive hours, and that was a rarity! We were physically and mentally challenged day and night. For a couple of months, I learned to sleep hard in the brief allotments they gave us. It amazed me that we could basically work out the entire day, learn new military tasks and, in the middle of the night, wake up for additional duty like fireguard or roving patrol. Before the sun peaked over the horizon, we awoke to the loudest, most unwelcoming bagpipes and shouting from drill sergeants to begin another day. It was painful, horrible, exhausting ... and *so much fun*. That non-military-bearing smile rarely left my face. I learned to love the absolute craziness of the Army. I smiled through it all. *Always Forward!*

A few months after graduating from boot camp, I crossed paths with my former drill sergeant. Even though time had passed, he still intimidated me!

We spoke briefly. I thanked him for being so motivating. He was the first soldier I idolized. He smiled and said, "Thanks for being that smiling face every day. You really brightened my days during the rough times." We parted with "Always Forward" and went our separate ways.

It's been nearly twenty years since that conversation, and it's never left me. I had no idea that my smile made a difference. If anything, I thought it just got me in trouble. I didn't even think about how tough it was for our drill sergeants and how demanding their schedules were (plus balancing a family life). I was so focused on the whirlwind of boot camp that I didn't even consider how challenging it must have been for them.

What I learned from that brief conversation was that even in the toughest, most physically exhausting, and sweaty (and stinky) situations, a small token of human kindness and connection goes a long way. Sometimes, we don't even know the joy we bring to others.

I stayed in the military for ten years. I deployed to Iraq. Challenges continued to get thrown my way, but I never lost my smile.

No matter what you do with your life — in a uniform or not — never forget that human connection can uplift those around you without even a word spoken. We may not all train and deploy to war, but we all have our own battles to fight that are no less significant. A smile or a simple act of kindness may have more of an impact on someone else's life than you realize. *Always Forward!*

— Liesl Marelli —

78

A True Reflection

*Owning our story and loving ourselves through that
process is the bravest thing that we'll ever do.*
~Brené Brown

I stood there trembling. I was the weakest I had ever been but also the strongest I had ever been. I stared down my dad. I said what my heart had felt for decades. It finally came out: "You should be proud to have me as a daughter."

He rolled his eyes and shrugged. It was the same reaction I had received from both parents my entire life

This time, however, it wasn't his reaction that mattered. What mattered now was finally having the courage to stand up for myself. I am lovable. I am worthy of being loved by my parents.

He still walked away, unconvinced that I was special.

Even though I had finally done it — the brave thing — the child inside me was still hurting. After all, we look to our parents as our first glimpse into who we are. When they kneel down and tell us, "You are smart," "You are kind," "You are beautiful," "You are wanted," or "We are proud of you," they are our first mirror, reflecting back to us who we are. We look to them to know we are wonderful and wanted. When we look to them and see disappointment, disapproval, and criticism, we start to wonder if that is who we are.

Their criticism over the years didn't align with who I felt I was in my heart. So that left me feeling confused. It was like I was looking into a broken mirror.

When I told my dad that I was an awesome daughter, I shattered that mirror into a thousand pieces. I would never look in that mirror again.

And now I was left standing at a doorway with shattered glass in every direction as my father walked away.

As the months go by, I still struggle to see who I truly am. But I know deep down that I am extraordinary, wonderful, and worthy. I know my parents' inability to love me is not a measure of how lovable I am. I've pored over books. I've done therapy. I've written unsent letters. I've written letters to myself with the words I needed to hear. I wrote a list of all the wonderful things about myself. Every amazing truth about me. All the remarkable things that make me beloved. It felt so good. That list sat in a file on my computer for months. But truth never does any good tucked away.

So, I printed my list with all the truths about who I am — pages and pages of all the unique and beautiful things about me. I taped them all over my mirror, covering the whole thing. Now, when I look into my mirror, I see my true reflection and my affirmations:

"You are wise."

"You have a fun sense of humor."

"You are strong enough to stand up for yourself."

"You are a good mother."

Then, I kneel down to my little girl and say to her:

"You are wise."

"You have a fun sense of humor."

"You are strong enough to stand up for yourself."

"You are an amazing daughter, and I am so proud of you."

— Katie Bergen —

79

A Mid-Mom Crisis

The greatest gifts you can give your children are the
roots of responsibility and the wings of independence.
~Denis Waitley

On a sunny Wednesday in May 2018, I sat across from my new therapist in her small, square office. Kim's slim legs were crossed at the ankles as she listened to me, the thirty-eight-year-old woman in a puddle on the brown couch opposite her. I cried through the entire hour-long appointment. I was depressed and anxious, confused as to how I — a competent, capable, educated woman — was able to slide so far, so quickly.

"I don't know what's happening," I told her, my voice heavy with frustration and exhaustion. I paused to blow my nose, adding to the pile of used tissues collecting in my lap. I was folded in on myself, my shoulders pushed forward by the weight of my ever-present anxiety. "I feel like I'm having a midlife crisis," I told her. As I said these words, I knew they were inadequate, but they were the only ones I could find to express my sense of being unmoored, adrift in the sea of my busy life. I rubbed my hand against the surface of the couch next to my leg, feeling its rough, raised texture.

Kim smoothed her skirt across her thighs before she responded gently. "Julie, I think you're a little young for a midlife crisis, but I think you may be having a mid-mom crisis."

My boys were nine and eleven at the time; the older one was about to start middle school. On the surface, perhaps, my angst seemed misplaced;

no one was leaving for college or moving out of our house. But feelings are unruly, popping up unexpectedly and unbidden, demanding our attention. Over the next year, Kim and I would circle this moment, this statement, unpacking its origins and implications as she helped me find my way back to myself.

When our children are small, their needs are immediate, consuming. Diapers, meals, tantrums, safety, hands are not for hitting. The important is forever sacrificed on the altar of the urgent. The fullness of these days lies not in their content but in their constancy; it's possible to be busy and bored at the same time. But, oh, they're beautiful days, full of wonder and awe and rhythm. Those early years of motherhood were the years I got to be my boys' best girl.

But parenting is a tricky business. Just as we're growing accustomed to this adoration, the children begin to grow into themselves. And though we always knew they were books to be read, not books to be written, it's still shocking. We know they are only meant to be ours for a season. We know we will have to let them go, that it will be a necessary, healthy part of the process. But this theoretical knowledge does nothing to prepare us for how to spend the rest of our lives letting them go, little by little. We can't possibly know in advance how to survive all the tiny heartbreaks: the moment when he no longer wants to hold our hand in public, the moment when she rolls her eyes at us, or when her traitorous teenage brain convinces her that we are the Queen of the Idiots.

On the day I sat across from Kim and gazed at the bright green leaves of the tree outside her second-floor window, my boys were beginning to make the turn, to pull away from me in tiny, nearly imperceptible ways. And I was grieving. But I dismissed that feeling, refusing to allow myself the space to acknowledge that a season was ending. I had invested over a decade of my life in these small people. Now what?

My mid-mom crisis happened right there, in a moment of suspension between dependence and independence. And it can be a beautiful moment when we begin to see our children's wings. There's an opportunity to create, to dream, to look forward to the next season with anticipation and joy.

But I didn't see an invitation to joy in that in-between moment. I had denied my feelings for too long, beginning with an anaphylactic reaction the previous November that had introduced a gnawing fear into my life: *This could all be gone anytime,* the fear whispered. *It's terribly precarious, this life.* Instead of acknowledging that this risk is unavoidable, part of the brutal truth of our humanity, I shoved that fear away and focused on controlling every variable I could find. I was ruthless and rational, and I denied my feelings — first, my fear, and later, my grief — distracting myself with productivity. I put a stopper in the bottle, but instead of dissipating, the feelings concentrated and multiplied. When their pressure reached its maximum, they spilled out, impossible to contain. I was a mess, an untethered balloon pumped full with the helium of anxiety. But, mercifully, when depression pulled me back down, I landed on Kim's couch.

Over the next year, Kim would help me find hope again, to believe that perhaps the best days weren't behind me. She reminded me that everything changes. She told me that my boys still needed me, would still need me, but in new ways. She pointed out the spaces in our lives and told me I could fill those with writing, reading, or something I hadn't yet considered.

If more is caught than taught, then the best thing I could do was to live my own days, to fill them with joy, to dream my own dreams. Because, as Kim pointed out, wasn't that what I wanted for my children? I wanted them to be creators of their own lives, to know their own power and agency. I wanted them to know resilience and grit and adaptation, and none of those would come without struggle. I wanted them to grow to be men who would embrace change by mining for what's good, even when life is painful and sad.

The mid-mom crisis was an invitation to adapt, to become the woman I was meant to be for the next season. That year taught me to feel, to hear my own voice again, to hold my life and my joys a little more loosely, and it all began on Kim's couch.

I may have been a mom, but I still had some growing to do.

— Julie Chavez —

80

I Am Bald and I Am Beautiful

Love yourself first and everything else falls into line.
You really have to love yourself to get
anything done in this world.
~Lucille Ball

I lost all my hair at age two due to alopecia. All I wanted growing up was to fit in. I would look at all the beautiful girls I was surrounded by at schools and in the media and think, *If I had hair, I would be beautiful, too.*

I wore a wig and was bullied and teased for it. I had no eyebrows, and my peers let me know it. They would call me "bald" or say, "Lindsay has no hair." They were right, so I just let them bully me. I felt like I deserved it, as if losing my hair due to this autoimmune condition was somehow my fault.

Sports became my escape, and I was fortunate to have innate athletic ability. I would race home every day and shoot hoops in my driveway for hours. I would pretend to make the game-winning shot. The crowd would go wild and chant my name. I never thought about my alopecia or bald head during these moments, but rather who I wanted to become and what I wanted to accomplish.

I started to gain recognition from others, but this time it was positive. I became known as the girl who was good at basketball, not just as the girl who didn't have hair. I was still bullied, but it began to bother me less because I had another distraction. I put all my time and energy into basketball and becoming the best player I could be.

I had big dreams. For the first time in my life, I felt like I could really do something, even with my alopecia. I became determined and wasn't going to let anything slow me down or hold me back from accomplishing my dreams.

I had a great high-school career, breaking countless school records, and received a scholarship to play in college. It was a dream come true. However, I still wasn't okay with my alopecia and rarely talked about it. College is a huge transition, and all I wanted was to be like everyone else. I was fearful of telling anyone, especially a guy, about my alopecia and having them walk away. I remember the first time I built up the courage to tell an amazing (or so I thought) guy about my alopecia. I was so nervous but optimistic at the same time.

However, my heart was crushed. He was shocked that I didn't have hair because I hid it so well. He told me, "I can't date someone who doesn't have hair." It broke my heart; it was one of my worst fears come true. I became angry about my alopecia and shut down. I didn't want to let anyone in again because it was the worst feeling. I continued to wear my wig all the time, no matter the weather or what I was doing. It was my security and way to hide from the world.

My senior year of college, I wanted to run the marathon in my town to check this athletic endeavor off my bucket list. I barely trained and thought it was simply just running. I was wrong in countless ways.

I had no idea at the time, but this 26.2-mile run would change my life and attitude in more ways than I could have imagined. During that run, something clicked inside me. I felt strong, fierce, and truly like Superwoman. I had never felt this way before, not even during the other sporting games I had played in. I will never forget the feeling of crossing the finish line, all the emotions I felt, and the way everyone celebrated me. I fell in love with the sport and knew I wanted to become a runner.

I began running marathons all over the country. I love to travel, and there is something so exhilarating about being in a new city, taking on the streets with my fellow runners all trying to accomplish the same goal. I loved the feeling I got from running and the training that went into it. I looked forward to my runs in the morning when the rest of the world was still sleeping. This was my "me time." It was my chance to reflect, dream big, and enjoy the sound of my feet on the pavement.

The more I ran, the stronger and more confident I felt. I slowly started to talk about my alopecia to close friends and even went on short errands without my wig.

Then one day, on a hot twenty-mile training run, something came over me. I ripped off my wig mid-run while tears welled up in my eyes. I couldn't believe what I had done. But, for the first time, I felt strong, beautiful, and brave, and I knew that I didn't need my wig. I felt like I was finally *me*, the person I was always called to be. It was a moment I had always prayed for.

I hung up my wig when I got home that day and didn't look back. I truly looked at myself in the mirror that day, full of sweat and all. But I saw true beauty and my beautiful green eyes. I saw someone who is kind, caring, empathetic and full of joy, not someone who doesn't have hair.

Two weeks later, I ran my first marathon bald. I set a personal record and was embraced, celebrated, and loved during that entire race weekend. I was scared, but I was surrounded by such positivity and support that I didn't even think of my bald head — just the desire to run.

Tears welled in my eyes as I crossed that finish line in San Diego. I was finally Lindsay.

Alopecia has been the greatest gift I never knew I needed. I know now I am beautiful and truly feel it. It is not what I look like that makes me beautiful, but being a good person, being kind, and always offering a smile and a helping hand to someone in need.

Yes, I am bald. And I am beautiful.

— Lindsay Walter —

Flying Nighties

I can be changed by what happens to me.
But I refuse to be reduced by it.
~Maya Angelou

The first nightgown was thrown to the side, then the second one, and finally the third and last of the spaghetti-strapped nighties were piled on my bed — all now unwearable. While trying on my summer nightgowns and worn-out nightshirts, I had to put my head down on the bed to get them over my head. Lifting my arms was not a comfortable or even possible option.

I glanced at my senior cat, Gracie. She was happy to have me home. Gracie had been left in the care of a neighbor and friend and had mostly stayed under the bed. Now, she steered clear of the flying nighties.

I was tired, and this experience was frustrating as well as exhausting. I felt as though my best self had left; I knew I would never be the same. My new image was now Woman Without Breasts. I was currently part of a population of women who had lost their breasts to a radical double mastectomy.

It was deep into September, an Indian summer night. I needed a cool and comfy nightie. This was my first night home after being away for twenty-two days at the hospital and nursing-care facility. It was neither wise nor my choice to be home alone in so much pain. I was scared.

After full-time nursing care and help that came at the press of a button, how could I manage way up in the hills of Santa Barbara on my own?

I recalled being handed a canvas bag before being discharged. The bag was full of donated items from some organization. I saw something hot pink, with the signature breast cancer ribbons, and a Velcro front closure. I would not be caught dead in anything with Velcro, but then again there was nothing about my situation that I would have chosen.

I still had not accepted the diagnosis, let alone the loss of my breasts. Hot pink is not in my palette of flattering colors, and the only Velcro I had ever worn was on athletic shoes. But there it was — this hot pink gown — and there I was, opening the Velcro and easing it over my arms without having to put my forehead on the side of the bed to try it on.

I was both resentful and grateful that this gown was specifically designed for women like me. I was struck by the reality that when my mother went through breast cancer she would not have had a pink-ribbon care bag or the dignified support that women dealing with breast cancer have today.

In my hands was a large, square piece of fabric with lots of room under the arms, which is so important when in pain and swollen. The sleeves did not even brush against my skin or raw scars. Comfort was the priority while I put all vanity aside, which caused me to feel even more frail.

I looked at myself in the mirror. I held out my arms. All I could see was one big square of shocking pink draped over a glassy-eyed, pale, square blob missing sensual, erotic breasts. Although I was by myself and had not been with a lover for a year or so, I stood there humiliated by who I had become. I stared at the largest underarm area I had ever seen. What I saw reflecting back was not the former sexy lover, the Hollywood stylist, the story editor, the film producer, or the wardrobe-image and interior-decor makeover specialist of Santa Barbara.

Instead, what I saw in my reflection was a weary woman whose face was drawn and sculpted. I also saw utter relief on my face to feel unrestricted in a garment with extra-large sleeves and Velcro clasps.

Gracie was now napping in the heap of nightgowns.

As I continued to stare in the mirror, I caught a look in my eyes I had never seen before… defeat. And shock. I closed my eyes to the horrifying reality that took over and tried tapping into my sensual mermaid essence.

I began my mermaid life as a young girl growing up on an island off Miami. It was my blissful escape — a place to ease all hurt in clear and warm salt water. Usually, I could bring that vision and sensation to mind. But it was blank. I was blank. I was a bone-tired shell in the heat of a sizzling night too spent to conjure up any magical thinking.

I turned from the mirror to focus on my almost twenty-one-year-old cat, a testament to being a tough survivor. She lifted her head to acknowledge me and stretched out in her "see how cute I am" way. I pushed the nightgowns off my bed and crawled under the sheet while snuggling up to my warm, furry friend and blocking out the noise in my head. I was soothed by the sound of deep purring and her soft fur on my face.

I avoided mirrors through many more nights of hot pink sleepwear with Velcro closures. The Velcro would have to hold me together. That, and the true friend by my side — resilience.

— Valerie Anne Burns —

Face Your Fears

Stronger Than We Think

The most difficult thing is the decision to act,
the rest is merely tenacity.
~Amelia Earhart

"I'm leaving for work, Mom. Love you!" my sixteen-year-old daughter, Julia, called as she hurried out the front door.

Twenty minutes later, my cell phone rang. When I answered it, all I heard was sobbing. My heart clenched. "Julia, honey, what's wrong? Are you okay?"

More crying.

"Baby, answer me. Are you okay?"

"Mom, a guy hit my car. It's really bad."

"Are you okay?"

"Yeah, but my car..."

"Where are you?" I interrupted.

When she told me, I realized she was less than five minutes from my husband's office.

"I'm on my way, honey," I said, "but I'm going to call Dad because he'll be able to get to you sooner than I can."

The next twenty minutes felt like hours. I grabbed my shoes, yelling for my ten-year-old son to do the same. We were in the car in less than a minute.

"She's okay. She said she's okay," I repeated over and over as I drove.

When I finally saw her, I hugged her tight. Then I looked at the other driver. "What happened?" I asked him.

"I fell asleep behind the wheel. I think I was going about seventy," he said casually.

Seventy miles an hour when the speed limit was forty-five. I could have choked him.

A woman who'd witnessed the accident had stopped and waited with Julia until we could get there. She put her hand on my arm and said, "He nearly pushed her into oncoming traffic. I don't need to tell you that this could have been much worse."

Tears filled my eyes as I looked at my sweet girl. I knew it could've been worse, but watching her standing in the street crying was still pretty awful.

By that night, it became obvious that Julia was not all right. She was dizzy and nauseous and had a terrible headache — classic signs of a concussion. The next morning, she could barely get out of bed because her neck and back hurt so much.

"It could have been worse," I reminded myself as she cried all the way to the doctor's office. I thought it was because she was in pain, but then I noticed that she was gripping the door handle so tightly that her knuckles were white.

The next few days were excruciating — for her, of course, but for me, too. I longed to make things better for her, but there was very little I could do. I rubbed her back. I made sure she took her pain pills. And I prayed. A lot.

I thanked God that Julia wasn't hurt more seriously. I was incredibly grateful that we'd be able to get back to normal and prayed for families whose outcomes weren't as positive as ours.

Four days after the accident, Julia seemed to be feeling better. "Let's go get some ice cream," I said cheerfully. I offered to take her to her favorite place.

But she shook her head. "I'm not hungry."

"Okay. I promised your little brother I'd take him, even if you don't want to go. We'll be back in a little bit."

"Wait, you're still going? Can you bring me something back?"

"I thought you weren't hungry."

She shrugged. "I changed my mind."

"Come with us, honey. It'll be fun to get out."

She shook her head vehemently, and I realized that she didn't want to ride in the car. Maybe getting back to normal wasn't going to be as easy as I'd thought.

The next day, Julia had a follow-up appointment with her doctor. As I put on my shoes, I heard her getting sick in the bathroom.

When she came out, she had tears in her eyes. "I'm not sick, Mom," she said. "I'm scared."

"To go to the doctor?"

"No. To ride in the car," she admitted quietly. "I know I don't have a choice, but I'm still afraid."

As I drove, Julia sat in the passenger seat gripping the door handle. A car got close to us — not dangerously so — but she screamed and grabbed my arm, squeezing so hard it hurt.

"It's okay. You're going to be fine," I said quietly. But I had to admit that her fear worried me. If she was this afraid to ride in the car, how would she drive by herself again?

At her appointment, her doctor cleared her to resume normal activities, including driving. But I could tell by the look on Julia's face that she had no intention of getting behind the wheel any time soon.

And, to be honest, I was relieved. If she didn't drive for a while, I wouldn't have to worry about her.

Later that day, I sat with Julia as she spoke on the phone with our insurance agent. She'd been so nervous, worried that the other driver would try to blame the accident on her.

But on the phone, she was poised and professional. She told the agent what had happened in a clear, concise way. With a start, I realized she sounded like an adult.

And adults drive cars. I realized that no matter how I felt about it, allowing Julia to give in to her fear wasn't the best thing for her. It wasn't the best thing for either of us.

When she hung up with the insurance company, I hugged her.

"You're stronger than you think," I said. "And tomorrow you're going to drive my car and meet your friends for lunch."

"Mom, I can't," she said.

"You have to, baby. Waiting isn't going to make it less scary. You just have to push through the fear and do it, and it will get easier each time you do."

I saw fear in her eyes, but I refused to acknowledge it. I also ignored the way my heart sped up when I thought about my little girl behind the wheel again. *We both need to do this,* I thought.

The next day, Julia drove my car to meet her friends. As I watched her leave with my keys in her hand, I felt nervous and proud at the same time. She texted me when she got to the restaurant, and I felt my heartrate return to normal.

"She's going to be fine," I told my husband. "She's stronger than she realizes."

He smiled at me. "You both are. I know it was hard for you to let her go."

The tears I'd been holding back all week flooded my eyes. I'd held them in, wanting to be strong for Julia. Watching her leave the house without me for the first time since the accident was frightening. But it was also necessary.

For both of us.

— Diane Stark —

83

On Laying Your Burdens Down

I can do anything when I am in a tutu.
~Misty Copeland

You started a pre-ballet class today. Last night, for a moment, I freaked out realizing this was the beginning of endless extracurricular activities. Of throwing things to the board and seeing what sticks. Of working to discover what you'll find interesting and possibly become passionate about.

I second-guessed your enrollment. Should we have started with gymnastics, karate, or something else significantly less girly? Never mind that you enjoy dancing and are pretty rhythmically inclined.

I didn't voice these thoughts, because I recognized it as overthinking and, more than anything, I was excited for you. Your excitement permeated the house, affecting every routine that generally feels mundane. I have never made breakfast smoothies with more enthusiasm.

This morning, I wanted to be as relaxed about time as I usually am, but I also wanted to be early. I didn't want you feeling rushed or on edge, so I had to keep my anxiety at bay. The truth is, I knew there wouldn't be many Black bodies in your class. I was hell-bent on ensuring that we wouldn't be stereotypically Black and late.

I fussed with your bun at least three times before we entered the dance studio. I was concerned that it wouldn't stay up because of the beads at the end of your braids. I have always enjoyed helping you accessorize your aesthetic. However, today your beads made me self-conscious. Again, I knew you'd be the only girl with beads in her hair. I didn't want them to make noise and risk the chance of having that be your identifying characteristic. Even now, I can recall a girl reaching out to touch them as you lined up to exit the studio.

I became overly aware of your appearance just before we left the car. Your great-grandmother passed me her travel-sized cocoa and shea butter mixture. I moisturized your face and put some of my lip gloss on you. When we finally walked inside — not without me seeking to remove lint from your hair and checking your bun one last time — I felt silly for not disregarding the dress code as other parents had. It called for bare legs, so you went without tights (though indoors) in the dead of winter… something I would never agree to in any other circumstance.

There were girls in tights, tutus, and color coordinated wraps that covered their arms. I comforted myself by stating aloud that you were a "hot body." It is true, though there was no reason for the general public to know that. No reason other than my sense of shame… of feeling like I let you down in some small way. You didn't even have on underwear, because I was worried about the way it peeked out from under your leotard.

Hours later, I am able to recognize that I was too invested in your physical appearance. Thankfully, it didn't detract from your experience. I fussed over you the same way my mother fussed over me. I know there is nothing unique about a mother saying this to her child, but Zora, I think you are so special. I am fearful of you existing in spaces where people won't see you that way… people with the authority or influence to impose their opinions on you and possibly have you adopt their thoughts as your own.

Today, as you stood in line with roughly fourteen other bouncy four-year-olds dressed in powder blue, my eyes saw nothing but you. They noticed when you were mistakenly skipped during one of the drills. They darted to the instructor, hoping she would notice, too. They noticed you choosing to keep quiet about it, and they communicated to my brain a small fear that you wouldn't assert yourself in larger spaces... when it really matters. My mind instantly processed the thought that an assertive Black woman is seldom valued in large settings, especially when they are filled with white faces.

Still, our present-day reality is this: you are only four, and this is merely your first dance class. You would definitely assert that you are four and a half, but that information is as trivial as what occurred today. In the grand scheme, this experience was but a blink in the vastness of your childhood. Yet, I know that small things have a way of adding up to something bigger. For this reason, I've already begun worrying myself about how you will handle the moments and mountains as they come.

Today, my mountains are the fear of you being overlooked or deemed unacceptable. The silver lining is that our mental mountains have no permanence beyond what we permit. So, no matter my personal hurdles, my hope for you is this: dance as if no one is watching or assessing your worth based on your appearance... especially if that person is me. Allow yourself to let your hair (or beads) down, and know that my worries were given to me by this world. However, they are not mine to keep. More importantly, they most certainly are not yours.

— Brandi Chantalle —

84

The Big Red Beast

Inaction breeds doubt and fear. Action breeds
confidence and courage. If you want to conquer fear,
do not sit home and think about it.
Go out and get busy.
~Dale Carnegie

After thirty-five years of marriage, I was a widow who had no clue how to survive on my own. I'd always had Bruce to count on. He mowed the lawn, vacuumed our huge in-ground pool, and tended to every little household repair, while I did the cooking, cleaning and laundry. I was comfortable fussing around the house, but now it was all up to me. Everything. My hands practically shook from the thought.

I looked out the window one day and groaned. We were having a full-fledged storm. Snow had already buried the walks and driveway, the mailbox was nearly covered, and big, chunky flakes continued to fall.

Another thing I'd never had to worry about: digging out. Bruce had always been the one to get out there and tackle the job. I stayed inside, making muffins and cocoa for when he came in all red-cheeked from the cold.

Like it or not, I would be the one to tackle the snow this time. I took a deep breath, drained the last of my coffee and unwrapped my hands from the warmth of the mug. With a fresh tray of muffins warming in the oven and a small pot of cocoa ready on the stove, I steeled myself for what was ahead. I tugged on my hat and coat, shoved my feet into boots, grabbed my gloves and trudged out to the ice-cold garage.

There it was: the snow blower I'd never planned to use. Mechanical things weren't my forte. I didn't even pump my own gas.

I approached the shiny red monster with trepidation. I was clearly no match for that motorized beast, but I had two choices: go back inside and wait for spring or find the courage to live up to this new challenge.

I pressed the button, and the garage door rolled open. Endless white blanketed everything. I shook my head. "I'll never be able to do this!" My body ached just looking at it. I wanted to run back inside and cook or clean something, but this was my job now.

I put on my magnifiers. My brow creased in concentration as I studied the diagram in the manual and attempted to match the parts to the contraption itself. After one last look, I let out a weary sigh and shoved my glasses back into my pocket.

It took all my strength to wheel the massive beast out to the driveway. I regretted not taking advantage of the free gym membership when I got my SilverSneakers card.

Gray puffs of breath floated about as I flipped the switch, adjusted the choke, jabbed the primer button, and yanked the starter exactly as the manual instructed. It rumbled a bit, and then belched a noxious mixture of oil and gas. My hopeful eyes watered and stung from the exhaust as it coughed and sputtered… then, nothing. My shoulders slumped at the silent machine and throbbed from yanking the endless cord. I remembered back to when this would have been a snap, but what used to be taut muscles now hung like empty sacks from under my arms.

Cold and tired, I stomped the snow off my boots, went back into the house and plopped down at the table. Defeated by a lousy hunk of metal! As I stared out the window, trying to find the beauty in snow-capped branches, an old Helen Reddy song came on Pandora. "I am woman, hear me roar…" When I was younger, I could take on the world. Now, with more years behind than in front of me, I had more of a meow than a roar.

After a muffin and some cocoa to warm me, I bundled up and went back out to tackle all that snow the old-fashioned way. I reached for the shovel that hung from a peg next to the rakes. It would take longer and probably send me to the couch with a heating pad later, but at least I knew how to manage a shovel.

Grasping the handle, I glanced over at the snow blower and scowled. What was wrong with me? Maybe I shouldn't give up so easily. There were plenty of women whose age didn't stop them, like the ballerina who was still en pointe in her seventies, another in her eighties who landed her would be assailant in the ER, and one running marathons in her nineties. Age didn't seem to matter to them. I was younger than all of them and couldn't even handle a snow blower, for heaven's sake.

I set aside the shovel and began to sing the song still playing in my head. "If I have to, I can do anything." It wasn't quite as melodic or confident as Helen Reddy's version, but it was infused with hope.

With focused determination, I marched back over to give it one more try. I flipped the switch, jabbed the primer button and declared with some degree of authority, "I can do this." I yanked the starter. Once, twice… nothing.

I stomped my booted foot. "I can do this," I repeated through gritted teeth. My arm ached, but I took a deep breath, let it out slowly and steeled myself for another tug. That's when the lumbering contraption roared to life. I punched a fisted glove in the air. "Yes!" Sporting a triumphant smile, I boldly sang, "If I have to, I can do anything…." With my shoulders back and my head held high, I pushed that thing up and down the long driveway as snow blew in high, icy white arcs. Fueled by victory, I cleared the entire driveway!

Tired but pleased, I returned Big Red to the garage, went into the house and peeled off my snow gear. I'd weathered the storm! That, I decided, was worthy of a second cup of cocoa and another muffin.

I sat at the table, the house silent around me, thinking how I was capable of more than I'd thought. It may not have been as grand a demonstration as those gutsy women I'd read about, but if I could tame that big red beast and clear eighteen inches of snow on my own, then I guessed I really could do anything. I lifted my mug high in the air. "I am strong. I am invincible. I am woman!"

—Susan A. Karas—

85

Adopting Faith

Feed your faith and your fears will starve to death.
~Author Unknown

ur church directory was finally being updated. Each family was to take a new group photo. Our two older children were not available, but our third and fourth children could do it. One was a senior in college and the other a senior in high school, but I cajoled them into saying yes. I signed us up for the last slot available and told the boys they'd better be there, or else.

Our session was on a Tuesday night, and I set alarms on my phone for Sunday, Monday, and during the day on Tuesday to remind me to remind them. I was going to get that picture if it was the last thing I did.

I lay down to sleep Sunday night thinking about coordinating outfits. "The guys all have white oxford dress shirts… I could iron those on Tuesday… I could wear something dark…" (It was not the most original idea, but I'm still trying to make up for the time I convinced everyone to wear overalls in our directory photo.) I was about to drift off when my cell phone lit up on the bedside table, and I absentmindedly read the screen. I didn't think about that directory photo again for quite a while because the message I read went something like this:

"You don't know me, but seventeen years ago I gave up a baby boy for adoption, and I think you adopted my son. I don't want to interfere with your family, but I would very much like to meet him if he'd like to meet me."

I read it a dozen times and instantly felt like a mama bear protecting her cub. Yes, we had adopted our youngest. And, yes, this was the name of his birth mother. But our adoption was closed, and the young mom wasn't supposed to know our names or where we lived. Yet, somehow, she'd tracked us down.

We've talked openly with Jonah about his adoption and his birth parents all his life. We told him they loved him and wanted him to have a better life, so they'd given us the unbelievable privilege of giving him the life he deserved. We didn't tell him about the substance abuse, domestic abuse, multiple drug arrests, and neglect that led to him being removed from the home. He was loved. His parents wanted a good life for him. That was true, and all that he needed to know. We'd always told him that if he wanted to find his birth mother when he turned eighteen, we'd do everything we could to help.

Even so, I imagined dozens of negative scenarios that could come from searching for his birth family. My logical mind knew his birth parents could also be lovely, loving people who'd add richly to his life. But all the mama bear in me knew was that someone could hurt my cub, and there wasn't much I could do about it.

I lay in bed — wide awake now — reading and rereading the message, trying to read between the lines. I thought about a day when Jonah was seven, and a tree fell on two of our cars during a hurricane. The insurance company told us it was our job to remove the tree before they'd pick up the damaged vehicles. Jonah and I watched as my husband and three teenage boys struggled to lift a huge pine tree, and Jonah mused, "Too bad I'm not under that tree, Mom. Then, you could pick it up." We all laughed, but it was true. I knew I'd lift a forest of trees to save my boy.

Now it was Jonah's senior year, a time to have fun with friends, date, make memories, and plan for college and life beyond. All summer, our house had been filled with his friends. I moaned about the cost of feeding two, three, or four extra teenage boys at every mealtime, but in truth we were thrilled to have them there and to see that Jonah was the hub of the wheel in his circle of friends.

Now, how was I going to drop a bomb like this on my happy-go-lucky guy? My first instinct was to forget I ever saw that message, not respond, and not tell anybody else about it. I couldn't even show it to my husband until the next morning. David is the levelheaded one in our marriage. He said not telling Jonah would be the same as lying to him. We'd have to tell him and let him decide what he wanted to do about it.

Of course, he was right. In my logical mind, I could put myself in his birth mother's shoes — carrying a baby for nine months at the age of fifteen, stuck in a violent relationship with no family support, and mustering the love to give him up to a better life. When Jonah was fifteen himself, I'd asked him whether he thought he was prepared to be a parent then, to help him understand why his mama had done what she did.

I could remove myself from myself long enough to know that meeting her could be a good thing for my Jonah. But my inner mama bear was so ready to fight anyone or anything that threatened my child that it was hard for my rational mind to get a word in edgewise. I thought of little else all day Monday. Around 3:00, I started getting my usual after-school texts from Jonah. "Can Matthew come over? Can Blake spend the night? Can Devon come hang out?"

I told him I'd like it to be just us — just for today — and his response was immediately, "What did I do?" That made me laugh because this kid honestly does little to cause his father or me to fuss at him — ever. I assured him it was nothing. I just wanted him to come home alone this one day. I calculated the time he'd arrive and brewed a pot of coffee (his favorite). I made my voice casual as he bounded through the front door: "Hey, Bud, you want some coffee?"

"Just tell me what I did wrong!" (Bless his heart.)

I said, "Well... You know how we always said we'd help you find your birth mom when you're eighteen? What if she found you first?" I handed him my phone to read the message, and the kid who has a clever retort for every situation was speechless. I assured him there was no right or wrong response, and whatever he decided to do, we'd support him 100 percent.

He said he just needed time to process the information. That was Monday afternoon. Our directory photo session was the next night. Jonah and I talked about it briefly Tuesday morning before school, but he still wanted time to process his feelings. Our photo session was at 8:00 that night, so our older son joined us for dinner before my three men donned their starched and ironed white shirts. I slipped into a "little black dress," and we headed out the door for church. At the last minute, I grabbed a favorite picture of our girls from the living room wall, a 16"x24" shot of them sitting barefoot on some garden steps. If David and I could hold it during our photo session, the whole family would be in the shot.

We got to church, and the boys raced each other up the steps to play foosball in the youth room. They don't get to see each other much during the school year and they had us laughing through dinner and the car ride to church with their shenanigans. Finally, it was our turn to be photographed. We coaxed the boys away from their foosball game, and they slipped in behind us, still jostling and clowning.

It always sounds strange when someone says God spoke to them. And standing there with our boys just over our shoulders and the portrait of our girls in front, I didn't hear God speak audibly. But very clearly in my heart, I heard Him say, "*This* is the family I chose for Jonah, and no one can take that away."

When Jonah came into our lives, we weren't looking to adopt. We didn't even know we wanted a fourth child. In fifteen years of marriage, we'd never discussed adoption. Then one day, when I was forty-three and David was fifty-three, God laid the idea of adoption on our hearts. From the moment we said "yes" to the idea, it was best-case scenario all around. God gave us a beautiful, healthy boy who looks just like his sisters and his dad. We're a musical family, and Jonah came to us with natural musical ability.

Our adoption was one of the smoothest the local foster-care system had ever seen. Jonah has been a healthy, happy, bright, delightful baby, child, and teenager. All his life, I've told him, "Before God created the world, you were my child. He just went about it a little differently than with your brother and sisters." Jonah is our son because God decided he would be. And nothing that happens or doesn't happen from here on out is going to change that.

—Mimi Greenwood Knight—

86

The Unexpected Gift

Hard days are the best because that's
when champions are made.
~Gabby Douglas

"**D**ad and Wes will be here when I wake up, right? Will they call tonight if they aren't going to be home? Do you know if they are on their way home now?"

As a young girl, I tended to get a little apprehensive about where the people I loved were. Dad and my older brother were out of state at a sheep show. I missed them and wanted them to get home before I went to bed. I knew that wasn't possible as Mom had told me many times throughout the day that they would be arriving very late.

Mom patiently reminded me, "Yes, you'll see them in the morning when you wake up. You'll spend all day with Dad and Wes tomorrow. Remember, I told you that they are on the road and will be home after midnight. Dad will call if there is any change in that plan."

As I look back now, I realize she knew that storms were coming in our direction, possibly severe thunderstorms, but she never let on that it was anything to be concerned about. That night, I drifted off to sleep in my parents' bed, stealing my dad's spot one last time before he got home.

Despite my nervousness, I went to bed on that hot, humid Sunday night excited to wake up the next morning, which happened to be my tenth birthday. That night, though, Mom woke me in the wee hours of the morning. "Leah, honey," she said. "We need to get up. It is storming, and we need to go downstairs."

She helped me sit up, and I became aware of the howling wind and the rain battering the bedroom window. Mom handed me a blanket and moved me toward the hallway. I sensed she was in a hurry.

Dad and Wes had gotten home, and now she moved me toward my brother's room to wake him. It was dark; the electricity had just gone out.

"Where is Dad? It's raining. Someone needs to shut up the hoop building," Wes stated as Mom moved us toward the stairs. He was always thinking about the farm and the sheep. He looked out the kitchen window. Mom grabbed his arm and moved him back to the stairs. She told us that Dad was shutting doors outside, and he would be right back.

We moved down the stairs carefully and, once in the basement, Mom had us go to the middle of the storeroom where there were no windows. After wrapping us in our blankets, huddled close together, she went back to the stairway door to get her phone and flashlights. When she opened the door, the air that hit our faces was something I will never forget. The wind now roared like a freight train. I remember hearing a soft "Oh, my God" from my mom. "I will be right back," she said over her shoulder.

My brother and I sat like statues in the dark, cold silence of the damp basement. Too afraid to speak, we both wondered where Dad was. The wind was so strong above us that we could feel the vibration in the basement. As we heard Mom coming back down the hallway, Wes remembered he had his phone and turned on the flashlight.

I could tell my mom was scared. She told us that glass and pine needles were scattered everywhere in the hallway at the top of the stairs. My parents' bedroom door was shut and vibrating as if it was about to explode. She had not even tried to get it open to retrieve her phone.

Mom told me to stay put, not realizing I was frozen with fear, while she went to the attached garage to see if she could spot Dad. We could hear only the sound of her footsteps coming and going and the slam of the garage door. It was nothing like we had ever experienced. While it was only minutes until Mom came back, it seemed endless.

I knew when she hugged us that she was very worried. She reassured us that Dad was probably in the barn and couldn't hear her because of the wind. She could not see much because the rain was so heavy. After a few minutes, she went back up and yelled his name again… no response. We were scared that something had happened to Dad.

Mom told me later that she knew the hoop building was all torn up, and she could see things flying through the air. She stood in the door of the garage trying to decide if she should go to the barn to find my dad or return to the basement with her kids. Her decision was to stay with us, knowing that if she went out in the storm, my brother and I might be faced with the tragedy of two parents being hurt, or worse.

The three of us huddled together in the basement, too scared to say what we were thinking. *What had happened to Dad?*

Then I heard the best sound ever: footsteps on the stairs. It was Dad! He came bursting through the door. He was pale as a ghost.

What a sight he was! He had just slipped on his work boots and run out to the hoop building in his underwear to shut the curtains like he had done so many times before. He was wet and cold and shaking. As my brother held up the flashlight, I could see Dad's blue eyes were so pale that they looked transparent. To this day, that shade of blue makes me think of that moment when I knew my dad was alive. He kept saying, "It is really bad, really bad." But to me, it couldn't be all that bad. My dad was with us, and he was safe.

As quickly as relief had come, it fled again. "Where is Max? Dad! Where is Max? Did you see him? Is he okay?" My brother was in a panic. Our beloved yellow Lab normally slept in the barn with his sheep friends. Mom stood up as if she was headed out to find him. My dad shook his head as if to say no one was going outside.

"I think Max is in the barn. You know he doesn't like to be in the rain." Dad tried to be confident, but we were anything but reassured.

The growling roar stopped, and the eerie silence almost seemed louder than the wind had been. We slowly emerged from the basement, daylight now allowing us to witness with our eyes what our ears had taken in.

Our house had been ransacked by Mother Nature. A huge forty-foot pine tree had crashed through the bedroom window, landing just inches from where my mom had been sleeping less than an hour before. Nails were scattered in the bed where I had slept. Glass covered the floor clear down the hallway. Thankfully, Mom had given us shoes before letting us come up the stairs. A huge piece of roof was ripped off just above where the tree had gone through the window. Across the hall in my bedroom, the west wall was torn loose at the corner as if it were a LEGO project that had been dropped, and water was dripping in around the window.

Like zombies, we wandered about the house; no one talking, no one giving directions. We all put on jackets and went outside in single file as if we had been sent on a mission of unknown purpose.

We stood in the driveway, looking in every direction, unable to believe what we saw. The air was completely still and very cool. There was not a sound to be heard. No birds chirping. No sheep calling out for their morning meal. But perhaps the best sound I will ever know came to my ears: the tags on my dog's collar jingling as he came around the corner of the barn. He was scared and shook as we all crowded around him. His tail did not wag. He only leaned into our legs and licked our hands. Physically unharmed, he regained his energy with our hugs and loving strokes.

Every pine tree that lined the west side of our property was broken or ripped out of the ground. The grain bins were twisted as if they were nothing but flimsy soda cans. The hoop building was ripped to shreds, the canvases laid motionless, and the entire south end had collapsed. The large piece of roof that had blown off the west end of our house was lying in the driveway right in the path where Dad had run to the house.

Dad stood, at first in silence, and then slowly shared with us the nightmare he had endured while out in the storm. He was in the hoop building when it started to tear apart. The wind was so strong that he could not stay standing. On his knees, he could see that the end of it was going to collapse, so he crawled the fifteen feet over to the barn where he lay until the wind slowed. He had heard Mom yelling his name and was yelling with all he had back to her. The wind acted as a concrete wall, holding back his plea, "Stay in the house!"

We remained clustered together as we continued to survey the damage the derecho of 2011 had brought to our home. The two hundred ewes huddled together out in the pasture as if they had no room to move. The lambs for the county fair were safe in their pens in the barn. Not one life had been lost. Not one animal was even injured despite being in what now looked like a war zone.

Looking out into the fields, we saw crops completely flattened. Debris from buildings and large pieces of canvas from the hoop building scattered the fields like litter after a sporting event. How would harvest, just two months away, even be possible? Farming was my family's livelihood. What would we do? As a ten-year-old, it was too much for me to process.

My parents started making phone calls to grandparents and neighbors. Despite the tremendous loss that we could see with our eyes, we continued to get the good news that no one, not one person, had been injured.

My mom looked at me with shock on her face. "Oh, sweetheart, it is your birthday! I am so sorry." She hugged me tightly, and my dad joined in. "We will celebrate your birthday sometime soon."

I hadn't remembered until that moment that I was ten. Interestingly, I felt wiser. I had wondered how it would feel to be ten years old, and I had never imagined it to be so profound. I truly felt like I was the luckiest girl in the world. While I may not have had a house that was sturdy, I had a home and a family that were very strong. The gift of perspective that I received on my birthday greatly impacted the person that I am today. I know there are storms that will need to be endured, some due to weather and some due to the trials of life. I also know that my family is strong and we, together, create a force that can withstand the greatest of storms.

— Leah Kaufman —

87

The Only One

In times like this, silence is complicity.
~Kamala Harris

My brown-hued skin stood out, especially in the white lab coat. It made me hyper-aware of all the contrast in the room. I noticed the longer than normal stares. I was the only one with kinks and coils. The only one with large lips and a nose not so straight. The only one who seemed unsure of herself.

I wondered if I would always feel like this. But then another thought followed, almost like a correction: *You're doing this to yourself; you're not that different.* I remembered some words I heard once; that "Black people always have a chip on their shoulder." Even though I felt Black people had every right to have said "chip," I wanted to be cautious of how I let my perceptions influence my interactions. I tried to let the thoughts go.

I sat at the lab bench with my group and began to survey the cells we were given. They were HeLa cells — used widely in science due to their "immortal" nature. And so began the thoughts again. *Am I the only one who feels uncomfortable right now?* These cells were taken without consent from a Black woman named Henrietta Lacks. Not to mention, profited off of and used in education without full acknowledgement of their unethical history. It felt wrong to perpetuate this injustice. I contemplated saying something but decided against it. Black women are already seen as problematic. I felt compelled to represent us well.

Much like the lab, I wanted to follow the procedure. Stay within the guidelines set by society. I was doing just fine in fact, until the girl across from me said something that stung. "This is so ghetto!" she exclaimed with a disappointed look on her face, referring to the beat down equipment we had to use.

Unbeknownst to her, it had taken me an hour and a half to trek from the ghetto I lived in to get to school that morning. The words stung and I was the only one who did not laugh in agreement. They had no idea what it meant to be taught in elementary school that you live in a government-created ghetto. To go to a "ghetto" high school. Or to be told that the hairstyles passed on by your ancestors, your community, or your way of speaking was "ghetto." See, when she said ghetto what she really meant (knowingly or not) was broken, inferior and undesirable. Sentiments that are so often ingrained in the minds of Black women, including mine.

It became clear then that this was not in my head. The life experiences that led me to that point were likely very different from my less melanated peers. And they would likely continue to be different in a career often saturated and controlled by non-Black men. However, *different* did not have to mean *insignificant*. At that moment, I knew that my voice was valid. That my perception mattered. That any silence or complicity or conformity would be a part of the problem.

And with that, I decided to make myself heard. Without code-switching or making my words more palatable. Without worrying about what to say, how to say it or how it would be taken. There was no room to tip-toe around the matter and quite clearly no one afforded me, or people like me, the same consideration.

With every ounce of respect and understanding that I could muster, I offered an account of my uneasiness from the moment that I stepped into the lab until then. The faces I was met with made it very clear that there was no malintent. They simply did not realize it. Several apologies came and I accepted, but it wasn't until I heard "thank you" that I felt content with what I had done.

I will never forget how it felt when that person shared that I enriched her point of view. It made the contrast between my brown skin and my white coat feel powerful and important. And for the first time in forever, I relished being the only one.

— Mariah RI —

88

Mirroring Light

At any given moment, you have the power to say:
This is not how the story is going to end.
~Christine Mason Miller

ixteen years old. The voice in my head was screaming at me… again. "You can't keep doing this. You're killing yourself."

For a while it had been a distant thought, a whisper in my ear. But honestly, I thought I knew what I was doing. It really did seem harmless at the time… at least I pretended it did.

That night, I was sitting cross-legged on my bedroom floor looking at myself in the mirror, tears streaming slowly, silently down my face. I was exhausted and had just thrown up my dinner… again. I was withering away, becoming smaller and smaller — not just in my body, but in my soul. I remember looking in the mirror that night and realizing that the light inside me had been dimming for a long time. That night, looking in the mirror, I saw something terrifying — I saw no light at all. I didn't know what to do.

The once tender whisper in my head had become a desperate, pleading, and petrifying scream. I was scared that I still wouldn't listen. I was scared that it would take my life for me to hear it.

I knew I could no longer trust myself. I was trapped in a cage of my own making. Looking at this hollow stranger in the mirror, entirely depleted of energy and spirit, I made a deal with the universe. If my dad happened to get up that very moment from the couch and walk past my room, I would tell him everything.

I heard a creak in the floor and felt a shift in the universe, an electrifying chill pulsating through my body. He stood up.

And I was paralyzed.

My hands shaking, my heartbeat throbbing, a magnificent drum set pounding in my ear, I found the light inside me again. With my voice barely audible, I heard my words penetrate my tears. "Dad, I have an eating disorder and I need help." My dad, stunned, soaked with a river of tears, responded, "I love you. We will get through this together."

Tears can catch you in their current. And tears can feel a lot like hope if you learn to ride the wave.

Everything changed after that moment. My days began to consist of therapy sessions, doctor appointments, blood tests, dietician sessions, meal checks and so on. I didn't know this at the time but recovering from an eating disorder takes a long, long time. I had to do so much work on myself before I even wanted to recover. There were many days when I regretted telling anyone. The eating disorder felt safe, familiar, like a friend. Recovery seemed scary, unknown, not real, impossible, not worth it.

Ten years later, I am a therapist, sitting in my office across from a sixteen-year-old client. She speaks softly, as though her words hold the power to destroy her. "I need help."

Her face dampened with tears, she tells me, "I'm scared that it's not possible, scared it's not worth it. My eating disorder is killing me. It's stealing my friends, my family, my spirit, my life… And I'm afraid I won't be able to stop it. But it also feels like my truest friend, like the safest home I've ever known. If it was gone, I think the overwhelming loneliness would consume me."

It's like looking into a time-warped mirror.

I take a breath and join her in the darkness. Sometimes when we're blinded to our spirit by our shadow weighted in fear, we need someone to shine a light for us, casting out the darkness and illuminating our soul.

I sit with her in silence for a moment, showing her that the screaming quiet of her mind is not a place that needs escaping, but instead a place to embrace, a place to envelop with curiosity, fearlessness, and, most of all, hope. Soon, she will look in the mirror and find the light that is deep within, waiting to burst through and blind with brightness. But for right now, in this moment, I will be her mirror.

I look into her eyes, glistening with desperation and fear and I feel my light shine through her, dispelling the darkness. I say, "We will get through this together. I cannot take the steps for you, but I can walk the path alongside you. I have walked it before and I know where it leads. I will light your path while you lead the way."

A shift in the universe, an electrifying chill. I look into her eyes, glistening now with a seed of something new. Her tears sowing the soil that will be her garden — her journey of recovery.

I look into this time-warped mirror. And the light is blinding.

— Maura Schauerman —

89

A Doubting Sort of Faith

*Faith is unseen but felt, faith is strength when we feel
we have none, faith is hope when all seems lost.*
~Catherine Pulsifer

Bedtimes, at least those of my five-year-old son Henry, are often the warm, aromatic soil where philosophical questions can grow and blossom into profound theological conundrums with dizzying speed. I suppose there's something about the calm darkness that surrounds him that provides clarity of thought and an absence of distraction, which leads, inevitably, down a rocky pathway girded by trenchant questions and far-too-deep-for-bedtime observations.

I recently learned from my wife that there's an additional reason for the plethora of interrogatories that flood my way as soon as the ceiling light goes off and the Darth Vader nightlight goes on. As it turns out — and who would have suspected this? — she gets bombarded with the standard investigative journalist's questions on a minute-to-minute basis during the day. Who, what, where, and when are unceasingly rocketed toward her from high-pitched voices on a wide variety of topics. She parries these blows as best she can while her maternal energy lasts. But it's the key question, the "Why?" — the basis for all philosophy and logic and science and literature and psychology — that she deflects with that tried-and-true redirection of, "You'll have to ask your dad."

And so, here we are, in the darkness, readjusting blankets and pillows, searching the house for Puppy (my three-year old's best friend and — according to him — the true cause of the mischief he inevitably finds himself caught up in), and making sure all water bottles have sufficiently fresh water for my children's high standards and refined palates. Oftentimes, I can get through these practical elements of bedtime without permanent damage, but as we head into our prayer time, I steel myself to enter the theological doors that automatically open.

Henry's seven-year-old cousin and best friend, Sawyer, received a terminal cancer diagnosis in March 2020 and died seven months later. As a result, Henry's questions are much harder now than they used to be before his cousin died. He used to ask questions like, "Why is Yoda green?" and "What is God's middle name?" They're hard questions in and of themselves, especially for the unprepared parent operating on insufficient REM cycles, but the answer to them could be just about anything, which would sufficiently satisfy his curiosity. But now that the reality of death has become such a devastating part of his young life, his questions tend to more readily explore much grimmer areas of his own thought process.

A few weeks ago, after we had finished our prayers and I finally settled the boys down for the night, I began my exit routine, which includes the requisite parental threats followed by affirmations of love and a series of "good nights" that can last far longer than needed.

"Dad?" I heard from the upper bunk as I turned to leave the room. "Dad, if God can do all things, why doesn't he bring people back to life?" Henry had sat up in bed, his soft onesie pajamas covered with tractors making him look so young, even as the question he'd uttered made him seem so old. I felt that sudden feeling in my chest that I often get when I know I'm being called on to provide answers to questions that not even the wisest rabbi or theologian can fully understand, let alone explain.

Of course, I didn't have a good answer. Not really. I'm not a seminary graduate, nor a pastor. I'm a sporadic Bible reader with an insufficient prayer life and a pathological aversion to the internal conflict that often accompanies my bouts of spiritual introspection. Perhaps by necessity, over the last year when I watched my young nephew fight brain cancer and lose, I've grappled more with doubts about God, Christianity, the Bible, hope, faith, heaven, hell, the efficacy of prayer, the reality of pain and suffering, and the distance from God that seems at times to be insurmountable. I'm a constantly struggling, often disloyal, and ever-frequent failure of a Christian, and I have not a single answer to the question Henry just asked me.

But I'm his dad, so he thinks I know.

My church background never seemed open to expressing doubts. When people raised doubts, it was in the past tense. They *had* been struggling with their faith, but now, at the point they feel comfortable raising that struggle in Sunday school or Wednesday night prayer meeting, they're past all that. They're confident in their faith once more. No one in my memory spoke about their current doubts, their current disbeliefs in what the Bible says, or their current and all-compassing anger at the God who "can do all things" but refuses to save the people we love. Doubts, while outright forbidden, nonetheless felt implicitly discouraged.

I don't want my son to feel the loneliness I often felt as a kid, alone with the doubts that only I seemed to have, alone with the spiritual deadness and apathy that only I experienced, alone with the dread of hell that caused me to pray again and again, night after night.

"I don't know, buddy," I finally replied. "I don't understand exactly why the Bible shows God bringing some people back from life and not others. We do know that death is simply part of our lives here on Earth, but that God's plan is not only for what we experience while we live on this planet but also for what happens to our souls after death."

"But why do people die?" he broke in. "Ughh, I hate that word!"

"What word?"

"'Die.' I hate that word so much!"

"I do, too, man," I said, placing my hand on his knee and giving it a squeeze. Far more than hating just that word, I hated a world that had made it necessary for him to even learn that word at age five. I hated that he knew a sense of loss so intimately, that he understood that pain so concretely, and all at a time when he should be consumed with wrestling matches with Daddy, or drawing preposterous pictures of poop as a lark, or pretending to be a spy or a baker or a Jedi for hours on end.

I brought up Adam and Eve, which we had studied in family devotions last year, and how they sinned in the Garden of Eden. "But, Dad," Henry said, "why did they sin? Why didn't God just tell Adam and Eve that he was in control of the universe and in control of the world and in control of them?" I took this question to mean, "Why would they sin if God had told them he was in control and they could trust him?"

"Well, he did, son. He told them that and showed them the world he had created for them and how that was an illustration of his power, love, and control over everything. But they sinned anyway."

I was losing steam. I could feel it. My answers felt fragile and insufficient in my mouth. I tried to bring the conversation back around to the foundational truth that I try to cling to myself — that God loves us, has a plan that we may not always see or understand, and that even amid suffering, pain and loss, God still cares for us, protects us, and blesses us in numerous and special ways. I hope it helped. He smiled a bit and settled back into his pillow, and yet another bedtime passed.

Yet his questions invariably echo my own. The words I tell him and the answers I struggle to articulate so often taste hollow. I can go days and weeks in relative peace, but not because I'm resting on the peace inherent in the principle of God's love. Rather, I'm at peace because I refuse to think about it. God's love is supposed to make me feel secure, right? Protected? Safe?

But it doesn't. I struggle to reconcile the truth of God's love with the truth of God's indifference. Or at least the perceived indifference, although that indifference feels evidenced to me by the lack of intervention in human affairs when I very much needed him to tag in and do something. So, I don't often rest in that love. Instead, I end up drifting off the beaten path that my denomination would prescribe and veer onto the *other* well-worn path that has been traveled by most of humanity throughout recorded history — a path strewn with doubts and anxieties and anger or disbelief toward God.

I still wonder, though. I still wonder whether there are truly two separate paths—one of absolute faith and one of unutterable doubt. This, I think, is where my religious background comes to play. If no Christians around me ever seemed to doubt and grapple and struggle with any of the things I was struggling with, then obviously it seemed that real Christians did not doubt or fear. Those feelings did not mark the true path of Christianity. I had to be on one or the other.

But I don't think that now, especially after this past year. As I move forward, my faith will ebb and flow; how can it not? My faith is the doubting kind, but faith it remains. Some days, it feels stronger; other days, I can't feel it at all. If we're honest, I suspect everyone who claims Christianity has a similarly doubting kind of faith. We don't choose between a path of faith and a path of doubt. There's only one path, and doubt follows reluctantly.

A few weeks after this particular bedtime, Henry approached me and asked, "Why is it so hard to love Jesus? I mean, I *like* Jesus, but it's hard for me to love him."

Like a wise, old therapist, I tried to gently turn that question back to him. "Why do *you* think it's so hard, buddy?"

He thought for a moment, his forehead furrowing in concentration. Then he said slowly, "Well, I think it's because I can't see him. I can see you and Sophia and Momma and Holden, and I love all of you, but I can't see Jesus."

That's it, isn't it? That's the truth that we can more readily accept at age five but creates such a storm of angst at age thirty-three (and fifty and seventy-five and one hundred). All of it—doubt, faith, love, fear, rage, anxiety—is ineluctably combined within us, and from that we try to reach in and grab that one bit of faith that still remains in the churning mixture. Most days, that's all I can do.

Henry talks about Sawyer almost every day. Some days, he breaks down in those same heavy sobs that I heard from him right after we told him that Sawyer had died. Some days, he's matter of fact about Sawyer's absence; other days, he tells me that he wished he had a time machine so he could go back to when Sawyer was still alive. He can't forget his cousin any more than he can travel through time. So, he remembers him every day.

The conversations I'll have with my boys will only get harder. Their questions will get more pointed, and their pushback will increase. They'll have doubts, just like I do. I pray that the doubts don't extinguish the faith altogether. I want them to understand that Christian faith is not something that is devoid of all doubt. But, more than anything, I don't want them ever to feel like they are alone in their fear or anger or struggles. I'm right there with them, fighting the same urge to abandon it all.

And so, boys, let's keep those difficult questions coming in the evening hours. I can't claim to know the answers, but at the very least we can ask the same questions, night after night, together.

— Jeremy R. Summerlin —

90

The Gift of Adversity

*The most successful people see adversity not as a
stumbling block, but as a stepping-stone to greatness.*
~Shawn Anchor

When I was five years old, I had a freak accident that left me standing in a bucket of my own blood. Thinking back to that day, all I can remember are glimpses of confusion, chaos, and excruciating pain. Had I been older, I might have been able to deal with the trauma better, but being a five-year-old, I was confused and terrified. For many years afterward, I feared that this accident had left me permanently "damaged" and thus unlovable.

Just weeks later, I found myself fleeing my homeland in an emotionally and physically devastating mass exodus. I was now a political refugee, destined for a dangerous boat ride out of war-torn Vietnam. My family and I were headed toward an utterly unknown future in America where we had to start over with much fear and uncertainty in our hearts.

Eventually, we resettled in California to slowly rebuild our lives. Finally, I thought my troubles were over. Boy, was I wrong. During my grade-school years, I was called a "f*cking gook" by a stranger sitting in a car and the "ugliest princess I have ever seen" by another stranger one unfortunate Halloween night. There was also an older neighborhood boy who bullied me with racial slurs and mean-spirited insults as I walked home from school. And then there was a fellow grade-school student who loved to trip me every time I walked past her desk, for no apparent reason other than to spitefully laugh at my self-conscious stumbling. Whenever she did, other kids would join in on the fun and laugh at me as well. I still remember how my face would flush from embarrassment.

When I wasn't being bullied, I felt humiliated about our difficult financial circumstances. Growing up, money was tight. At the beginning of each school year, teachers routinely asked us about the family trips we had taken the summer before. While other children would gush about their fun trips to all sorts of cool destinations, I had no such stories to share. I would lie, fabricating trips we had never taken. And when other students showed off their new clothes for the school year, I would sink further into my seat, knowing that I was wearing the same cheap clothes from the year before. Once, my grandmother fashioned a homemade "raincoat" out of a thick, clear plastic material for me. While I knew that it was meant to protect me from the rain, there was no way I could wear it without being subjected to taunts from the other children. Every rainy day, I hid my raincoat from everyone for fear of the ridicule that was a staple of my young life. I grew up with very low self-esteem.

Nevertheless, even in the darkest moments of my childhood, I still believed that there was a happier future out there, a possibility for a new beginning. Hope came to me in many forms throughout my life. Whether it be a friendly smile from a kind student or a blossoming new friendship I hadn't expected, hope always walked alongside me, even at times when I didn't realize it was there. I truly believe that I survived my childhood and eventually grew up to become a confident adult because I never lost hope for a better tomorrow.

Today, people frequently tell me that I am brave, strong, and resilient. If I possess any of these traits, it's because I was given a gift a very long time ago: adversity. I truly believe that adversity is just an opportunity to triumph. Considering the adversity I faced, I had the choice to try to overcome it or to allow it to overcome me. Although it certainly has not been easy, I have chosen the former. And in the process of trying to overcome the challenges I faced, I became stronger.

On the same note, adversity has taught me many valuable lessons in life. For instance, when I recall how unlovable I felt because of my childhood accident, I remind myself of the value of unconditional love, which I searched for and found with my husband. When I look back at the hardships that followed me as a child, I realize that those experiences gave me much needed perspective on life and gratitude for the blessings I have today. When I remember the degradation that I was subjected to as a child, I am reminded of the importance of being kind to everyone I meet. When I think about how ugly I felt after my ill-fated Halloween incident, I understand that true beauty comes from within. Adversity is truly a gift because it has been such a great teacher and guide in my life.

Five years ago, I decided to follow my passion and become a writer. While my words may not change the world, end hunger, or create world peace, I have always hoped that they would touch people and be a source of inspiration and strength that they need to deal with their own hardships. Today, every time someone refers to me as brave, it flatters me greatly. It also motivates me to continue sharing my stories, hoping that whatever courage I have becomes infectious to those who need strength for whatever journey they are embarking on.

Last year, a young woman who had read one of my stories messaged me on social media. She told me that she was bullied daily as a child and suffers from low self-esteem to this day. She went on to say that she hoped to be as brave as I am. I thanked her for her kind message and wished her the best in finding her own courage. It is my heartfelt wish for this young woman to find the self-love and confidence she needs to heal her past wounds and live her best life possible. Until then, I will keep writing my stories in the hopes of being a source of inspiration and comfort to her and women like her everywhere.

People often say that what doesn't kill you makes you stronger. Along those lines, a childhood friend once referred to me as a "little warrior" because of all the traumatic things I faced in my life: bullying, racism, cultural displacement because of war, accidents, and extremely low self-esteem. I believe there is a little warrior inside all of us, who is ready to triumph over adversity and reign victorious.

— Kristen Mai Pham —

Chapter 10

Loss, Grieving, and Healing

The Obituary

If we want to write to heal, our words matter —
especially our positive words.
~Sandra Marinella, The Story You Need to Tell

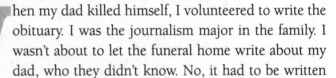

hen my dad killed himself, I volunteered to write the obituary. I was the journalism major in the family. I wasn't about to let the funeral home write about my dad, who they didn't know. No, it had to be written by someone who understood the elements of a proper obituary and who would mention that he golfed, rooted for the Cleveland Indians, and dug English post-punk band The Fall.

My mom and I found my dad on the last day of spring semester during my freshman year, a Wednesday. I needed to have 300 words on his life and legacy e-mailed to *The Star-Ledger* by 3:00 P.M. on Friday. I procrastinated, and only started writing the thing at 11:59 P.M. on Thursday.

My base was the kitchen table where I used to do homework in elementary school. Consequently, I approached the obituary as a regular assignment. I re-read the fake Betty White obituary I had written earlier that year for a class exercise, even substituting my dad's name, but clearly that wasn't working. I abandoned the celebrity obituary treatment, so instead I searched old issues of *The Star-Ledger* to see how the common folk were eulogized in print. I found nothing save for sentimentality.

At 3:00 A.M. I had a blank page, and only twelve hours until the deadline. So I word vomited the facts: Michael V. Pedalino died on May 21, 2014. A lifelong Nutley resident, Michael attended Nutley High School. He became a high-school teacher at Passaic Valley Regional High School and later Hillside High School. He is survived by his wife of 23 years, Maria (née Rano); his daughter, Alana; his father, Vincent J. Pedalino; his sister, Marilyn Milano and her husband, Don; his brother, Vincent Pedalino and his wife, Mary; brother-in-law, Thomas Rano and his wife, Debbie; and his in-laws, Francis and Anna Rano. He was predeceased by his mother, Rose.

The pain began when I started injecting my dad's personality and history into the piece. He loved animals, especially his cats, Misty, Splash, and Diego. He went to college for an industrial-arts degree and special-education certification. It was adding in the trifecta — his favorite hobby, sports team, and band — that sucker-punched me. When I broke, the sky did, too. Sobs mingled with thunder, and thunder mingled with gasps of, *How could you be so stupid, Dad?* and *How could you leave us like that?* It was all very cinematic in the most clichéd ways.

Writing this obituary was the hardest thing I had ever done and may ever do. It forced me to acknowledge that my dad was dead, and come to terms with the unfairness of his mental illness. It was catharsis in its rawest, scariest state. It was also absolutely necessary because before then I had refused to cry, to feel, to hurt. Giving myself over to emotion and two and a half boxes of Kleenex was healing, not weak.

I finished the obituary around 11:00 A.M. It ran in *The Star-Ledger* for three days. My byline wasn't on it, but I had gotten my first clip published in a professional news outlet. I felt a surreal sense of pride when I saw it in print; I proved I was worth my salt as a journalist by following the standard obituary format while also writing my dad a damn good obituary.

I took comfort in being able to read the obituary in the paper, and I knew that feeling remotely fine indicated I was moving forward with my life. And though it would be months until I'd forgive my dad for his suicide and adjust to a single-parent household, I was also proud everyone knew I was the daughter of the man with the memorable obituary: the golfer who rooted for the Cleveland Indians and dug The Fall.

—Alana Pedalino—

92

Messages in His Books

A great soul serves everyone all the time. A great soul
never dies. It brings us together again and again.
~Maya Angelou

My husband bought books like some women buy shoes. Long before I knew him, he had amassed a vast library of books — sales, marketing, consulting, leadership, biography, sports, religion, spirituality. And after we were married, he continued to buy them. Following seminars or outings at the mall, he'd come home with another shopping bag full of books. He'd cram the new books into the already packed ceiling-high shelves in his office, often wedging the books sideways above the upright ones.

"Even if you get just one idea from a whole book," he said, "it's worth it."

In one of those famous compromises of marriage, I learned to live with the growing collection of books, keeping my sniping comments down ("When will you ever read them all?") and occasionally dusting or straightening them.

After his passing, when I could finally stand to enter his office, I yielded to an insistent need to weed, straighten, and streamline everything. So, I tackled his bookshelves.

As I did, I discovered books behind books behind books and

titles I'd never even seen in our many years together. To my surprise, a random title in marketing or sales or spirituality caught my eye, and then another and another. Instead of putting them in the box to give away, I started piling them up in a corner to read or at least skim.

I collected quite a pile, and one lunchtime I picked one to read. Opening it, I saw what I'd forgotten — his habit of marking up the pages. And I felt again my irritation at the excess. Not the occasional bracket or asterisk, but strings of exclamation points, stars, curlicues, arrows, and marginal notes: "Important!" "Take note!" He underlined entire paragraphs twice, three times, even four times, and with colored markers. I could hardly read the printed page through the notes.

The ink markings weren't enough. He also stuck Post-its on page after page. Often, there were so many Post-its that the book bulked to twice its thickness. He also dog-eared pages, a taboo for many of us.

In my own books, I cherished the unsullied page. Once in a while, I might draw a modest, light bracket at an especially gorgeous, evocative, or memorable phrase or sentence. Or I gently placed a Post-it next to a particularly meaningful passage. Whenever I saw a turned-down corner anywhere, even in a dentist office magazine, I unbent it.

But here, in my husband's books that went back twenty, thirty, sometimes forty years, I stared at the uncontrolled pen markings, some faded almost beyond legibility; the multiple Post-its straining the bindings; the turned-down corners about to flake with age. I sighed with annoyance at what I felt was desecration of the books.

Despite my disapproval, though, they pulled me in. I read one musty, marked-up book after another. And I saw something.

All those markings and wads of Post-its were his way of teaching himself. In his career, he was a superb seminar leader, trainer, teacher, and consultant for companies and individuals. That's how I'd met him. A friend whose business he'd miraculously gotten off the ground suggested I contact him. Our first meeting was a "conference" for his help with my writing and editing business.

Through the books and their ever-proliferating markings, I could trace his thinking, his development, his growth, his voracious zest for learning, his hunger for knowing and always improving. Only now, after his passing, did I understand him.

I kept reading, or rather mining, those books, his writing making me uncomfortable. He put dates down, too — of his readings, re-readings, and re-rereadings. To reinforce and cement the thoughts, at the bottoms of pages or ends of chapters, he summarized what he was reading. "I am worthy of it all." "I attract what I need." "Concentrate on what you want."

These messages leapt out at me. Many years old but ever new, they were messages I needed. To my shock, next to the dates, some of the Post-its had my name on them. He was thinking of me, my worries, my concerns, my needs, and wanted to give me the comfort and help he'd gotten from the books.

I wept.

Through those old books, the ceaseless markings, the blizzards of Post-its, and my name on so many, I feel my husband's presence. He is here. In his books, he continues to support me, guide me, encourage me, and love me.

— Noelle Sterne —

93

The Coloring Book

If you do not enjoy a moment, you lose it forever.
If you enjoy it, it is yours forever.
~Debasish Mridha

We were gathered at the kitchen table as we did every afternoon when we got home from school. Matt had just started first grade, Mike had started sixth, and I had started freshman year of high school. My mother, who always sat with us, rolled up to the table, my grandmother pushing her.

"Mom, I colored in school today!" exclaimed Matt, dumping his colored pencils from his backpack onto the table.

"Matt, that's great. What did you color? Let me see what you did." My mother squinted her eyes through her thick glasses as Matt held up his artwork. She brought the artwork close to her face.

"This is great. So beautiful!" she said, and Matt beamed. "Hey, we should all color. Matt, tear us out some pages from that book."

He did so and placed one in front of each of us. My mother was given a coloring page with fairies. She asked my grandmother to roll her closer to the table and reached to pick out a pencil.

I was fourteen and it seemed a bit childish to sit there with my family and color. But I had seen the concentration in my mom's face as she picked out her first pencil and the way she lit up when she saw Matt's coloring. This was no time for pride. I looked down at the forest scene in front of me and then glanced up at my mother. I knew my minutes with her were precious and limited. My eyes started to burn with the salty sting of tears, so I distracted myself by shading in the grassy ground of the page.

Mom was entering her sixth year of chemo treatment. She had an aggressive stage IV breast cancer that had metastasized to her brain. She had undergone numerous radiation treatments and brain surgeries, the last couple of which had left her confined to a wheelchair. All her treatments had caused vision issues, so she relied on thick glasses to see. She also had problems with fine motor coordination. The thing was, if you spoke to her, you would forget all this. Her personality was preserved, and she was still herself through and through. She embodied life more than anyone I had ever known, and her smile could still light up a room despite the growing number of physical limitations she had.

I knew her prognosis was not good. I learned it through the years of watching her battle this illness. I heard the sympathetic whispers of people in the neighborhood when they saw us, and my school was making me speak with a social worker to help me through my mom's illness and eventual death. I wasn't sure how much my younger brothers understood, but they seemed to spend as much time as they could with her, so I think they knew deep down.

Mom settled on different shades of purple. She leaned over her coloring page, fiercely coloring in a large area, the pencil markings not staying in the lines at all. Matt looked over at her.

"Mom, that's so nice!" he exclaimed. My brother had inherited her smile and her joyful attitude.

She beamed. She held up her artwork the way he had. "I tried my best. I know it's not neat, but look, I got most of it in the lines! And look at this nice purple. I love purple!" We all took a minute and looked at her coloring page. Then we all showed ours in a kind of impromptu show-and-tell. They were all winners, she said.

She passed away the following year after fighting cancer for six-and-a-half years. It was a devastating loss for our family. Our mother was our glue and our beacon of light. She was also beloved by our friends and our community; our neighbors felt the loss too, as if she were a member of their own families.

In her last days, when she was confined to her bed and slowly losing consciousness, my mother told us that she had fought for us, wanting to be there for as many milestones as she could. Little did she know that we cherished these seemingly small moments with her just as much as we cherished her being there for the big ones.

Coloring books are sometimes short and sometimes long. Sometimes, they are filled with meticulous shading and coloring; other times, they are empty — just lines of black and white. Sometimes, the coloring isn't perfect; it reaches outside the lines. But the colors are brilliant either way.

My mother's life was one of those coloring books that was short but full of blues, greens, purples, yellows and every shade of every hue. The pages in the last part of her life had scribbling outside the lines, but that just shows the determination of the artist to continue coloring even when it was hard. She continued to fill out the book until the very end, not leaving a single page blank and leaving us with these beautiful pages to look back on.

— Cristina Vergara —

94

The Junk Drawer

My father didn't tell me how to live;
he lived, and let me watch him do it.
~Clarence B. Kelland

hen Dad passed away, my brother and I procrastinated, but eventually we rummaged through the contents of the storage shed. Undaunted by cobwebs and
mouse droppings, we tackled each box as an explora-
tion until the label "Junk Drawer" appeared in the dark back corner.

In my youth, searching through that drawer had usually consumed more time than the sought item was worth. The drawer held
the handheld pencil sharpener, the one binder clip we owned, and
a tiny screwdriver to adjust our sunglasses on days when we finally
got around to it.

Our treasure chest, the junk drawer, started as the place to store
batteries and extra shoelaces. One shoestring held lost-then-found
buttons waiting to be needed, expecting the dreaded day when a
hanging thread would appear while hurriedly dressing for work. The
one time I did need a button, I found it dead center on the string, so
I had to remove half the buttons to get the one I needed.

As my brother and I cleared the storage shed, we looked at that
box and remembered the day Dad had moved from his house in the
forest to a smaller abode in town to accommodate health concerns.
All the contents of the junk drawer had been dumped into a box. I
wondered why anyone would pack and label junk, only to store it

Loss, Grieving, and Healing |

for seven years. I found myself laughing as I went through the junk drawer turned junk box.

There were old keys that must have opened something some time, photos of unknown faces, long-expired coupons, and several pairs of dollar-store reading glasses.

However, the real find appeared at the bottom of the cardboard box, wedged under the flaps: a small, plastic baggie holding a gold-plated tooth and a row of three gold veneers. Really!? Who saves their teeth? I slipped them into my pocket for later examination, thinking there must be something I was missing, some secret nobody shared.

Days later, I took the gold pieces and some jewelry to the pawnshop across town. I was pleasantly surprised to sell it all for $400.

I especially enjoyed the shock in my brother's eyes when I handed him his half. I explained that this portion of our inheritance came from the junk drawer and suggested we spend it all on lottery tickets.

He responded, "That's what Dad would have wanted."

With cash in hand, we headed to the nearest convenience store. We each picked out $200 worth of scratch-off lottery tickets. As the line behind us grew with customers expecting a quick stop, I overheard several disgruntled remarks, so I offered an explanation.

"Sorry, but our dad died and left $400. This seemed like the best way to spend it."

Nobody said another word.

In fact, the lady behind the counter became much nicer and offered suggestions about which tickets had the highest payouts. I hadn't realized there was a science to gambling.

My brother won all his money plus a little. I've been scratching tickets for two days and have $79 to show for my investment. During our gaming experience, we laughed and shared stories. Who could have imagined the visions from the past that lived in the junk drawer or the memories created from spending the inheritance?

If we don't earn the entire $400 back, we will still be a little bit richer through the process.

— Brenda Mahler —

95

When the End Is the Beginning

There will come a time when you believe everything is finished. Yet that will be the beginning.
~Louis L'Amour

Five Days After

Vertigo. It's a seasonal thing for me, which returns with the allergies that come every spring and fall. Fluid builds up inside my sinuses, and I get vertigo. When I stand up too fast or lie down too quickly, it happens. The room spins, my mind reels, I get a feeling of dizzy disorientation as to whether I'm up or down, and it takes a moment to re-orient myself and feel "normal" again. I've learned that there's nothing I can do for it, just let it happen and let my body do what I know it can do: recover. Soon, my balance returns, and I am on my way (or off to sleep) again.

Today, five days after the Camp Fire came through Paradise and literally leveled my hometown, leaving us all with nothing but ashes and memories, I have the mental version. Vertigo. I see the photos but can't really comprehend that this is what is left of my town. Disorientation. I can't process what I am seeing. It isn't a destroyed block, or area, or side of town; it's… everywhere.

One or two random structures stand among the streets and streets of ash and concrete slabs, an occasional burned-out vehicle, part of a brick wall, a fireplace chimney. It boggles the mind to see, and that doesn't even begin to describe what it does to the emotional part of the brain. I can't even name my feelings. I understand better what war looks like from the inside now. But our enemy wasn't an "other," a political adversary or a foreign entity bent on destroying our way of life. It was… fire. Fire and wind and dry, dry land.

It happened so fast. We had hours at best to get out of its way. We left everything; many left with just the clothes on their back. We landed in a respite location, somewhere, and said to each other, at least we have our family, our pets, each other. Some had to leave beloved animals behind and just escape; some didn't make it out at all.

We used technology, cell phones, social media, and e-mail to find each other, checking in, sharing our stories. Stories of fleeing on foot, abandoning our cars and running for our lives; some sheltering in place in abandoned buildings, lying down, covered with fire blankets by firefighters and soaked down with water in case the fire swept through before we could get out.

Stories of strangers helping strangers, pulling neighbors out of homes, picking up people on foot and driving together to safety. Many are horrifying, but many are hopeful and illustrate the kindness of humanity. All the stories are exactly what the experience was: Surreal. A nightmare in real life. A war zone. Words fail. Thought process, logic, and balance are suspended by the stories, the photos, the… reality. And so… emotional, physical, mental, spiritual vertigo.

So, I wait for my mind, my spirit, to re-orient itself so that I can begin what I know I must do: regain my balance and recover.

Five Weeks After

Two steps forward, one step back. One step forward, four steps back. Crazy, cruel dance, grief, recovery, capricious in its behavior. I know I must get through the next days, the next weeks, months. But — I don't want to.

I feel like I'm in the middle of the aftermath of a mass shooting. Friends, strangers, nearly everyone around me is… gone. It was a wildfire, not a shooting, but still, grief and devastation are everywhere. Yet here I am. I "survived." My house… survived. It looks like it always did, this house I loved and put my heart into. Yet, in the past five weeks,

I have often wished that it was destroyed with all the rest. Today, the day the town is reopened, finally, for residents to enter and see what is left, I, too, come "up the hill" to see it all at last.

My neighbor arrives to see her "house" for the first time. It is a pile of ashes and rubble, drywall and ash, concrete and debris, soaked by days and days of rain, making a fine, clay-like substance that smooshes, collapses, as we walk through it, looking for… what? A keepsake perhaps, a mug, a special ring, something that survived this cataclysmic event that ripped the fabric of our lives into this… wreckage. We hug. She begins to cry, and then I cry, too, again, feeling her loss with her, knowing how devastating it all is, but not experiencing it completely for my house is, eerily, completely intact, right across the street.

Survivor's guilt, they call it. I feel it and understand it. But sometimes, right now, it is jealousy, unbelievably so. People have received insurance checks, financial compensation for their destroyed lives, their "totaled" homes. Many have paid off mortgages and moved away already or plan to soon. They have lost everything and will grieve those losses for a long time.

In a new location, they can move forward, move on, in their new place, new community, new life. They will surround themselves with normalcy as they wade through their loss, their grief. That, in itself, is surreal, the normalcy. People just living their lives because… they can. I've experienced that, too, when I have lost a loved one. Some days, you forget, just for a moment, that the loss even happened until… you remember. But you can, and you must, take a step every day toward recovery because it's how you mend. Chop wood, carry water, the old Zen master's advice says, until you can do more.

But this time, this loved one — it surrounds me now. It will be, for a time, like living with the decomposing body of the thing that died: my neighborhood, my favorite places, my daily routine. My town. It doesn't sound like a lot to have to deal with, does it? After all, I have my house, my "things." I can hole myself up inside and, once utilities are restored, pretend nothing has changed. Except, no, everything has changed. And I'd trade my "stuff" in a heartbeat to have my town back. Now, I want to give it all away to someone who lost everything.

Loss, Grieving, and Healing |

And I know that even that won't be enough.

So, I look to what I can do since we are staying here, to help with what remains, to rebuild, to grow. Neighbors and friends who still share this zip code, people I know and those I don't know yet, the ones who are staying, will be the new pioneers for this new town. No, it will never be the same. But the building, the rebuilding, must begin. It will take time, work, and patience. So. Much. Patience.

So, begin we must. Mother Nature has already started her task: Green shoots are coming up in the midst of the ashes. And that is what we must do, too… rise from the ashes, a new Paradise. The phoenix, the bird that rises from the ashes, will be our example, our inspiration.

We. Will. Rise.

— Ginny Brown —

96

The Healing Garden

The glory of gardening: hands in the dirt, head in the sun, heart with nature. To nurture a garden is to feed not just the body, but the soul.
~Alfred Austin

When my husband Randy died in late fall, deciding what to do with his garden was way down on the list of necessary tasks. During the first few months, I cried with our daughters, ordered death certificates, planned a memorial, cried with my family, celebrated a quiet Thanksgiving, panicked over not having bought Christmas presents, cried with my friends, and diligently chipped away at stacks of paperwork.

As the calendar turned to a new year, the often rainy days and long nights compounded my grief. I found myself exhausted at the end of February, my mental and physical reserves depleted.

Then the daffodils bloomed.

Years before, Randy had planted dozens of these lemon-yellow bursts of color in strategic places around our yard. To him, they served as beacons of hope, a promise that light and warmth would soon replace cold and dark. Looking at those daffodils, I thought about how Randy had considered our garden a living work of art, strategically choosing plants so we'd see new blooms every month.

Then I noticed all the weeds. I needed to get to work.

At first, I felt overwhelmed. Randy's illness had lasted a couple of years, a time when he didn't have energy for yardwork the way he had before. The neglect showed.

Invasive species had taken root and spread. Shrubbery had gotten leggy. Weeds were sprouting everywhere. My daughters suggested I hire a service to clean everything up. But I wanted to do the work myself. In some way, I *needed* to do the work myself.

Randy had always found that working in the garden was a pleasure, an antidote to his structured corporate life. Many days he came home from work, changed into old clothes, and headed out the door to mow or prune or just "piddle around," as I called it. No matter how cold or wet it was, the fresh air and physical activity energized him.

I discovered that working outside helped me feel close to him, and I often asked him questions I wished he could answer: How much fertilizer should I use on the roses? Where do I clip the hydrangeas to get the same beautiful, huge flowers you did? Are these new shoots weeds or something we want to keep?

At times, I felt crushed by it all, certain my efforts could never be good enough. Somehow, every time I reached a low, the outdoors responded to lift my spirits. For several days, an orange dragonfly followed me around the yard as I worked, reminding me of Randy and his orange jacket. The buzz from honeybees and bumblebees gorging on pollen created a comforting thrum in my ears. Song sparrows trilled a mating call, squirrels chittered from high in the maples, and gentle breezes carried the scent of dirt teeming with earthworms and organisms too small to see. The work was quiet and comforting.

Spring turned to summer, and as the days grew warmer and lighter, my list of urgent garden chores got shorter. The vegetables were planted, the strawberries harvested, the weeds held at bay. I started to relax on the back deck without scanning the yard for areas needing attention. It felt good, this sense of accomplishment.

Yet, a touch of the bittersweet tinged my enjoyment. Working in the yard kept my hands busy and my mind focused on the task in front of me. Relaxing left me time to dwell on my loss. I still had questions for Randy, but now they turned more wistful: *Can you see* how I've tended your garden? Do you know I picked the first ripened figs from the tree you planted? Have you noticed our prolific blueberry crop? Are you with me still?

As the weeks passed, though, I felt the seeds of healing begin to take root in my heart. My thoughts of Randy focused less on the sadness of his last months and my life without him, and more on the happy years of our early courtship and marriage, and the decades we raised our daughters. I noticed that I laughed more, cut flowers to bring inside, and paused after plucking a ripe tomato from the vine, breathing deeply of its warmth and grassy scent.

When neighbors and friends complimented the beauty in our yard, saying, "Randy would be so proud," I'd reply, "Yes, I believe he would." He always celebrated my success, always cheered the loudest when I worked hard to achieve something. Looking over his former domain, I felt gratified that my efforts this time helped preserve what he created and helped carry on the work he did before me.

When summer became fall and nearly a year separated me from Randy's passing, I turned my attention to "putting the garden to bed," as he used to say. It's necessary work, taking out the withered tomato vines, raking the leaves from the lawn, teasing sunflower seeds from spent flowers and leaving them for the squirrels to eat. But while a fall and winter garden may seem fallow, I now know it holds plenty of life. The lush abundance of spring and summer may be gone, but under the leaf piles and deep in the soil and down to the roots of every living thing rest the kernels of what is needed to emerge from a quiet repose, ready to thrive again.

— Cindy Hudson —

97

Surviving Beyond the Shadow

I am not a product of my circumstances.
I am a product of my decisions.
~Stephen Covey

The day my son Nick was born, losing a child became my biggest fear. When you love someone that vastly, the idea of them no longer being in your world is unbearable. Eighteen years and two months after that day, I was suddenly forced to face that fear. Were it not for my fifteen-year-old daughter, Anna, I wouldn't have made it past the first few weeks.

People around me said things like, "I couldn't survive that," and, "I don't know how you do it." But I had Anna, whom I love every bit as much as I love Nick, and she deserved to have a whole mom, not a shadow mom.

A shadow mom is what I was becoming, though. I couldn't eat. My days were filled with sorrow and tears. My immune system began to suffer, and I found myself shivering with fever on the couch one day. Anna looked at me and asked, "Mom, can someone really die of a broken heart?"

Her words struck hard and deep. She wasn't just asking a general question; she was asking if she was going to lose me, too. And that was one thing I couldn't let happen. I loved this girl more than anyone in this world. Despite feeling pulled in two, with half my heart here on

Earth and half my heart in heaven, I realized I had to choose. That meant actively working to heal so I could be here for Anna.

At Nick's memorial service, a dear friend and fellow artist gave me a box of random materials for creating mixed-media art, an art form she had introduced me to the year before. "You are going to need to do art to get through this," she wisely told me as she handed me the box.

I pulled out the box and began to create. Unlike the paintings I normally did, mixed media didn't require careful planning. I didn't have to have an image of a finished piece in my head. I could allow myself to follow my instincts and emotions, and just pour myself out onto the canvas. Tearing paper, burning the edges, and gluing them down in whatever pattern felt right. Adding colors: angry reds, mourning blacks, sorrowful blues. I piled on papers, paints and miscellaneous trinkets.

With each piece of art I created, I felt myself shift a little more from shadow to solid.

I dug through Nick's belongings and found some old posters with images from his favorite video games and movies. I tore them in creative ways, combined them with materials from the art box, and worked them into a large piece that I framed and hung in my dining room where I could see it every day while I moved on to other projects.

Before long, I was able to move away from purely mixed media as my mind regained some clarity. Painting lured me now — specifically, a series inspired by the lyrics of a song. Shortly after Nick's death, we discovered he'd particularly loved and connected with the song "Illusion" by the band VNV Nation. While listening to more of their music, I'd stumbled onto another song, "Beloved," and the words spoke strongly to me, specifically targeting my grief. I read through each verse, and images emerged in my mind that captured their meaning and the emotions they brought out from me.

The first painting was entirely black and white. An empty, snow-covered forest. The second, just a touch of green and a lone, pale-yellow butterfly were added to the monochrome. In the third painting, a little more color and an open field, the butterfly ever so slightly larger and brighter, with hints of orange. Then, fourth, mountains and a blue sky, the butterfly now showing yellow, orange, and red. The fifth painting featured a huge fluffy cloud and an even bluer sky, as the butterfly found a branch to land on. The sixth, a sunset, vibrant with fiery reds and oranges, and the blue fades, the butterfly silhouetted and hanging from a blade of grass, a shadow overcome by light. Finally, painting seven: soaring through the skies, a phoenix with butterfly-shaped wings, representing rebirth.

The series hangs on my living room wall, a constant reminder of the beginning of a process that will continue for the rest of my life. I still find myself creating art that reflects my grief. But, more and more often, I can paint images purely for enjoyment as the shadow fades and my life solidifies. And Anna no longer worries about losing me to a broken heart. Instead, she has become quite the artist herself and brightens my days even more with her own creations.

—Kat Heckenbach—

98

On Family Heirlooms

A mother's love is like an everlasting bed of roses,
that continues to blossom. A mother's love bears
strength, comfort, healing, and warmth.
~Ellen J. Barrier

I learned about adornment from my mother. Long before the phrase "Black girl magic" was coined, she showed me the ways of enchanted women. She wore her nails at a length not suitable for corporate America. They were multicolored and eye-catching. The clacking of her gold bangles announced her arrival before she entered a room.

She also fought lupus with the strength of a heavyweight. My usage of past tense affirms that it was a fight she did not win.

After she passed, her belongings were divided among a slew of aunts. They laid claim to what belonged to her. My grandmother was thoughtful enough to set a few things aside for me. At age nine, I couldn't understand that I was receiving the remnants of a person who had perished. I did not yet know the worth of sentimental value.

But at age twelve, I received her gold bangles. I call this moment my "glow up." I felt equal parts B-girl bad and royal. I came from humble beginnings, but wearing my mother's jewelry made me feel worth something. My father would later indulge my growing apprecia-tion of material things. After serving his second term in prison, he was finally tasked with raising one of his children. He made no qualms about spoiling me and steadily noted the importance of "looking good as a unit."

My senior year of high school, someone broke into our house. I am sure this was done in response to a personal vendetta. My father's hustle didn't put him in the business of making long-term friends, so our house was riddled with bullets. Our dog, a Pitbull appropriately named Gotti, was shot and stabbed. It must be noted that he lived through this ordeal and further earned the right to his name. Nonetheless, my mother's bangles were stolen from the house.

I cannot put into words the anger I harbored toward my father. His lifestyle already meant I had grown accustomed to his absence, but now I was also robbed of a connection to my mother. I had not yet grown into the understanding that they were only things—that my connection to her was not at all reliant on my wearing something that was hers.

Some time ago, my husband thought he had misplaced a necklace he wears daily. It's a cartouche necklace that belonged to his deceased mother. He told me just before it was time to read our daughter a bedtime story, and he later admitted that he debated whether or not he should tell me. As members of the dead mother's club, we try not to trigger each other's "mommy moments." That's the term we use to identify when our hearts long (more significantly than usual) for our mothers.

It's also a well-known fact that I am a crier. So, after he admitted he couldn't find her necklace, I instantly remembered the anxiety caused by misplacing my mother's things. I can recall being in high school when one of her bangles unclasped itself and left my wrist feeling just a wee bit lighter than usual. I spent the rest of the school day with my eyes glued to the ground. I had no time for small talk during lunch. I was on the hunt for a piece of me that had gone missing. My close friends knew this was not to be taken lightly. Their eyes were also glued to the ground.

Needless to say, when my husband lost his mother's necklace, I cried. It was not because I was triggered into reliving my own mommy moment but because I remember the weight of losing something that belonged to her. It had plagued me for months.

It has been nearly two decades since my mother passed. However, my husband lost his mother all of four years ago, and I found myself wanting to rush his grieving process. I wanted to force a realization it took me years to unfold. Still, I was fully aware that I couldn't say, "It's all good. It's just a necklace." In the moment, when you've lost something that represents a connection you're still fighting desperately to maintain, brushing it off isn't a feasible response.

It is not enough to say he is still his mother's son. I am still my mother's daughter but all that counts for nothing when you want something tangible to hold onto. Nevertheless, I know that in reality my husband is still his mother's son, whether he has her things or not. I am still my mother's daughter. The proof of that is bone-deep and not so easily misplaced.

— Brandi Chantalle —

99

Finding Peace Rocks

Gratitude is like love or fresh air —
you can't get too much of it.
~Danielle LaPorte

"Cool rock," I said to the car mechanic. He stopped typing my car's complaints into the dusty keyboard and looked at the golf ball–sized rock next to his fraying mousepad. In the background, hydraulic lifts hissed and impact wrenches rattled, but all my focus was on the painted rock.

"It's cool, isn't it? I found it right outside that door," he absently gestured left. "I walked out, and there it was... just sitting there waiting for me." His face showed disbelief, maybe even a little wonder. My stomach flipped. I'd forgotten about this one. I'd forgotten I'd left that colorful rock several months earlier.

It had started simply as a way to cope. Our hurting hearts and empty hands needed something to do.

From the beginning, Roger's diagnosis had been serious. "Aggressive," they'd labelled it. My beloved brother-in-law fought through endless appointments and clinical trials to gain as much time as possible. As treatment options dwindled, Roger found solace in creativity. Everything from music to mobiles, paintings to poetry filled his time. When hospice services began, he hunched over Oreo-sized rocks, colorfully painting them pink, green, blue, orange, white, and yellow, and then hand-lettering one word: Peace. He longed to remind himself, and everyone else, that peace rocks, and decided everyone attending his memorial should have one.

In the silent days following the service, my daughters and I tried to find solace of our own. Aged ten and thirteen, they'd never known grief like this before. Uncle Roger wasn't only their favorite uncle; he was their best listener, cheerleader and king of silly games. Losing him disoriented all of us. Seeing their grief broke my heart all over again. To distract us while keeping his memory near, we decided to paint peace rocks of our own.

In time, our collection covered half the dining table. We began carrying them with us and randomly leaving them places. Peace rocks appeared on fence posts, gas pumps, building ledges, library shelves, public benches… wherever it felt right. One night, we left several by an ATM. When my daughters realized security cameras captured our caper, fits of giggles overtook them. They joked about my "suspicious" behavior and how I'd look in an orange jumpsuit. They created a mock police interrogation where I implored, "But, officer, I was only leaving a peace rock!" With animation and great embellishment, they re-enacted the story to their dad when we arrived home. It was the most we'd laughed in weeks. It felt like medicine.

That night, something returned: joy. I felt my kids' joy restitch our wounded hearts. These rocks, I discovered, held the magic of healing.

Sitting in the mechanic's garage months later, I looked at the peace rock I dimly recalled leaving ages ago and realized how difficult those early days had been. I'd forgotten how painting rocks as a family seemed like the only thing that helped. I was also shocked not only by being reunited with one I'd left behind, but also by the attendant's reverent reaction to it. For a long time, I'd been invested in painting them to heal *our* pain; I never gave a thought to how *receiving* a peace rock might feel.

"I guess you were supposed to find it, huh?" I said. He looked at me for a moment, but his mind seemed far away.

"Yeah." He paused, picked it up and looked closely at the rock. "I guess so. I keep it right there every day. It's my reminder…" His voice trailed off. He shrugged a little, set it back down, and then shook his head as if to clear it. He returned to pecking the keyboard one finger at a time.

I sensed there was more to his story. Maybe he had just lost someone special, too. Or perhaps finding the rock gave him peace of mind when he needed it most. I'll never know. I'm just glad it meant something to him.

My heart pounded a little as I realized that none of this would've happened without Roger. We missed him — we always would — but his creativity taught me a lot about traveling through dark times. By learning how to cope, we inadvertently helped each other. If sharing a few painted rocks can do that, then it's better than anything I'd ever expected.

— Katie O'Connell —

100

Recovery

The pain passes, but the beauty remains.
~Henri Matisse

T he stifling summer night's heat closed around me. I had tossed and turned since 10:00 P.M. when I finally shut down my day and crawled into bed. I was exhausted, sore, listless and adrift in a sea of sadness.

Oh, for blessed sleep. *Please, Lord, let tonight be different. Please let me rest. Please don't make it another punishing night of sleepless tossing and turning.*

I had insisted that my husband make the trip home when I learned he was ill. Three thousand miles and an indescribable emotional distance away were not acceptable. Two days after Christmas, his plane landed, but he didn't come through the doors at Baggage Claim. The kids and I panicked.

We raced back upstairs to the service desk to ask if he'd been aboard.

"Yes, ma'am. He boarded in Albuquerque and changed planes in Chicago. He was on the plane."

In 1983, airlines permitted non-travelers access to arrival and departure gates. I sprinted, kids in tow, to American Airlines Gate 2. There, he sat in a wheelchair alone in a corner, weak and exhausted. His pallor was ghostly gray. I ran to him. Our older son pushed the wheelchair through the airport, and our younger son and daughter collected his luggage. The boys lifted him into the car. We drove directly to the hospital.

Nine days later, his heart failed, and he gasped his last breath.

Family and friends swarmed around me and the children. After the funeral and a twenty-one-gun salute at the cemetery, the American flag was presented to me according to protocol. The casket was lowered. The crowd left the cemetery. In the ensuing days, we accepted hugs, phone calls, cards with notes, some with money, all heartfelt and sincere.

Then I was alone.

The following week, I visited the Social Security office to apply for benefits. After twenty years of marriage, on the line asking marital status, I wrote: Widowed. In my mind, I added: Single mother of three adolescents.

I was empty.

Where are the instructions for raising a family alone? What does one do? How does one carry on?

Six months later, I thought I'd made some good decisions. I knew I'd made some bad decisions. I chose to remain in the same house, despite knowing finances and memories would be a struggle. In that house, he'd lain beside me so many nights, talking and making plans about things we'd do, how we would raise the kids, and our hopes for the future. We'd loved, laughed, doubted. We'd felt assured we were right and wondered if we were wrong. We even dared speculate how we might spend our retirement. Now I lay alone, trying to predict my future without him. I couldn't.

Tick-tock. I looked at the clock — again. 11:45. I slipped out of bed and crossed the room. Leaning on the windowsill, I gazed into the brilliant night sky. Thousands of stars winked at me through the treetops. The muted roar of a distant jet broke the silence. I watched the contrail draw a straight line across the sky, connecting the dots, one star to another. I watched it drift away.

A gentle breeze carried the fragrance of roses and lilacs into the room. I remembered the clean aroma of his aftershave. Tears dropped onto my cheeks. Night sounds distracted me for a time — bullfrogs in the pond, tiny scampering feet across the stone walkway, an occasional snarl.

Beyond the edge of the yard, moonlight shone golden on the lake. Ripples played across the reflection, drawing a watery pathway directly toward me. Beckoning. I tiptoed into each child's bedroom, stood over them for a moment, and watched them sleep. Oh, for the peaceful, trusting sleep of childhood. One by one, I smoothed their hair back over their foreheads and allowed my hand to linger on each cheek for just a moment before lightly kissing my children with all the love I had in my heart.

I eased the back door closed behind me and then stood still for a moment, allowing my eyes to adjust to the darkness. I wondered if I dared leave the children alone in the house while indulging myself — just this once. Drawing on my deep faith, I convinced myself it would be all right — just this once.

Padding through the dew-covered grass to the end of the yard, I stepped onto the dock where the boat was moored. I loosened the ropes securing each end of the pontoon and climbed aboard. I turned the key in the ignition and pushed the throttle forward gently until the propeller sputtered in the water. While the engine warmed, I looked back at the house to make sure no lights had been turned on.

I slowly throttled up the power and backed away from the dock, out of the canal and into the lake. I guided my floating island into the golden reflection of the moon and felt ethereal.

One turn around the dark perimeter of the lake revealed that I was afloat alone. I felt strangely relieved for the first time in months. Here, in control of my vessel, I was free. Free from the pain and the sadness and the difficulties that had overwhelmed me since January.

Could I really begin to recover? Would my children really be all right? Would life really return to normal — a new normal, to be sure, but normal?

Steering the boat into calm waters on the opposite side of the lake, I could see the dark space where the house stood. Solitude and peace descended upon me while still allowing me to watch for any sign that I should return home immediately.

Turning off the ignition and lowering the anchor, I crawled onto the back seat of the boat where I found a threadbare blanket. When I stretched out my arm, it fell upon a small cushion he had left on the boat the previous summer. It was old and tattered but so comforting now. I curled up on the seat, tucking my feet under me and pulling the blanket even closer, cocooning myself. His cushion cradled my head, and the stars stretched to eternity above me.

Was he up there? I hoped he would continue to watch over us.

Sleep came as the moon began to fade and midnight slipped away.

When I woke, a brilliant crimson sunrise was creeping over the horizon.

The stifling heat was gone, and in its place the refreshing chill of dawn nudged me to meet the day.

I had slept, deeply slept, for the first time since January. The house remained dark. Draped in the blanket, I slowly piloted the boat across the lake to the dock. I stowed the cushion and blanket, tied the boat to its mooring, removed the key from the ignition, and dropped it into the floating plastic container he'd bought.

"Never leave the boat without putting away the key," he'd instructed.

I crossed the lawn and entered the house silently. I visited each child once more and watched them begin to stir from their peaceful sleep.

I knew that everything was going to be all right. Sometime between midnight and dawn, recovery had begun.

— Judith Eassa —

Triumphing Over Tragedy

*Only people who are capable of loving strongly can
also suffer great sorrow, but this same necessity of
loving serves to counteract their grief and heals them.*
~Leo Tolstoy

One cold November morning, my husband of almost thirty-eight years, Sid, died suddenly in his sleep. I felt like my shattered heart could not possibly go on beating without him.

I remember lying alone in the dark that night begging God to take me, too. But when the sun came up, I was still breathing. I knew that, somehow, I would have to crawl out of the deep hole of grief that totally engulfed me.

Looking back, I realize that joining a grief support group and receiving some individual counseling were vital first steps for me. I was given comfort and understanding, plus the skills I needed to deal with my sorrow and move ahead.

My counselor asked me a key question. If I had died first, would I want my husband to spend the rest of his life unhappy? Of course not. I needed to do what I would want him to do.

It was hard to begin to believe that I could ever be happy again. Grief counseling helped me see that the best way to honor my husband would be to go on with my life as a contented, productive person.

Before I could imagine life without Sid, I had to take my negative, sad feelings and turn them into positive thoughts. That didn't happen right away. A few months after Sid's death, I began actively battling the most vicious enemy I had ever faced: grief. I had to change my outlook or sorrow was going to defeat me.

As my counselor wisely advised, "Be grateful for what you had. Don't focus on what you lost." It was a slow, difficult process, but I learned to treasure all the good years I had with my husband. Even though our lives together were tragically cut short, I had many happy memories to sustain me. I started to count those blessings and be grateful for them.

I remembered reading about a mother who lost her teenage son to leukemia. A friend asked the mother if she had known the outcome, would she have still chosen to conceive that child? Of course, the answer was yes.

Despite the horrendous pain endured after she lost her son, her life was enriched by his loving presence. Like that grieving mother, I wouldn't have changed a thing. In fact, I was lucky. Some people never get the chance to experience such love.

As my attitude slowly shifted and I became more and more positive, I started to think about the possible. The journey through grief was leading me down a different path, but maybe life could be good again. Was it possible some real joy might be ahead?

For that to become a reality, I needed to accept the fact that, as unfair as it was, I had no choice. I had to take a fork off the road I had traveled with my husband. It was often painfully difficult, but I needed to imagine exciting possibilities ahead rather than lamenting what might have been.

A strange thing happened as I stumbled along. I encountered roadblocks that I had never dealt with before, like handling financial issues. At first, I was terrified of these new responsibilities. But soon I discovered there were unexpected benefits in meeting new challenges.

As I conquered each unfamiliar task, it empowered me. I gained confidence and put things in perspective. I couldn't change the fact that I had lost Sid, but I could meet the challenges head-on, tackle them and emerge as a stronger, better woman.

I learned to trust my own instincts and listen to my heart. I also felt like I had Sid in my heart to help me face the many unexpected struggles I encountered as a widow. He was always there encouraging me to move forward into a new life.

Dealing with Sid's death also taught me to embrace every day and appreciate the simple pleasures. I found passion for new endeavors and cherished my relationships like I never had before. I woke up each morning grateful for another chance to appreciate everything and everyone around me.

I would never have chosen to lose Sid, but I learned so much as I inched forward on the road to recovery. I grew as a person and optimistically established and achieved new goals. Working hard to overcome my deep sorrow enabled me to turn my life around and find a different yet satisfying life.

The journey through grief never really ends, and life after a death is never the same. But I discovered that I had the power to make sure loss did not define me. I found purpose again and inspiration in treasuring the past, living for today and looking forward to tomorrow.

We can turn even the most horrible adversity into opportunity. Armed with memories in our hearts, we can triumph over tragedy. I remind myself every day that Sid is just a smile away, telling me to always believe that almost anything is possible.

— Melinda Richarz Lyons —

Meet Our Contributors

Kirsten Alexis is a California-based outdoor adventure enthusiast and content creator. She received her Bachelor of Arts from UCLA in 2010 with an emphasis on photography and media. She enjoys hiking, skydiving, paddle boarding, snowboarding, cross-country skiing, kickboxing, and fitness. She hopes to one day publish a book.

John Apel graduated from the University of Colorado Boulder with a business degree in 2021. He currently works in risk and financial advisory for a consulting firm, but he plans to write fiction and nonfiction outside of work until the day he makes a living as an author.

Angela Ayres graduated from Wilberforce University with a B.S. in Business Management and is a retired paralegal. She volunteers as a special education advocate and co-authored a children's book with her son Stephen entitled *Rainbow Zebra* that deals with the subject of bullying.

David-Matthew Barnes is a bestselling author of fifteen novels, three collections of poetry, seven short stories, five produced screenplays, and more than sixty stage plays that have been performed in three languages in twelve countries. He writes in multiple genres, primarily young adult, romance, thriller, and horror.

Katie Bergen is a wife and mom of two living in Canada. She loves coffee, wine, writing and travelling. She hopes to use her words and voice to inspire others to know their worth and live confidently in who they are.

Tamra Anne Bolles received her Bachelor of Arts in journalism from the University of Georgia and her Master of Education from Georgia State University. She has taught for the Cobb school district for twenty-one years. Tamra enjoys yoga, kayaking, hiking and researching genealogical history. She hopes to visit Ireland one day.

Cynthia Briggs embraces her love of cooking and writing through her nostalgic tales and recipes. She enjoys reading, reviewing books, speaking to women's groups, coaching budding authors, and writing for various publications. Reach Cindy through her blog cynthiabriggsblog.com or e-mail her at cynthiabriggsbooks@yahoo.com.

Ginny Brown lives in the town of Paradise, CA with her husband of thirty-seven years. Their extended, blended family includes six amazing and creative humans, all adults now, and two grand-dogs. She is a retired community college teacher and high school career counselor.

Lori Bryant lives in California. She and her husband have pastored thousands of people toward healing and living their best life. She is a storyteller, speaker, author, and minister. Her passion is her family. Her primary mission is to love God and love people. She has contributed to previous titles in the *Chicken Soup for the Soul* series.

Nathan Burgoine is a former bookseller turned writer who lives in Ottawa, Canada with his husband, Dan, and their rescued Husky, Max. Though he usually sticks to short fiction, his first gay YA novel, *Exit Plans for Teenage Freaks*, was a finalist for the Prix Aurora Award.

Kellie Burley has recently revived her passion for writing and has found the process to be incredibly healing. Kellie lives in Massachusetts where she is Auntie Kiki to seven nieces and nephews, is an inside sales manager at a software company, and can be found practicing yoga or enjoying time with loved ones on Cape Cod.

Valerie Anne Burns graduated from the Hollywood school of hard knocks and is a makeover specialist for home and wardrobe. She's had essays from her book *Caution: Mermaid Crossing* published in HerStry/Libretto and facilitated her workshop at a retreat in Italy. Valerie lives in Santa Barbara where she's survived breast cancer.

After graduating from art school, **Jack Byron** worked as a freelance illustrator. As a gallery artist whose work has been shown throughout the United States, Jack has also worked with Los Angeles-based Savage

Interior Design and has had several of his art essays published, in addition to his stories in the *Chicken Soup for the Soul* series.

Nikki Campo works as a writer and is a mother to three young children in Charlotte, NC. She received her MBA from Harvard Business School in 2006. Her essays and humor have appeared in *The New York Times*, *The Washington Post*, *Good Housekeeping*, *Charlotte Parent*, McSweeney's Internet Tendency, and elsewhere.

Brandi Chantalle is an educator, author, and public speaker. She facilitates workshops that prioritize the healing/experience of BIPOC, particularly women. Motherhood inspired her upcoming book *Love Notes for Our Daughters*. Brandi enjoys the outdoors, live music, and pretending she isn't too sleepy to indulge in a good book.

Julie Chavez writes to explore the joys and impossibilities of mothering and modern womanhood. She's an elementary school librarian living in sunny California with her husband and two teenage sons. Her forthcoming memoir, titled *Little by Little*, will be published in the coming year.

Pastor Wanda Christy-Shaner is a semi-retired minister. She has been published in five *Chicken Soup for the Soul* books and four magazine features. Wanda is a fur mom who enjoys crazy things such as, recently, sky diving. In her spare time she does animal rescue and oversees Good News Only on Facebook.

Cj Cole has served the Eastern Shore of Virginia as a radio morning show host and a newspaper advice columnist for nearly twenty years. She finds great happiness in sharing stories with *Chicken Soup for the Soul* readers.

Steve Coney lives in Endicott, NY with his daughter Maybellene. Since age eighteen he has published dozens of articles and stories in local newspapers, national magazines and websites. He loves his daughter, music, mystery novels, and baseball.

Morgan Cruise is a children's book author, artist, and high school English teacher originally from Memphis, TN. In another life, she could have been a leader of the free world, but for now she settles on taking week-long road trips, dancing in the mirror like no one is watching, and learning new recipes for her air fryer.

Lakeyshia N. Crummel resides in Harrisburg, PA with her husband and children. She enjoys faithfully serving at her church and encouraging others with the love of Christ by sharing her story as often as she can. She plans to write books of inspiration based on her life experiences and how God has worked in her life.

Amber Curtis resides in Philly with her cat, Sombra. She is blessed to have been published in the *Chicken Soup for the Soul* series multiple times and hopes her story sparks kindness. Outside of running, working, and deepening her faith, she is working on her first novel. This story wouldn't be possible without her mom, who taught her true generosity.

Darcy Daniels is Mom to two amazing daughters, Wendy and Penny. She loves to read, do yoga, tend her vegetable garden, and travel with her family. She talks to strangers, wins random things in raffles, and gives away leftovers to neighbors. The best decision she ever made was to marry her college sweetheart, Michael.

Lorri Danzig's poetry and personal essays have been published in many journals and anthologies. She is the creator of Let it Shine Journeys from Ageing to Sage-ing, programs that guide elders in finding joy and meaning. She writes often on the spiritual journey of dementia and caregiving. E-mail her at lbdanzig@lorridanzig.com.

Michele Ivy Davis is a freelance writer and photographer. Her stories and articles have appeared in a variety of magazines, newspapers, and law enforcement publications, and her debut novel, *Evangeline Brown and the Cadillac Motel*, received national and international awards. Learn more at www.MicheleIvyDavis.com.

Diane DeCaprio is writing a memoir about her POTS journey with the hopes of helping others to not just survive but thrive during tough times. She continues to follow her passion for martial arts and is a second-degree black belt and instructor. Learn more at www. standingonfaith.blog.

A Cleveland native with a B.A. in journalism from Duquesne U., **Kristine Meldrum Denholm** is a writer with work published in *USA Today*, *The Washington Post*, *Family Circle*, and dozens more. She's poured her heart, soul and rock-and-roll into her debut novel, and is now at work on her second book.

A Cleveland native, **Joan Donnelly-Emery** graduated from Syracuse University with a musical theatre degree, then performed regionally and in national tours, even at various theme park shows in Orlando, FL. She now enjoys a quiet life with husband Alan in Franklin, TN, gardening and screaming for her beloved Cleveland Browns.

Judith Eassa's writing endeavors began with Writing Your Life Story, an adult ed. session by author Cynthia F. Reynolds. Now retired, when not on her pontoon boat, gardening, birdwatching or making memories with family, Eassa writes at her rural home on a lake in S.E. Michigan. Her memoirs and a novel are current projects.

Maria Victoria Espinosa is originally from Argentina. She has published stories both in English and Spanish. She's an avid traveler and outdoors lover. She lives in Davis, CA with her husband and three children.

Cheryl L. Forshey is a published author whose short stories have been published in twenty-five publications, including several in the *Chicken Soup for the Soul* series. "Daddy's Day," "Making Sarah Cry" and "The Most Beautiful Flower" are just a few of her most popular titles.

ReBecca Gardea holds a Master of English and Creative Writing degree. She lives in Texas with her husband and children, but loves to travel, especially to Italy where she grew up. After teaching high school English for seventeen years, she is currently taking a break to stop and smell the roses and to focus on her writing.

Josh Granovsky is a screenwriter from Toronto, Canada. He graduated with a B.A.H. in Film Studies from Queen's University and is currently pursuing an M.F.A. in Screenwriting from the University of Southern California. This is his second story published in the *Chicken Soup for the Soul* series.

Randi Grant is a digital marketer who loves writing and learning new things. She lives in Southern California with her husband Steve, daughter Logan, and Goldendoodle Lucy. A breast cancer survivor at thirty-three, Randi wants to inspire others to be proactive about their health. E-mail her at randigrant@yahoo.com.

Elizabeth Harsany has been teaching high school English for over thirteen years. Originally a native of Oklahoma, she currently resides in Michigan where she has taught for the past eleven years. She and her husband Joshua have a five-year-old son, Zachary, and a newborn baby girl, Fiona.

Sharon Haston has written stories and poems ever since she was a child. Her family nickname is Dilly Daydream, as she loves to lose herself in a world of imagination. In real life she is a civil servant who also loves reading, walking, and travelling.

Kat Heckenbach graduated from the University of Tampa with a bachelor's degree in biology, went on to teach math, and then home-schooled her son and daughter while writing and making sci-fi/fantasy art. Learn more at www.katheckenbach.com.

Lori Hein is a freelance writer and the author of *Ribbons of Highway: A Mother-Child Journey Across America*, the story of a 12,000-mile cross country road trip the author and her children took after 9/11. Lori has contributed to other titles in the *Chicken Soup for the Soul* series.

Laura Wheatman Hill lives in Portland, OR with her two children where she writes about everything and teaches English and drama when not living in an apocalyptic dystopia. She has been published by *CNN*, *Real Simple*, *Parents*, and others. You can find her at laurawheatmanhill.com/ and on Twitter @Lwheatma.

Cindy Hudson lives in Portland, OR with her two daughters and a cat named Zipper. The author of *Book by Book: The Complete Guide to Creating Mother-Daughter Book Clubs*, she enjoys writing about the things that inspire her: family life, her community, reading, and family literacy. Learn more at CindyHudson.com.

Pamela Jane is an author of over thirty children's books, and an essayist whose work has appeared in *The New York Times*, *The Wall Street Journal*, the New York *Daily News*, *Writer's Digest*, *The Independent*, and *The Writer*. Her popular Halloween book, *Little Goblins Ten* is now out in paperback (Harper).

Heather Martin Jauquet is a reading specialist turned SAHM to her four children. When she isn't writing, she's running, reading, or crocheting. This is her third story published in the *Chicken Soup for the Soul* series. You can find her musings on HeatherJauquet.com or on Facebook at The Discombobulated Mommy.

Susan A. Karas considers her greatest accomplishment winning the Guideposts Writers Workshop Contest. She's been writing for them ever since. She's also a regular contributor to the *Chicken Soup for the Soul* series. Susan shares her home with her teacup Maltese, Bentley. She enjoys gardening, reading, and spending time with her children and grandchildren.

Leah Kaufman was raised on a farm in rural Iowa. She is attending college with the goal of majoring in Early Elementary Special Education. Her ideal job is to teach in a classroom of children with varying educational needs. She enjoys outdoor adventures and playing cards/board games with family and friends.

Steven M. Kaufman received his journalism degree from Long Island University-C.W. Post Campus in 2002. A person who stutters, with Asperger's, Steven works for the federal government and lives in the suburbs of Maryland. He enjoys freelance writing, traveling, hockey, and catering to the demands of his black cat, Lucky.

L.A. Kennedy writes short stories and creates work in clay, mache and pen and ink in her studio while supervised by one or more of her three cats: Tortie, Marble and Willy. Her ongoing project is the fixer-upper house bought after losing the family home to a wildfire in 2018. E-mail her at elkaynca@aol.com.

Mimi Greenwood Knight is a freelance writer, gardener, beekeeper, and recent empty nester living on a hobby farm in South Louisiana with her husband, David. She's blessed to have thousands of essays and articles in print in national and regional magazines, anthologies, and devotionals including more than thirty in the *Chicken Soup for the Soul* series.

Whitni Kostboth has a college degree, but her degree in "life experience" has proved to be more beneficial. She is a stay-at-home mom with a wonderful husband and daughter who make her life a constant adventure. She's published one children's book with plans for more.

Shelby Krommenacker has held positions for David Letterman's final season as well as Country Music Television in Nashville, TN. On

Saturday nights, you can hear her on Nashville's Rock Station, 102.9 THE BUZZ. Learn more at www.shelbykrom.com.

Sharon LaCour grew up in New Orleans and most of her writing takes place there or in the Deep South. Her essays and short fiction can be found in numerous journals including the Arkansas and Xavier Reviews. She lives in the Midwest where she has worked as a piano instructor for over thirty years. E-mail her at sharonannlacour@gmail.com.

Ingar Lammers is a mostly stay-at-home mom to three kids and resides in Colorado. In addition to writing, she also has a passion for running and inspiring kids to develop a love for it as well. Ingar would love to write her own book one day and encourage others by sharing her own story of survival.

Barbara LoMonaco is the Senior Editor for the *Chicken Soup for the Soul* series and has had stories published in many titles. She graduated from USC and has a teaching credential. She lives in Southern California where she is surrounded by boys: her husband, her three grown sons and her two grandsons. Thankfully, her three lovely daughters-in-law have diluted the mix somewhat, but the boys are still in the majority.

Melinda Richarz Lyons received her Bachelor of Arts in journalism from the University of North Texas. Her articles have appeared in many publications. She has also authored four books and lives in Tyler, TX.

Brenda Mahler retired from public education after thirty-four years. Supported by a Master of Education, she fulfilled her passion to support America's youth. She is a mother of two and grandmother of four. Brenda enjoys traveling and writing short stories that inspire others.

New Jersey native **Liesl Marelli** joined the U.S. Army following September 11th. During her ten years of service, she was deployed to Al Ramadi, Iraq in support of Operation Iraqi Freedom. Her time in uniform transformed her life. She is a mother of two awesome kiddos and lives in Florida. She would like to dedicate her story to DS Batalon.

Gold Meadows is a passionate singer, actress, and narrative writer. Her love for writing developed through poetry as a girl and grew after becoming a reporter for her local newspaper. She is now a regional manager for a sports company in Los Angeles. Gold loves observing colors in nature and spending time with family.

Paula W. Millet is a retired educator and now, a writer of novels. Holding a B.A. in Communication and an M.A. in Humanities, she has always been fascinated by the human experience. Originally from South Louisiana, she currently lives in suburban Atlanta. Learn more at paulamillet.com.

Lauren Morton is a freelance writer from Salisbury, MD who focuses on the connectivity between identity race and society. Her work has appeared in *OM*, *Aaduna*, *Midnight & Indigo* and *Luxe Radar Media*. She is a graduate of Salisbury University with an M.A. in Conflict Analysis & Dispute Resolution and a B.A. in Sociology.

Amy Mullis writes essays and hoards hand sanitizer in upstate South Carolina. Newly retired and seeking to find herself, she most often finds herself socially distancing in the express line at Walmart. She has had stories previously published in the *Chicken Soup for the Soul* series and received honorable mention in the Erma Bombeck Writing Competition.

Katie O'Connell writes, teaches, and cheerleads others in their writing process. A lover of all things creative, her work appears in several publications and other titles in the *Chicken Soup for the Soul* series. Katie believes in the healing power of stories and writing from the heart. Learn more at heartwiredwriting.com.

Molly O'Connor is a graduate of creative writing at Carleton University and Algonquin College. She is a published author of nine books: *Snow Business*, *Trevor Tractor*, *Morty the Street Bus* and *Stuck on Me* (children's), *Fourteen Cups*, *Wandering Backwards*, *When Secrets Become Lies*, *While She Was Gone* and *Whispers Never Spoken* (adult).

Nancy Emmick Panko is a retired RN from North Carolina who has contributed eighteen stories to the *Chicken Soup for the Soul* series. Award-winning author of two novels, *Guiding Missal* and *Sheltering Angels* and recently released *Blueberry Moose*, Panko is a member of NC Scribes and The Military Writers Society of America.

Ree Pashley lived and worked in Canada for twelve years before moving to Tanzania, East Africa. Now, she is a mom to eight awesome kids and spends her days changing diapers, writing, and hiking. She dreams of climbing Mount Kilimanjaro and diving around Mafia Island one day.

Lisa Pawlak is a three-time cancer survivor, award-winning freelance writer, and mother of two very tall and incredibly bright young men. In her free time, she loves to draw, read, hike, and eat cookies.

Alana Pedalino has earned recognition from ACES: The Society for Editing, the 92nd Street Y Unterberg Poetry Center, MDDC Press Association, University of Maryland MFA Program in Creative Writing, and Folger Shakespeare Library. She works in publishing and loves to kayak and travel. Follow her on Twitter @AP_Style_.

In the rare moments when **Kristen Mai Pham** is not binge-watching *Cobra Kai* or sharing Corgi videos, you may actually find her writing. Her next big project is to publish a debut book, a collection of short stories from her life. E-mail her at kristenmaipham3@gmail.com or follow her on Instagram at @kristenmaipham.

Sarah Prager is the author of three books for young people about LGBTQ+ history: *Queer, There, and Everywhere*, *Rainbow Revolutionaries*, and *Kind Like Marsha*. She has written for various publications, including *The Atlantic*, *The New York Times*, *NBC News*, and *National Geographic*. Learn more at sarahprager.com.

Dorian Leigh Quillen is a licensed professional counselor and author of three books, including, *Captured by Grace: The Jamie Jungers story*. She is a magna cum laude, Phi Beta Kappa graduate of the University of Oklahoma, with a B.A. in Journalism and an M.Ed. in Community Counseling. She enjoys cycling.

Brian Rashid is the CEO of Brian Rashid Global, a bilingual branding, marketing, and communications company that creates digital strategies and content that sell in a 2020 world. Brian has delivered two TEDx talks, and has a daily YouTube and Facebook Show, *BTV*, that gives an up close and personal look into life as a modern-day CEO.

Amanda ReCupido is an author whose writing has appeared in publications such as *McSweeney's*, *Forbes*, and on stages around Chicago.

Lexcee Reel is a pseudonym for Kimberly Lucas who is a native of Bailey, NC. She is an educator who is also a wife, mom, glam-ma and godmother of some uniquely, wonderful souls. Reel enjoys reading, writing, and traveling. She's authored several written works in addition to a small collection of film.

Mariah RI received her Honors Bachelor of Science from the University of Toronto in 2021. She enjoys travelling, writing, baking, cooking, being outside and spending time with friends and family. Her dreams are to become a physician and author, work with underserved communities, and teach.

Teri Rizvi is the founder and director of the Erma Bombeck Writers' Workshop at the University of Dayton. Her debut book, *One Heart with Courage: Essays and Stories* (Braughler Books, 2021) benefits the workshop's endowment fund.

Donna L. Roberts is a native upstate New Yorker who lives and works in Europe. She is an Associate Professor and holds a Ph.D. in Psychology. Donna is an animal and human rights advocate and when she is researching or writing she can be found at her computer buried in rescue cats.

Nicko Rochell received her B.A. in Communications, with honors, from Lindenwood University. Through her writings, she hopes to inspire others with empowering words of hope and love. She resides in St. Louis, MO and is mom to one incredible son. She loves to read, write, travel, and spend time with family and friends.

Angela Rolleman is a social worker, writer, speaker, trainer, and entrepreneur. She is founder of Mission: Empowerment, a company that provides personal and professional development seminars and events. Angela loves animals, reading, travelling, and spending time in nature. Learn more at www.angelarolleman.com.

Debra Rughoo is a writer from Toronto with a Bachelor of Arts in English and Communications Studies. Her work has appeared in the *Chicken Soup for the Soul* series, as well as in newspapers and magazines in Canada and the U.S. She enjoys travelling, sports, stand-up comedy, questionable reality TV shows, and chocolate.

Maura Schauerman is a marriage and family therapist specializing in the treatment of eating disorders, anxiety, and depression. Being fully recovered from an eating disorder herself, Maura has a passion for helping others fulfill their desire to live a full and authentic life of freedom and recovery.

Regina Schneider holds a Master's in Counseling and Special Education. She has experience writing both fiction and non-fiction. In her private life she is on the staff of three cats — Ollie, Lulu and Missy. For entertainment she enjoys coloring and jigsaw puzzles.

Santa **Dan Short** has enjoyed the privilege of sharing the true "spirit of Christmas" with children and their families for more than twenty-five years. He is known as the North Pole city Santa at the spectacular Oklahoma City seasonal retail venue where he has heard the wishes of more than 10,000 "very good children" each year.

Erin Solej, valedictorian of Felician College class of 1997, is a teacher, writer, and mother of Lucas and Hanna. She has been published in *Chicken Soup for the Soul: Just for Preteens*, *Chicken Soup for the Soul: Christmas Magic*, and *Chicken Soup for the Soul: Messages from Heaven*. She is currently seeking publication of her first novel. Follow her on Instagram @ewritermom.

Stephanie Sprenger is a writer, mother, and music therapist living in Colorado with her family. She is the Executive Producer of Listen To Your Mother Boulder and co-editor of The HerStories Project, a writing and publishing community for Gen X women at midlife. Learn more at stephaniesprenger.com.

Suzette Martinez Standring is an award-winning author of *The Art of Column Writing* and *The Art of Opinion Writing* and has been writing an opinion column since 2007. She gives writing workshops and especially loves novice and terrified writers. Learn more at www.readsuzette.com.

Diane Stark is a wife, mother, and writer. She is a frequent contributor to the *Chicken Soup for the Soul* series. She loves to write about the important things in life: her family and her faith.

Noelle Sterne (Ph.D.) has published over 600 essays, writing craft, and spiritual articles, fiction, and poems. Her book, *Challenges in Writing Your Dissertation*, grew from her academic editing and coaching practice. Her book *Trust Your Life* helps readers reach lifelong dreams. Fulfilling her own, she is completing her third novel.

Jeremy R. Summerlin is a lawyer and writer living in Greenville, SC. When not at work, he answers questions from the tiny squatters who live in his house and eat all his snacks.

Born on the beautiful island of St. Croix in the U.S. Virgin Islands, **Cassandra Ulrich** received a Bachelor of Arts in Mathematics, with honors, from the University of the Virgin Islands and a Master's in Computer Science from Penn State. She is married and has two sons. She enjoys singing, learning new languages, and writing.

Cristina Vergara is a nurse practitioner currently working with cancer patients. In her free time, she enjoys running, hiking, trying new food, and baking. She lives in New York City with her husband Andrew and their adorable three-legged dog named Riley.

Lindsay Walter is a freelance writer, marathon and ultra-marathon runner. She grew up in Wisconsin and currently resides in North Carolina. She lost her hair at age two due to the autoimmune condition alopecia. She loves everything about health and fitness, and aims to inspire others to be proud of who they are and to dream big.

Dr. Tracy Robinson Whitaker is a faculty member at the Howard University School of Social Work. Her writing explores her evolving relationships with the world, those she loves, and herself. She lives in Laurel, MD with her husband and son. She finds joy in laughter and seeks to create it whenever possible.

Chandra Thomas Whitfield is an award-winning freelance multimedia journalist whose work has appeared in *The New York Times*, *The Washington Post, Essence, Ebony,* NBCNews.com and *The Huffington Post.* As a Leonard C. Goodman Institute for Investigative Reporting Fellow, she produced the award-winning "In The Gap" podcast.

Audrey Wick is a writer and English professor at Blinn College in Texas who survived a brain aneurysm rupture in 2019. She believes the secret to happiness includes lifelong learning and good stories, but travel and coffee help. She has journeyed to over twenty countries and sipped coffee in every one of them. Learn more at audreywick.com.

Dr. Natasha Williams is a Registered Psychologist, Radical Self-Care and Leadership Expert, Clinical Director of Allied Psychological Services and the President of the Association of Black Psychologists in

Toronto, Canada. In her spare time, Dr. Williams enjoys fitness, fine dining, and travelling.

Danielle M. Wong is an award-winning author from California. Her debut novel, *Swearing Off Stars,* won an Independent Press Award, an International Book Award, and a Benjamin Franklin Award. Danielle's work has appeared in *Harper's Bazaar,* *The Huffington Post,* and *Writer's Digest.* She is currently writing her next novel.

Kelly Wright is a national award-winning journalist. He is seen nationally on the nightly news program, *The World Tonight with Kelly and Nayyera,* which airs on BNC (Black News Channel). Throughout his career, Kelly has covered top stories globally. He is also a recording artist and inspirational speaker.

Marvin Yanke is a licensed social worker and life coach. His keys to life are… Gratitude: I cried when I had no shoes, then I met a man who had no feet; Love: Being kind is more important than being right; and grandkids: Silly Grandpa! Learn more at www.MarvinYanke.com or e-mail him at MarvinYanke@gmail.com.

Jenine Zimmers owns and operates Mind Your Biz Jewelry, an Etsy shop offering handmade and vintage designs (mindyourbiz.etsy. com). She is also a reality TV trivia nerd, a New York Islanders fan, and a covert stealer of your French fries. Please check out her novel, *Fatty,* now available online.

Meet Amy Newmark

Amy Newmark is the bestselling author, editor-in-chief, and publisher of the *Chicken Soup for the Soul* book series. Since 2008, she has published 178 new books, most of them national bestsellers in the U.S. and Canada, more than doubling the number of Chicken Soup for the Soul titles in print today. She is also the author of *Simply Happy*, a crash course in Chicken Soup for the Soul advice and wisdom that is filled with easy-to-implement, practical tips for enjoying a better life.

Amy is credited with revitalizing the Chicken Soup for the Soul brand, which has been a publishing industry phenomenon since the first book came out in 1993. By compiling inspirational and aspirational true stories curated from ordinary people who have had extraordinary experiences, Amy has kept the twenty-eight-year-old Chicken Soup for the Soul brand fresh and relevant.

Amy graduated *magna cum laude* from Harvard University where she majored in Portuguese and minored in French. She then embarked on a three-decade career as a Wall Street analyst, a hedge fund manager, and a corporate executive in the technology field. She is a Chartered Financial Analyst.

Her return to literary pursuits was inevitable, as her honors thesis in college involved traveling throughout Brazil's impoverished northeast region, collecting stories from regular people. She is delighted to have come full circle in her writing career — from collecting stories "from the people" in Brazil as a twenty-year-old to, three decades later, collecting stories "from the people" for Chicken Soup for the Soul.

When Amy and her husband Bill, the CEO of Chicken Soup for the Soul, are not working, they are visiting their four grown children and their three grandchildren.

Follow Amy on Twitter @amynewmark. Listen to her free podcast — Chicken Soup for the Soul with Amy Newmark — on Apple, Google, or by using your favorite podcast app on your phone.